EXPANDING THE VIEW

EXPANDING THE VIEW

Gustavo Gutiérrez and the
Future of Liberation Theology

Edited by
Marc H. Ellis & Otto Maduro

ORBIS BOOKS

Maryknoll, New York 10545

Copyright © 1988, 1989, 1990 by Orbis Books

"Expanding the View" by Gustavo Gutiérrez appeared in the Fifteenth Anniversary edition of *A Theology of Liberation*, © 1988 by Orbis Books. The remaining essays appeared first in *The Future of Liberation Theology: Essays in Honor of Gustavo Gutirrez* © 1989 by Orbis Books.

Published in the United States of America by Orbis Books, Maryknoll, NY 10545
Manufactured in the United States of America

Library of Congress Cataloging-in-Publication Data

Expanding the view : Gustavo Gutiérrez and the future of liberation
  theology / edited by Marc H. Ellis & Otto Maduro.
      p. cm.
  Includes bibliographical references.
  ISBN 0-88344-690-1
  1. Gutiérrez, Gustavo, 1928–   . 2. Liberation theology.
I. Ellis, Marc H.   II. Maduro, Otto, 1945–
BT83.57.E96   1990
230'.046 – dc20   90-37128
                                                          CIP

Contents

Preface

MARC H. ELLIS

In July 1988 over one hundred theologians and activists from around the world gathered at Maryknoll to celebrate two significant historical events: the twentieth anniversary of the Latin American episcopal conference at Medellín, Colombia, which consolidated and furthered the participation of the Catholic church in the historic project of the poor in Latin America; and the fifteenth anniversary of the publication of the English translation of Gustavo Gutiérrez's *A Theology of Liberation*, the seminal work of Latin American liberation theology. On a more personal note, those assembled celebrated Gutiérrez's sixtieth birthday in a special tribute to his life and work as a pioneering figure in the development of liberation theology.

If the month featured numerous celebrations, including the recognition that liberation theology had in twenty years become a global phenomenon, it also was a time to look at the future and the possibilities to be found within the continuing development of liberation theology. Yet, the celebrations of both the past and of future hopes were shadowed by the ongoing suffering and struggle of the peoples represented, among them theologians from El Salvador, South Africa, the Philippines, China, India, and minorities from within the United States—Hispanics, African Americans, feminists.

In greeting Gutiérrez, Elie Wiesel, the Jewish Holocaust survivor and Nobel laureate, reflected on this suffering:

> I feel very close to Gustavo Gutiérrez, even though we have not met one another. We share a common passion for Job—whose situation intrigues and saddens us at the same time—and a need to believe that God has not abandoned creation. Some theologians would describe our approach as "liberative." And indeed, why not? I feel at home with the term "liberation." Because we are created in the image of God, we human beings ought to be free just as God is free. And, like God, we should want to be vehicles of freedom for others. Or, to put it another way, those persons are truly human who recognize themselves in the freedom of others, and who measure the extent of their own freedom by its relationship to that of their fellow human

beings. It was in order that we might be free that God chose to create us. Persons who live in fear, in oppression, in hunger, in misery, are not free. What remains free, however, is their thirst for freedom, their desire to free themselves—the part of them that God, as only God can do, loves to enlighten in the fulfillment of hope.

Yes, I feel very close to Gustavo Gutiérrez. Along with him, I believe that God is not an abstraction but a living presence. To the prisoner, God represents memory; to the starving, a smile; and to the wandering exile, a companion on the way.

The mystical tradition teaches us that even God is in exile. In the process of freeing the oppressed from their oppression, and the humiliated from their shame, we are likewise freeing God.

Wiesel's words remind us of Gutiérrez's own challenge, presented in his commentary *On Job*:

It needs to be realized, however, that for us Latin Americans the question is not precisely "How are we to do theology after Auschwitz?" The reason is that in Latin America we are still experiencing every day the violation of human rights, murder, and the torture that we find so blameworthy in the Jewish holocaust of World War II. Our task here is to find the words with which to talk about God in the midst of the starvation of millions, the humiliation of races regarded as inferior, discrimination against women who are poor, systematic social injustice, a persistent high rate of infant mortality, those who simply "disappear" or are deprived of their freedom, the sufferings of peoples who are struggling for their right to live, the exiles and the refugees, terrorism of every kind, and the corpse-filled common graves of Ayacucho. What we must deal with is not the past but, unfortunately, a cruel present and a dark tunnel with no apparent end.

In Peru, therefore—but the question is perhaps symbolic of all Latin America—we must ask: How are we to do theology while Ayacucho lasts? How are we to speak of the God of life when cruel murder on a massive scale goes on in "the corner of the dead"? How are we to preach the love of God amid such profound contempt for human life? How are we to proclaim the resurrection of the Lord where death reigns, and especially the death of children, women, the poor, indigenes, and the "unimportant" members of the society?

The success of the conference led nine months later to the publication of fifty essays representing voices from twenty-four countries in a volume titled *The Future of Liberation Theology: Essays in Honor of Gustavo Gutiérrez*. The response to this volume has been enthusiastic and many have requested an abridged and thus more accessible edition, particularly for use in course adoptions. Thus, we present this paperback edition, with a poignant greeting from Cardinal Paulo Evaristo Arns, and fourteen of the original essays, chosen, with difficulty, as representative of the ongoing discussion regarding liberation theology. We have also included Gustavo Gutiérrez's introduction to the fifteenth anniversary edition of *A Theology of Liberation* as a way of providing the framework for the ensuing essays.

Gutiérrez's essay also sets the tone for the rest of the volume, less as a definitive look at liberation theology and more as an exploration of its diverse and expanding vistas. Because of the significant impact of liberation theology, these essays also take on a meaning beyond the specific genre of liberation theology and point to future trends and possibilities for the global theological enterprise.

At the close of his essay, Gutiérrez writes of the ever-evolving expression of theological discourse within the constant of affirmed tradition. That is why it is possible for him, over the course of years, to nuance certain themes in his theology and give greater emphasis to others. Yet throughout Gutiérrez's theological writing, as I think is evident in the essays by other contributors as well, is a relationship with God and neighbor infused by commitment and love. This, then, is why Gutiérrez can see his theological writings, characterized by suffering and struggle, as a love letter to God. Few of us present at the celebration will forget the solidarity and friendship shared together, and it is a pleasure, long after the event, to offer a broader audience a taste of the future we so eagerly discussed and continue to hope for.

Introduction

CARDINAL PAULO EVARISTO ARNS

When the Apostle Paul was talking to the community of Corinth, he introduced all the themes we ought to recall on this occasion, when we want to recognize the effort, the dedication, and the influential service of one of our brothers, an evangelist and theologian. The cross of Jesus is the fount of the Spirit's wisdom on the noble road of the praxis of love, in the poverty of Christ.

The whole church in Latin America must thank the Lord for the gift he chose to give us through the person and mission of our brother and friend, Fr. Gustavo Gutiérrez, the evangelist and theologian of the poor. His evangelical dedication has been shown often and in a variety of ways. The content of his books and articles, his lectures and courses, was born out of a proclamation of the gospel, taken directly to the poorest.

Fr. Gustavo Gutiérrez realized the urgency of taking the good news to the poor. From the beginning of his pastoral life he took up his position in the field of struggle and witness. Who is unaware of the value and influence of the *cursos populares* he organized in Lima? There the suffering of the poor, the cries of the oppressed, the generosity and struggles of women swelled and grew to become a clear sign of the kingdom of God and an appeal to discernment. The living water of the Spirit gathered and rose until the word shot dazzlingly forth, insisting that the task of witness and theological reflection consists in going to "drink from our own wells." It is the well of wisdom that plants its tent among the poor. And it is there that the prophets, evangelists, and doctors have to go to seek the newness of the gospel in our generation and in our society.

The evangelist's effort was matched by his charism as a theologian and doctor. In this capacity he saw, however, that his discernment would be fruitful and lively only if it was always rooted in the unity of the church. He saw that fidelity to the church was the prerequisite for the growth and maturing of a task full of new challenges and vitally important to the poor.

As a result the fruits were not slow in coming. Fr. Gustavo's ecclesial service and fidelity were shown most clearly and significantly at the conference of the Latin American episcopate at Medellín in 1968. Who does not remember the prophetic force of the young theologian during that memorable event, which has determined the direction of evangelization in Latin America over the last twenty years?

The seed grew. It became a tree that gave shelter to all efforts in a reflection taking into account the new phenomenon of the poor as the basic historical subject of Latin American history. And who does not also recall the faithful, humble, even hidden, efforts of our theologian brother at the Puebla assembly? The prophetic and pertinent sanction of the perspective of evangelization based on the preferential option for the poor found in Fr. Gustavo one of its warmest and most eloquent defenders.

I think that the pastoral and theological work of this friend of ours brought something new to our lives and mission. When the newness of the gospel touches us and penetrates to the very life of the churches, a common first reaction is reserve and, very often, fear. Those in positions of authority either keep silent or wait to see the results. They are not always the first to accept the offered newness.

One thing I should like to do here is to bear witness to the ecclesial quality of this newness, to which our theologian proclaimed and witnessed. What he was the first to say strongly and with conviction grew out of an overall ecclesial climate. At that moment he interpreted the signs of the times in Latin America and devoted himself with all his strength to make all this reach the heart of the church's life and mission. Happily, he succeeded. In this way, the theologian's principal role was to hear what the Spirit is saying to the church through the cry of the poor and oppressed, and to see all the energies of the people of God in the perspective of liberation, which is the effective name today for the transforming power of the gospel (cf. Rom. 1:16–17). It would be worthwhile to reflect on some aspects of this newness proclaimed to us with all the love and dedication of a disciple who discovered and experienced the power of the call to follow Jesus in the way of the cross so as to reach the fullness of communion with the God of life.

We all agree that the action of thousands of women and men changed direction and outlook once they were made aware of the irruption of the poor into the life of society and the church. The poor were always with us, and at our side. Nevertheless, it was a silent presence and very often an unnoticed presence. One of the great merits of liberation theology was to call attention to the situation and to the cry of the poor as a new historical phenomenon: the irruption of the poor into society and the church is a sign of a *new historical subject* that we are seeing emerge, take form, and search for alternatives.

This fact will not fail to have an effect on the way we analyze society, look for new social models, and also look for a new way of living the ever-demanding newness of the gospel. Indeed, this new historical subject is the bearer of the newness that provokes a deep conversion and change, not merely on the individual level, but also on the community and collective level both in society and in the church. The irruption of the poor into our history is a force that summons us to the urgent task of evangelical discernment. And this discernment points to the presence of the spirit of the kingdom of God, which is revealed in this "historical power of the poor, the little ones, believers and oppressed."

Another point that calls our attention is that the poor lead us to the core of the truth that sets us free. However, this truth cannot be a naively peaceful systematization, based on the false security of a system, however brilliantly constructed. Truth is found in a continuing search, and in the midst of a hostile world built on lies and slavery. Theological discernment starting from the struggle of the poor for liberation has shown us that the search for truth is not just a matter of clarity of ideas and concepts. This experience takes place and is validated in the practice of love for the "little ones."

In this perspective, theological discernment reaches the limits of radicalness because it starts from the experience of nothing other than the absoluteness of the God of life. The hostile world of lies, which destroys the lives and liberty of the "little ones," manufactures a false image of God and constructs a set of ideas that turn into an ideal of death and disintegration.

Unfortunately, this stealthy activity of falsehood can even influence the way we seek to describe and proclaim the transcendence and the coming of the true God of life. To the extent that we keep our distance from the suffering and the struggle of the poor, we build up a particular image of God and a system of ideas that, in their certainty and assurance, are the projection of our own unjust and life-denying interests.

Fr. Gustavo Gutiérrez, in his profound meditation on the book of Job, drew our attention at an opportune moment to the fact that a radical experience of contemplation of the God of life and the prophetic power of his message will always be the product of the suffering of the innocent poor. This is the vocation, the task, of theology as the century draws to a close, to carry on looking for its strength in this experience of the God whose presence is revealed in the process of the liberation of the great majority of the peoples of our Latin American countries.

Only someone who has understood this dimension of theological discernment can appreciate, and see with pleasure, the unity of the venture of theology. Theology is one. It has one subject and central axis of judgment, the God of life, the God who comes to bring freedom and in the process is revealed as Father, Son, and Spirit of life, freedom, and love.

The unity of this judgment shows that we therefore need to practice an active and militant reading of the Bible. And the important thing in this reading is to go to the roots of the historical process in order to expose its most decisive contradictions and look for ways forward, which come from the very life of God and the historical praxis of Jesus Christ. And the unity of judgment, at this depth, shows also that the way we read and analyze the Bible as the sign and testament of the God who is coming is the same as the way we analyze the structures and contradictions of a particular social system.

Finally, the theological enterprise shines with full force when it presents itself courageously as the wisdom of the cross. Even today, many persons are still looking for signs and wonders. They want magical or mechanical formulas to transform nature. They put their trust in the logic of technology, of economics, of winning power at any price. But the person who has discovered the force of the gospel's newness from contact with the poor realizes that the wisdom that confounds the powers of the world is the wisdom of the cross.

The important thing, however, is to see how theology shows the unity and the connection between the cross of Christ and the cross of millions of poor and marginalized persons who continue to challenge us in everyday life and in the structures of our existing society. Wisdom is the image of the Son who is the word of the Father. Consequently, the task of theology is to read and reveal this image stamped by the Spirit of life on the process of the liberation of the poor. It then comes as no surprise that theology inevitably bursts forth in a rich and fruitful spirituality rising out of the communion and praxis of the poor in their search for life and freedom.

This spirituality is a call to conversion and a search for the real will of God. It is a search for the Spirit who leads us to abandon the idols of this world and wait for the coming and revelation of the Son of God in the twisting course of our present history.

The dynamism of this spirituality is found in the process of liberation itself. It is the Easter challenge of the passage from the world of law to life in the freedom of the Spirit. The experience of the Spirit and the experience of freedom occur in a single act. The Lord, we remember, is Spirit, and where the Spirit is, there is freedom.

The mission of spirituality is to proclaim and build the life of the new human person, the collective life in the alliance of freedom. To encounter the Spirit is to realize that it was for freedom that Christ set us free.

But life in the Spirit is life in the power of the gospel. It is the present force to transform and justify. The struggle for justice, to win dignity for our oppressed sisters and brothers, which is a common task, opens the paths to "justification": the transformation of the contradictions of history and society into transparency and into the calls of the Spirit. The same Spirit, united with the Son, is gradually shaping an egalitarian and friendly human race that continually cries out as a proclamation to the whole world, "Abba!" In this way this spirituality culminates in a life as sons and daughters, in a spiritual childhood whom the theologian we are honoring here stressed so much as a basis for an authentic theology and of the experience of life as a disciple of Jesus.

In a word, the great appeal that Fr. Gustavo Gutiérrez has been sending out over the last twenty years to the men and women of North and South is the word that he met among the Amerindians of Peru—*pachacuti*! We might translate it as: "Be converted, believe in the good news to the poor, and dedicate yourselves to changing our society to liberate the poor."

This is the revolution that comes from the gospel. And it is this which, enlightened and fired by the word that our brother proclaims to us, we wish to see accomplished, from hope to hope.

PART I

LIBERATION THEOLOGY
AFTER TWENTY YEARS

1

Expanding the View

GUSTAVO GUTIÉRREZ

In 1968 the Latin American bishops wrote this description of the new phase of history that was dawning among us:

Latin America is obviously under the sign of transformation and development; a transformation that, besides taking place with extraordinary speed, has come to touch and influence every level of human activity, from the economic to the religious.

This indicates that we are on the threshold of a new epoch in this history of Latin America. It appears to be a time of zeal for full emancipation, of liberation from every form of servitude, of personal maturity and of collective integration [Medellín, "Introduction," 4].

This was a vision of a new historical era to be characterized by a radical aspiration for integral liberation. However painful the Latin American situation is (and it was painful in 1968), the vision is still valid. During the intervening years much has happened to change the history of the region and bring it across the threshold of which the bishops spoke and into an ever-accelerating process.

All this creates a new challenge for those who are trying to draw inspiration for their lives from him who "dwelt among us" (John 1:14). The perspective given by faith should help us see what is at stake in the present stage of history. In this context the bishops at Medellín observed:

We cannot fail to see in this gigantic effort toward a rapid transformation and development an obvious sign of the Spirit who leads the history of humankind and of the peoples toward their vocation. We

This essay appeared as the introduction to the Fifteenth Anniversary edition of *A Theology of Liberation* (Orbis Books, 1988).

cannot but discover in this force, daily more insistent and impatient
for transformation, vestiges of the image of God in human nature as
a powerful incentive. This dynamism leads us progressively to an even
greater control of nature, a more profound personalization and fellowship, and an encounter with the God who ratifies and deepens
those values attained through human efforts [Medellín, ibid.].

My reason for beginning with these lengthy citations is that they express
so well both the historical situation of liberation theology and the perspective of faith in which it interprets this situation. (The name and reality of
"liberation theology" came into existence at Chimbote, Peru, in July 1968,
only a few months before Medellín.)[1] Ever since Medellín, the development
of liberation theology in Latin America has been accompanied by a continual awareness that we have entered into a new historical stage in the life
of our peoples and by a felt need of understanding this new stage as a call
from the Lord to preach the gospel in a way that befits the new situation.
Both of these factors condition the thinking of liberation theology, requiring
that it maintain a twofold fidelity: to the God of our faith and to the peoples
of Latin America. Therefore we cannot separate our discourse about God
from the historical process of liberation.

In the years since Medellín there has been an inevitable clarification of
this theological undertaking. Liberation theology has been welcomed with
sympathy and hope by many and has contributed to the vitality of numerous
undertakings in the service of Christian witness. At the same time it has
stimulated an interest in reflection on the Christian faith—an interest previously unknown in Latin American intellectual circles, which have traditionally been cool toward Christianity or even hostile to it. The years have
also brought serious and relevant critiques that have helped this theological
thinking to reach maturity. On the other hand, the theology of liberation
has also stirred facile enthusiasms that have interpreted it in a simplistic
or erroneous way by ignoring the integral demands of the Christian faith
as lived in the communion of the church. Finally, there has been the fore-
seeable resistance of some.

There are various reasons for these several responses. But rather than
point out the responsibilities of others, let me say simply that it is not easy
to deal with sensitive and conflictual themes—like the very reality we are
attempting to penetrate with the eyes of faith—and to find immediately
and for good the clearest and most balanced formulas in which to express
theological reflection on these themes. All language is to some extent a
groping for clarity; it is therefore necessary to deal respectfully with other
persons and with what they think they find in works written from this
theological perspective. Readers have rights that authors neither can nor
ought to deny. At every stage, therefore, we must refine, improve, and
possibly correct earlier formulations if we want to use language that is

understandable and faithful both to the integral Christian message and to the reality we experience.[2]

Recent years have witnessed an important debate on the theology of liberation in the context of the Catholic Church. It has meant some painful moments at the personal level, usually for reasons that eventually pass away. The important thing, however, is that the debate has been an enriching spiritual experience. It has also been an opportunity to renew in depth our fidelity to the church in which all of us as a community believe and hope in the Lord, as well as to reassert our solidarity with the poor, those privileged members of the reign of God. The theological labor must continue, but in pursuing it we now have some important documents of the magisterium that advise us about the path to be followed and in various ways spur us on in our quest.[3]

The passage of time has caused essentials to become clearer. Secondary elements have lost the importance they seemed to have at an earlier period. A process of maturation has been under way. But the temporal *factor* is not the only one affecting the course of liberation theology during these years. There has also been a *spatial* extension. Within the different Christian confessions and their respective traditions, thinkers have adopted the liberation perspective suggested by the message of God's reign. In this development, theological influences (which in some cases were evidently nonexistent at the beginning) have played a less important role than the impulse given by a situation of fundamental oppression and marginalization that the Christian conscience rejects and in response to which it proclaims the total gospel in all its radicalness.

Black, Hispanic, and Amerindian theologies in the United States, theologies arising in the complex contexts of Africa, Asia, and the South Pacific, and the especially fruitful thinking of those who have adopted the feminist perspective—all these have meant that for the first time in many centuries theology is being done outside the customary European and North American centers. The result in the so-called First World has been a new kind of dialogue between traditional thinking and new thinking. In addition, outside the Christian sphere efforts are underway to develop liberation theologies from Jewish and Muslim perspectives.[4]

We are thus in the presence of a complex phenomenon developing on every side and representing a great treasure for the Christian churches and for their dialogue with other religions. The clarification I mentioned earlier is thus not limited to the Latin American context but affects a process and a search that are being conducted on a very broad front today.

These considerations should not make us forget, however, that we are not dealing here solely with an intellectual pursuit. Behind liberation theology are Christian communities, religious groups, and peoples, who are becoming increasingly conscious that the oppression and neglect from which they suffer are incompatible with their faith in Jesus Christ (or, speaking more generally, with their religious faith). These concrete, real-life movements are what give this theology its distinctive character; in liberation theology, faith and life are inseparable. This unity accounts for its prophetic vigor and its potentialities.

It is not possible, when speaking of liberation theology, to pass over in silence this broad movement of Christian and religious experiments and commitments that feed reflection. In these pages I must nonetheless deal especially with the Latin American world, for it is the world closest to me and the one in which I have made my own contribution and experienced my own development.

Now that twenty years have passed since the beginning of liberation theology, it may be appropriate to review the ways in which it has found expression and the paths it has followed. I shall not try to rewrite past essays, such as those in this book, in the light of my present concerns and perspectives. I do, however, think it important and useful to call attention to what I regard as the most important points, to anticipate ambiguous interpretations, revise and make more accurate certain formulations I now consider unsatisfactory, leave aside what time has undermined, and point out some of the new and promising themes developed in recent years. The task is an extensive one; it has been begun and is underway. My intention here is to indicate some important points in that program.[5]

The "new epoch in the history of Latin America, " of which Medellín spoke, continues to be our vital context. In the language of the Bible, we are in a *kairos*, a propitious and demanding time in which the Lord challenges us and we are called upon to bear a very specific witness. During this *kairos* Latin American Christians are experiencing a tense and intense period of *solidarity, reflection*, and *martyrdom*. This direct, real-life setting enables me to go more deeply into the three points that I have for some time regarded as basic to liberation theology and have also been the primary ones in the chronological development of this theology: the viewpoint of the poor; theological work; and the proclamation of the kingdom of life. I should like to explain here what is permanent in each of these, the enrichments each has received, the development and maturation that time has effected, and the resultant evolution of ideas in the theological perspective that I have adopted.

A NEW PRESENCE

What we have often called the "major fact" in the life of the Latin American church—the participation of Christians in the process of liberation—is simply an expression of a far-reaching historical event: *the irruption of the poor*. Our time bears the imprint of the new presence of those who in fact used to be "absent" from our society and from the church. By "absent" I mean: of little or no importance, and without the opportunity to give expression themselves to their sufferings, their comraderies, their plans, their hopes.

This state of affairs began to change in Latin America in recent decades, as a result of a broad historical process. But it also began to change in Africa (new nations) and Asia (old nations obtaining their independence), and among racial minorities (blacks, Hispanics, Amerindians, Arabs, Asiatics) living in the rich countries and in the poor countries as well (including Latin American countries). There has been a further important and diversified movement: the new presence of women, whom Puebla described as "doubly oppressed and marginalized" (1134, note) among the poor of Latin America.

As a result of all this it can be said that:

The powerful and almost irresistible aspiration that persons have for liberation constitutes one of the principal signs of the times that the church has to examine and interpret in the light of the gospel. This major phenomenon of our time is universally widespread, though it takes on different forms and exists in different degrees according to the particular people involved. It is, above all, among those who bear the burden of misery and in the heart of the disinherited classes that this aspiration expresses itself with the greatest force [*Libertatis Nuntius*, 1, 1].

Liberation theology is closely bound up with this new presence of those who in the past were always absent from our history.[6] They have gradually been turning into active agents of their own destiny and beginning a resolute process that is changing the condition of the poor and oppressed of this world. Liberation theology (which is an expression of the right of the poor to think out their own faith) has not been an automatic result of this situation and the changes it has undergone. It represents rather an attempt to accept the invitation of Pope John XXIII and the Second Vatican Council and interpret this sign of the times by reflecting on it critically in the light of God's word. This theology should lead us to a serious discernment of the values and limitations of this sign of the times.

A Complex World

"Dominated peoples," "exploited social classes," "despised races," and "marginalized cultures" were formulas often used in speaking of the poor in the context of liberation theology (there was repeated reference also to discrimination against women). The point of these formulas was to make it clear that the poor have a social dimension. But the turbulent situation in Latin America has caused many to place an almost exclusive emphasis on the social and economic aspect of poverty (this was a departure from the original insight). I am indeed convinced that it is still necessary to call atttention to this dimension of poverty if we are to do more than touch the surface of the real situation of the poor, but I also insist that we must be attentive to other aspects of poverty as well.

As a matter of fact, the increasingly numerous commitments being made to the poor have given us a better understanding of how very complex their world is. For myself, this has been the most important (and even crushing) experience of these past years. The world of the poor is a universe in which the socio-economic aspect is basic but not all-inclusive. In the final analysis, poverty means death: lack of food and housing, the inability to attend properly to health and education needs, the exploitation of workers, permanent unemployment, the lack of respect for one's human dignity, and unjust limitations placed on personal freedom in the areas of self-expression, politics, and religion. Poverty is a situation that destroys peoples, families, and individuals; Medellín and Puebla called it "institutionalized violence" (to which must be added the equally unacceptable violence of terrorism and repression).

At the same time, it is important to realize that being poor is a way of living, thinking, loving, praying, believing, and hoping, spending leisure time, and struggling for a livelihood. Being poor today is also increasingly coming to mean being involved in the struggle for justice and peace, defending one's life and freedom, seeking a more democratic participation in the decisions made by society, organizing "to live their faith in an integral way" (Puebla, 1137), and being committed to the liberation of every human being.

All this, I repeat, goes to make up the complex world of the poor.[7] The fact that misery and oppression lead to a cruel, inhuman death, and are therefore contrary to the will of the God of Christian revelation who wants us to live, should not keep us from seeing the other aspects of poverty that I have mentioned. They reveal a human depth and a toughness that are a promise of life. This perception represents one of the most profound changes in our way of seeing the reality of poverty and consequently in the overall judgment we pass on it.

The same period, meanwhile, has seen a converging process in which we have become more aware that there is a racial problem among us. One of our social lies has been the claim that there is no racism in Latin America. There may indeed be no racist laws as in some other countries, but there are very rigid racist customs that are no less serious for being hidden. The marginalization of Amerindian and black populations, and the contempt in which they are held, are situations we cannot accept as human beings, much less as Christians. These populations themselves are becoming increasingly aware of their situation and are beginning to claim their most basic human rights; this new attitude carries the promise of fruitful results.

The racial question represents a major challenge to the Christian community, and one to which we are only now beginning to respond.[8] The approaching five-hundredth anniversary of the evangelization of Latin America should be the occasion for an examination of conscience regarding

the immense human cost historically connected with that evangelization—
I mean the destruction of individuals and cultures. Such an examination
will help us define a commitment of the church to races that have for
centuries been neglected and mistreated. The bold efforts of Bartolomé de
Las Casas and so many others past and present are there to point a way
we must follow in accordance with our present historical situation.

I referred above to the conditions in which women live. We in Latin
America are only now beginning to wake up to the unacceptable and inhuman character of their situation. One thing that makes it very difficult to
grasp its true character is its hiddenness, for it has become something
habitual, part of everyday life and cultural tradition. So true is this that
when we point it out we sound a bit like foreigners bent on causing trouble.
The issue was hardly raised at Medellín. Puebla, however, did initiate
reflection on it (see 834–49 and 1134). A growing number of persons are
committed to the restoration of women's rights, even as we realize more
and more clearly how intolerable the situation of women really is.

The situation of racial and cultural minorities and of women among us
is a challenge to pastoral care and to commitment on the part of the Christian churches; it is therefore also a challenge to theological reflection. In
this area we have a long way to go, but a good beginning is being made as
cultural and racial and feminist themes are addressed more and more frequently in liberation theology. The most important part will have to be
played by persons who themselves belong to these groups, despite the difficulties in the way of their doing so. It is not possible for others simply to
stand up and effectively play the part of a protagonist. But the voices of
these groups are beginning to be heard, and this development is promising.
This will certainly be one of the richest veins to be mined by liberation
theology in years ahead.

In this whole matter I have found it very helpful to enter into dialogue
with theologies developed in settings different from our own. Through
direct contacts with Christian groups in other countries and continents (as
well as through meetings with those who are trying to reflect theologically
in those contexts) I have learned much about situations different from the
Latin American. At the same time, I have gained a better understanding
and appreciation of aspects of our people that had been clear in theory
but had little or no consequence in practice. As a result, I have come to
see with new eyes our racial and cultural world, and the discrimination
against women.

Perhaps the most important fruit derived from dialogues among Third
World theologians (organized principally by the Ecumenical Association of
Third World Theologians—EATWOT) and from related activities has been
a better and deeper understanding of the world of the poor. Closely connected as we are with our peoples, we brought to these meetings a desire
to speak about the world from which we come, with its experiences and its
thinking, but little by little we learned that it was more important to listen

to what others had to say about their respective situations. Captivated as we are by the life and death of the poor of Latin America and by the riches to be found in the Christian communities that come into existence there and bear witness—even to the point of martyrdom—to the Lord in their midst, we have perhaps tended to focus our attention too much on these things. I must admit, therefore, that from these contacts with these other theologians I have grown in hope and have become more sensitive to the suffering of human groups geographically and culturally far removed from us.

The predominant characteristics of this complex and widespread world of the poor are, on the one hand, its unimportance in the eyes of the great powers that rule today's wider world and, on the other, its vast human, cultural, and religious wealth, and especially its capacity for creating new forms of solidarity in these areas.

All this takes us far from the simplistic position we were perhaps in danger of initially adopting in analyzing the situation of poverty. A fundamental point has become clear: it is not enough to describe the situation; its *causes* must also be determined. Medellín, Puebla, and John Paul II in his encyclical on work and, more recently, on social concerns, as well as in other writings, have made a forceful analysis of these causes. Structural analysis has thus played an important part in building up the picture of the world to which liberation theology addresses itself. The use of this analysis has had its price, for although the privileged of this world can accept the existence of human poverty on a massive scale and not be overawed by it (after all, it is something that cannot be hidden away in our time), problems begin when the *causes* of this poverty are pointed out to them. Once causes are determined, then there is talk of "social injustice," and the privileged begin to resist. This is especially true when to structural analysis there is added a concrete historical perspective in which personal responsibilities come to light. But it is the conscientization and resultant organization of poor sectors that rouse the greatest fears and the strongest resistance.

The tools used in this analysis vary with time and according to their proven effectiveness for gaining knowledge of social reality and finding solutions for social problems. Science is by its nature critical of its own presuppositions and achievements; it moves on to new interpretive hypotheses. It is clear, for example, that the theory of dependence, which was so extensively used in the early years of our encounter with the Latin American world, is now an inadequate tool, because it does not take sufficient account of the internal dynamics of each country or of the vast dimensions of the world of the poor. In addition, Latin American social scientists are increasingly alert to factors of which they were not conscious earlier and which show that the world economy has evolved.

Problems like unpayable foreign debt, to give but one example, are drawing attention, sharpening awareness of what lies behind them, and refining the available analytical tools (it is worth mentioning here that Medellín in

1968 called attention to the dangers of foreign indebtedness; see "Peace," 9d). It is in fact impossible to deal effectively with the poverty experienced in Latin America without following the development of the most urgent problems and without attending to factors that enable us to locate these problems in a broad and complex international context.

All this requires that we refine our analytical tools and develop new ones. The socio-economic dimension is very important but we must go beyond it. In recent years there has been an insistent emphasis, and rightly so, on the contrast between a Northern world developed and wealthy (whether it be capitalist or socialist) and a Southern world underdeveloped and poor. This approach yields a different view of the world scene, one in which it is not enough to focus on ideological confrontations or give a narrow interpretation of opposition between social classes. It also brings out the radical opposition that is the setting for the confrontation of East and West.[9] Diverse factors are making us aware of the different kinds of opposition and social conflict that exist in the modern world.

As far as poverty is concerned, an important transformation is undoubtedly taking place in the social analysis on which liberation theology depends to some extent. The change has led liberation theology to incorporate beneficial perspectives and new sources of knowledge from the human sciences (psychology, ethnology, anthropology) for its study of a reality that is intricate and shifting. To incorporate does not mean simply to add on without interrelating. Attention to cultural factors will help us to enter into mentalities and basic attitudes that explain important aspects of the reality with which we are faced. The economic dimension itself will take on a new character once we see things from the cultural point of view; the converse will also certainly be true.

There is no question of choosing among the tools to be used; poverty is a complex human condition, and its causes must also be complex. The use of a variety of tools does not mean sacrificing depth of analysis; the point is only not to be simplistic but rather to insist on getting at the deepest causes of the situation, for this is what it means to be truly radical. Responsiveness to new challenges requires changes in our approach to the paths to be followed in really overcoming the social conflicts mentioned earlier and in building a just and fraternal world, as the gospel calls upon us to do.

If we were simply to adopt the traditional approach, we would be taking the course that has always been taken in the social sciences in their contribution to analysis. But we also know that the sciences and, for a number of reasons, the social sciences in particular, are not neutral. They carry with them ideological baggage requiring discernment; for this reason the use of the sciences can never be uncritical (see the Introduction of *Libertatis Nuntius*). In consequence, both the scientific outlook itself and the Christian conception of the world call for a rigorous discernment of scientific data — discernment, but not fear of the contributions of the human disciplines.[10]

We need to make an unruffled but critical use of mediations that can help us to understand better where and how the Lord is challenging us as we face the life (and death) of our brothers and sisters.[11]

Opting for the God of Jesus

Important though it is to acquire a substantial knowledge of the poverty in which the vast majority of Latin Americans live and of the causes from which it springs, theological work proper begins when we try to interpret this reality in the light of Christian revelation.

The meaning given to poverty in the Bible is therefore a cornerstone of liberation theology. The problem of poverty is an ancient one in Christian thought, but the new presence of the poor to which I have referred gives it a new urgency. An essential clue to the understanding of poverty in liberation theology is the distinction, made in the Medellín document "Poverty of the Church," between three meanings of the term "poverty": real poverty as an evil—that is something that God does not want; spiritual poverty, in the sense of a readiness to do God's will; and solidarity with the poor, along with protest against the conditions under which they suffer.

This is the context of a theme that is central in liberation theology and has now been widely accepted in the universal church: the preferential option for the poor. Medellín had already spoken of giving "preference to the poorest and most needy sectors and to those segregated for any cause whatsoever" ("Poverty," 9). The very word "preference" denies all exclusiveness and seeks rather to call attention to those who are the first—though not the only ones—with whom we should be in solidarity. In the interests of truth and personal honesty I want to say that from the very beginning of liberation theology, as many of my writings show, I insisted that the great challenge was to maintain both the universality of God's love and God's predilection for those on the lowest rung of the ladder of history. To focus exclusively on the one or the other is to mutilate the Christian message. Therefore every attempt at such an exclusive emphasis must be rejected.

During the difficult decade of the 1970s this attitude gave rise to many experiences and resultant theological reflections in the Latin American church. In the process, formulas intended to express commitment to the poor and oppressed proliferated. This became clear at Puebla, which chose the formula "preferential option for the poor" (see the Puebla Final Document, part 4, chapter 1). It was a formula that theologians in Latin America had already begun to use in preceding years. The Puebla Conference thus gave it a major endorsement and importance.

The term "option" has not always been correctly understood. Like every term, it has its limitations; the intention in using it is to emphasize the freedom and commitment expressed in a decision. The commitment to the poor is not "optional" in the sense that a Christian is free to make or not make this option, or commitment, to the poor, just as the love we owe to all human beings without exception is not "optional." Neither, on the other hand, does the term "option" suppose that those making it do not themselves belong to the world of the poor. In very many instances, of course, they do not, but it must be said at the same time that the poor too have an obligation to make this option.

The expression "preferential option for the poor" had an important and significant predecessor. I refer to John XXIII's statement, a month before the opening of Vatican II, that the church is called upon to be a church of the poor. The reader will probably be familiar with the passage: "In face of the underdeveloped countries, the church is, and wants to be, the church of all and especially the church of the poor" (address of September 11, 1962). Let me say only that we have here two aspects of the church's life that are both demanding and inseparable: universality and preference for the poor.

In recent years the central teaching authority of the Catholic Church has issued important documents that echo the outlook of the Latin American church and use the expression "preferential option for the poor." John Paul II has used it repeatedly.[12] It is also to be found in the second Instruction of the Congregation for the Doctrine of the Faith on liberation theology (*Libertatis Conscientia*, 68). In addition, the extraordinary Synod of Bishops held in 1985 spoke as follows in its final report:

> Following the Second Vatican Council the church became more aware of its mission in the service of the poor, the oppressed, and the outcast. In this preferential option, which must not be understood as exclusive, the true spirit of the gospel shines forth. Jesus Christ declared the poor blessed (Matt. 5:3; Luke 6:20), and he himself wished to be poor for us (2 Cor. 8:9).[13]

The experience and thinking of the Latin American church have undoubtedly played a very important role in this growth of consciousness.

At both ends of the spectrum of positions on these subjects, there are those who claim that the magisterium has been trying to substitute "preferential love" for "preferential option." It seems to me, however, that any doubt on this point has been removed by John Paul II's encyclical *Sollicitudo Rei Socialis*. Speaking of "characteristic themes and guidelines" of the magisterium in the recent years, the pope says:

> Here I would like to indicate one of them: the option or love of preference for the poor. This is an option or special form of primacy in the exercise of Christian charity to which the whole tradition of the church bears witness. It affects the life of each Christian inasmuch as he or she seeks to imitate the life of Christ, but it applies equally to our social responsibilities and hence to our manner of living, and

to the logical decisions to be made concerning the ownership and use of goods [*Sollicitudo Rei Socialis*, 42].

In the final analysis, an option for the poor is an option for the God of the kingdom whom Jesus proclaims to us; this is a point that I myself have developed and discussed in depth on various occasions.[14] The entire Bible, beginning with the story of Cain and Abel, mirrors God's predilection for the weak and abused of human history. This preference brings out the gratuitous or unmerited character of God's love. The same revelation is given in the evangelical Beatitudes, for they tell us with the utmost simplicity that God's predilection for the poor, the hungry, and the suffering is based on God's unmerited goodness to us.

The ultimate reason for commitment to the poor and oppressed is not to be found in the social analysis we use, or in human compassion, or in any direct experience we ourselves may have of poverty. These are all doubtless valid motives that play an important part in our commitment. As Christians, however, our commitment is grounded, in the final analysis, in the God of our faith. It is a theocentric, prophetic option that has its roots in the unmerited love of God and is demanded by this love. Bartolomé de Las Casas, who had direct experience of the terrible poverty and decimation of Latin American Amerindians, explained it by saying: "God has the freshest and keenest memory of the least and most forgotten."[15] The Bible has much to say to us about this divine remembering, as the works of J. Dupont, among others, have made clear to us.

This same perception was confirmed by the experience of the Christian communities of Latin America and reached Puebla via the document that the Peruvian bishops prepared for the CELAM meeting. Puebla asserted that simply because of God's love for them as manifested in Christ "the poor merit preferential attention, whatever may be the moral or personal situation in which they find themselves" (no. 1142). In other words, the poor deserve preference not because they are morally or religiously better than others, but because God is God, in whose eyes "the last are first." This statement clashes with our narrow understanding of justice; this very preference reminds us, therefore, that God's ways are not ours (see Isa. 55:8).

There have certainly been misunderstandings of the preferential option for the poor, as well as tendencies, sociological and spiritualist, to play it down, and this on the part both of those who claim to favor it and those who are expressly opposed to it. It can be said, nonetheless, that the option is now an essential element in the understanding that the church as a whole has of its task in the present world. This new approach is pregnant with consequences; it is also, we must say, only in its beginnings.

THE ROLE OF REFLECTION

The rich, troubled, and creative life that the Latin American church is living as it tries to respond to the challenge set for it by the new presence of the poor calls for a deeper understanding of its own faith in the Lord Jesus. For a long time, as a result of a Latin American cultural tradition imposed by colonization, theology as practiced among us simply echoed the theology developed in Europe. Latin American theologians had recourse to European theology without any reference to its intellectual and historical context, with the result that their theology easily became a set of abstract propositions. Or else they made a painful effort to adapt European theology to a new reality, but were unable to explain the reasons for its themes and priorities or for the development of this kind of thinking, as long as the effort was undertaken in a North Atlantic framework.

The quest for models or guidelines outside itself was long characteristic of Latin American thinking, and indeed still is in some circles. But the urgency and rich resources of the commitment that many Christians were beginning to make to the process of popular liberation during the 1960s raised new questions based on Latin American reality, and they pointed to new and fruitful ways for theological discourse. Liberation theology is one manifestation of the adulthood that Latin American society, and the church as part of it, began to achieve in recent decades. Medellín took note of this coming of age and in turn made a major contribution to its historical significance and importance.

All this reminds us that this theological perspective is explicable only when seen in close conjunction with the life and commitments of Christian communities. This connection was present at the historical beginnings of liberation theology in the 1960s and is still fully operative today. It is the basis for the familiar distinction between the two phases of theological work: Christian life and reflection in the strict sense. The way in which a people lives its faith and hope and puts its love to work is the most important thing in God's eyes and is also, or ought to be, the most important in discourse about God and God's saving will.

I have already pointed out the important role played in Christian consciousness by the irruption of the poor into our history. In the development of liberation theology our awareness of this new presence has made us aware that our partners in dialogue are the poor, those who are "nonpersons"—that is, those who are not considered to be human beings with full rights, beginning with the right to life and to freedom in various spheres. Elsewhere, on the other hand, the best modern theology has been sensitive rather to the challenge posed by the mentality that asserted itself at the European Enlightenment; it is therefore responsive to the challenges posed by the nonbeliever or by Christians under the sway of modernity.

The distinction between these two approaches is not an attempt to juxtapose two theological perspectives. It tries only to be clear on their respective starting points, to see their differences, and then correctly to define relationships between the two. If we follow this line, we will avoid yielding to a tendency found in some academic settings: the tendency to regard liberation theology as the radical, political wing of European progressive theology. Such a view of liberation theology is clearly a caricature for any-one with a good knowledge of the subject. It is true, of course, that in a world of increasingly rapid communication it is not possible to do theology in a manner free of all contacts and influences; it is, however, both possible and necessary to be clear on the perduring basis and inspiration of our theological thinking. Only on that condition can there be dialogue among the various theologies that share a concern to speak of God in our day.

The Life of a People

One of the first statements of my way of understanding the theological task was that liberation theology is "a critical reflection on Christian praxis in light of the word of God." The point of this was not to try to reduce the riches of a quest to a short definition, but rather to point out a path to be followed.

In many and very different ways the Bible shows us that the doing of God's will is the main demand placed on believers. Karl Barth echoed this thought when he said that "the true hearer of the word is the one who puts it into practice." In liberation theology I accepted this traditional datum of Christian revelation because I was moved by the witness of those who were beginning to commit themselves ever more fully to the process of freeing the poor from the various servitudes from which they suffer

This commitment reflected the experience of the oppressed themselves, who were beginning to become the agents of their own destiny. During the 1950s and 60s we saw the first steps being taken in conscientization, and we saw the poor beginning to organize themselves in the defense of their right to life, in the struggle for dignity and social justice, and in a commit-ment to their own liberation. As a result, they were beginning to play a major active role that would become stronger with the passing years and that is still intensifying today amid advances and regressions. Many Chris-tians played a part in this process. It is therefore wrong to say that theo-logical thinking on liberation originated in the middle classes and that only years later did it open itself to the experience of the poor themselves. No, this experience played its part from the outset—at the level it had reached at that time. To be ignorant of this is to be mistaken about what happened at that time or even to give an explicitly false picture of it; the facts reject any such interpretation.

The praxis on which liberation theology reflects is a praxis of solidarity in the interests of liberation and is inspired by the gospel. It is the activity of "peacemakers"—that is, those who are forging shalom. Western lan-guages translate this Hebrew word as "peace" but in doing so, diminish its meaning. Shalom in fact refers to the whole of life and, as part of this, to the need of establishing justice and peace. Consequently, a praxis motivated by evangelical values embraces to some extent every effort to bring about authentic fellowship and authentic justice. For faith shows us that in this commitment the grace of Christ plays its part, whether or not those who practice it are aware of this fact.

This liberating praxis endeavors to transform history in the light of the reign of God. It accepts the reign now, even though knowing that it will arrive in its fullness only at the end of time. In this practice of love, social aspects have an important place on a continent in which socio-economic structures are in the service of the powerful and work against the weak of society. But in my understanding of it, "praxis" is not reducible to "social aspects" in this narrow sense. The complexity of the world of the poor and lowly compels us to attend to other dimensions of Christian practice if it is to meet the requirements of a total love of God.

In saying this I am not trying to make the Christian commitment less demanding and radical, but only to bring out the breadth of vision and the courage needed if we are to enter into the world of the poor and respond to their varied aspirations for justice and freely given friendship. As I have traveled this road, I have learned much in recent years; various experiences of being a part of the world of the poor have brought me to a less theoretical knowledge of that world and to a greater awareness of simple but profoundly human aspects of it, apart from which there is no truly liberating commitment.[16] The struggles of those who reject racism and machismo (two attitudes so deeply rooted in the culture and custom of peoples and individuals), as well as of those who oppose the marginalization of the elderly, children, and other "unimportant" persons in our society, have made me see, for example, the importance of gestures and ways of "being with" that some may regard as having little political effectiveness.

In addition, the experience of these years has shown me that generous solidarity with the poor is not exempted from the temptation of imposing on them categories foreign to them and from the risk of dealing with them in an impersonal way. Sensitivity to these and other dangers is part of a human and Christian praxis whose truly liberating effects extend to those also who are trying to carry on such a praxis for the benefit of the poor and exploited. If there is no friendship with them and no sharing of the life of the poor, then there is no authentic commitment to liberation, because love exists only among equals. Any talk of liberation necessarily refers to a comprehensive process, one that embraces everyone. This is an insight that has been repeated again and again since the beginnings of liberation theology and that in my own case has become much more firmly established and has acquired a much greater importance with the passage of the years.

Christian life is commitment in the form of an acceptance of the gift of the reign of God. It is also, and necessarily, prayer. There is no life of faith that does not have its contemplative dimension. The Latin Americans who are struggling for justice are also persons who believe and hope. They are oppressed persons, but also Christians who, like Mary in her Magnificat, remember their obligations of thankfulness and of surrender to God in prayer.

This outlook is characteristic of the faith of our Latin Americans. They cultivate a form of prayer that the modern mind is likely to regard as primitive if not downright superstitious. But, although it is true that various factors play a part in this way of living the faith, it would be a serious mistake to stop at a superficial analysis and not to discern the profound sense of God that this prayer manifests in ways that are perhaps not very enlightened but that are not therefore any less legitimate. Deeply rooted as it is in this popular devotion, while also drawing nourishment from the wellspring of protest against repression and the demand for freedom, the prayer life of the Christian communities that are engaged in the process of liberation possesses great creativity and depth. Those who have claimed from time to time that Latin America has been losing the spirit of prayer have shown only that they themselves are remote from the everyday life of the poor and committed sectors of our peoples.

Those working at a theology of liberation in the Asian context have likewise tried to bring out the deeply contemplative side of that continent on which ancient and magnificent religions of the human race have left such a profound imprint. Aloysius Pieris, theologian of Sri Lanka, describes the Asian peoples as both poor and religious.[17] Both of these conditions point the way to a radical and complete liberation.[18] Meanwhile, black theology in the United States has drawn fruitfully on the liberating and religious perspectives that find expression in black music.[19] Theology done in the African context has likewise always been open to the cultural riches of the African peoples; religion is an essential element of this cultural treasure.

Prayer is a privileged way of being in communion with Christ and of "keeping all these things in our heart," as his mother did (see Luke 2:51). The Gospels tell us of various occasions when the Lord went apart to pray. Contemplation was an essential part of his life. At one of the most difficult times in his experience, he rebuked his disciples for having been unable to persevere with him during his final prayer, which had turned into a difficult struggle for him. Luke tells us that he was "in an agony" as he struggled for his life, so that his sweat "became like great drops of blood" (22:44-45). Our communion with the prayer of Jesus must reach this point of "agony"—that is, of combat (that is what the Greek word *agōnia* means). But this requirement is not difficult for those to understand who are putting their own lives on the line as they share the lot of the stripped and impoverished of Latin America.

Those, therefore, who adopt the liberation perspective must have the sensitivity that is needed for understanding and cultivating the celebratory and contemplative dimension of peoples who find in the God of their faith the source of their demand for life and dignity. Nothing could be further from my mind, however, than to defend in this context the kind of spiritualism that serves as a refuge from the troubles and sufferings of daily life. I am referring rather to the desire and determination to live simultaneously, and to the reciprocal enrichment of each, two pursuits that the Western mind often separates. The Western mind persistently applies this dichotomy in interpreting both the more spontaneously unified behavior of other peoples and cultures, and the theological efforts made in that context.

I am, of course, not speaking of syntheses that are fully successful and without defects, but rather of a process whereby one achieves a diversified presence that is open to a variety of experiences and that progresses only amid setbacks; that develops gradually and deploys creativity. It is a matter of honesty to recognize this fact, as well as of respect for those who bear this witness. We find ourselves, then, in the presence of a process that locates us at a point at which it is impossible to separate solidarity with the poor *and* prayer. This means that we are disciples of Christ, who is both God and a human being.

What we see here is an authentic spirituality—that is, a way of being Christian. It is from this rich experience of the following of Jesus that liberation theology emerges; the following constitutes the practice—at once commitment and prayer—on which liberation theology reflects. The increasing number of Latin American theological works on spirituality in recent years are not as it were an appendix to works on other themes; they represent rather a deeper penetration of the very wellspring from which this kind of theological thinking flows.

The work done on spirituality will help to develop, more than has hitherto been done, a traditional aspect of theology (one whose existence was acknowledged at an early date in the perspective I am adopting here)— namely, its function as wisdom. Discourse on faith is knowledge that brings with it a taste for its object; it is a spiritual tasting of the word of the Lord, and, as such, it nourishes our life and is the source of our joy.

In liberation theology the way to rational talk of God is located within a broader and more challenging course of action: the following of Jesus. Talk of God supposes that we are living in depth our condition as disciples of him who said in so many words that he is the Way (see John 14:6). This fact has led me to the position that in the final analysis the method for talking of God is supplied by our spirituality. In other words, the distinction of two phases in theological work is not simply an academic question; it is, above all, a matter of lifestyle, a way of living the faith. Being part of the life of our people, sharing their sufferings and joys, their concerns and their struggles, as well as the faith and hope that they live as a Christian community—all this is not a formality required if one is to do theology; it is a requirement for being a Christian. For that reason, it also feeds the very roots of a reflection that seeks to explain the God of life when death is all around.

The Locus of Reflection

The historical womb from which liberation theology has emerged is the life of the poor and, in particular, of the Christian communities that have arisen within the bosom of the present-day Latin American church. This experience is the setting in which liberation theology tries to read the word of God and be alert to the challenges that faith issues to the historical process in which that people is engaged. Revelation and history, faith in Christ and the life of a people, eschatology and praxis: these are the factors that, when set in motion, give rise to what has been called the hermeneutical circle. The aim is to enter more deeply into faith in a God who became one of us, and to do so on the basis of the faith-filled experience and commitment of those who acknowledge this God as their liberator.[20]

The major challenges to which theology must respond will come, therefore, from the demands of the gospel as seen today in the development of an oppressed but Christian people. Since liberation theology is a critical reflection on the word of God received in the church, it will make explicit the values of faith, hope, and love that inspire the praxis of Christians. But it will also have to help in correcting possible deviation on the part of those who reject the demands for participation in history and the promotion of justice that follow from faith in the God of life, and also on the part of those who run the risk of forgetting central aspects of Christian life, because they are caught up in the demands of immediate political activity.

Because liberation theology takes a critical approach, it refuses to serve as a Christian justification of positions already taken. It seeks to show that unless we make an ongoing commitment to the poor, who are the privileged members of the reign of God, we are far removed from the Christian message. It also wants to help make the commitment to liberation increasingly evangelical, effective, and integral. Theology is at the service of the evangelizing mission of the Christian community; it develops therefore as an ecclesial function. Its task is one that locates it within the church, for it is there that it receives revelation and there that it is nourished by the charisms of prophecy, government, and teaching that reside in the church and guide its efforts.

It is clear from what I have been saying that when I call reflection in the strict sense a *second* stage of theological work, I am by no means saying that is *secondary*. Discourse about God comes second because faith comes first and is the source of theology; in the formula of St. Anselm, we believe in order that we may understand (*credo ut intelligam*). For the same reason, the effort at reflection has an irreplaceable role, but one that is always subordinate to a faith that is lived and receives guidance within the communion of the church.

The first stage or phase of theological work is the lived faith that finds expression in prayer and commitment. To live the faith means to put into practice, in the light of the demands of the reign of God, these fundamental elements of Christian existence. Faith is here lived "in the church" and geared to the communication of the Lord's message. The second act of theology, that of reflection in the proper sense of the term, has for its purpose to read this complex praxis in the light of God's word. There is need of discernment in regard to the concrete forms that Christian commitment takes, and this discernment is accomplished through recourse to the sources of revelation.[21] The ultimate norms of judgment come from the revealed truth that we accept by faith and not from praxis itself. But the "deposit of faith" is not a set of indifferent, catalogued truths; on the contrary, it lives in the church, where it rouses Christians to commitments in accordance with God's will and also provides criteria for judging them in the light of God's word.

For all these reasons, a principal task of "reflection on praxis in the light of faith" will be to strengthen the necessary and fruitful links between orthopraxis and orthodoxy. The necessity of this circular relationship between the two is a point frequently underscored in liberation theology; as is always the case in dealing with essential dimensions of one and the same reality, it is not possible to accept the one and belittle the other. More than that, any attempt to focus on only one means the loss of both; orthopraxis and orthodoxy need one another, and each is adversely affected when sight is lost of the other.[22] The polemical manner in which this subject is sometimes treated (whether for or against the union of orthopraxis and orthodoxy) should not make one forget that fidelity to the message of Jesus requires one not to impoverish or mutilate it by choosing where no choice is possible. In a key passage of Mark's Gospel (8:27–33) he speaks in an incisive way of the necessity of this enriching circular relationship.[23] Theology as critical reflection must make its contribution to this profound unity.

Starting from Christian praxis (commitment and prayer), theology seeks to provide a language for speaking about God. It deals with a faith that is inseparable from the concrete conditions in which the vast majority and, in a sense, even all the inhabitants of Latin America live. Among us the great pastoral, and therefore theological, question is: How is it possible to tell the poor, who are forced to live in conditions that embody a denial of love, that God loves them? This is equivalent to asking: How can we find a way of talking about God amid the suffering and oppression that is the experience of the Latin American poor? How is it possible to do theology "while Ayacucho lasts"?[24] As the church, the assembly of the disciples of Jesus, we must proclaim his resurrection to a continent scarred by "inhuman" (Medellín, "Poverty," 1) and "antievangelical" (Puebla, 1159) poverty. As I said earlier, in the final analysis poverty means death. Liberation theology had its origin in the contrast between the urgent task of proclaiming the life of the risen Jesus and the conditions of death in which the poor of Latin America were living.

Theology done in such a setting has something in common with all theology: dialogue with the prevailing culture or, in our case, with the various cultures to be found in Latin America. This dialogue has barely begun, and it has a long way to go. In conducting it, we will be greatly helped if we adopt the view of theology as wisdom, which I mentioned above—that is, if we see theology as knowledge shot through with the "savored" experience first of God but then also of the people and culture to which we belong. In the contributions that I myself have been able to make to liberation theology, my frequent references to Felipe Guamán Poma de Ayala, César Vallejo, José Carlos Mariátegui, and José María Arguedas, among others, have had the purpose precisely of communicating some of this "savor." These men are all Peruvians who have experienced their own time in depth; they have been deeply involved in the sufferings and hopes of our peoples and have been able to express, as few others have, the soul of the nation, its Amerindians and mestizos. But, I repeat, this is an area in which far more remains to be done than has so far been accomplished.

This approach makes it urgent that we acquire a better understanding of our history. A people that knows the past that lies behind its sufferings and hopes is in a better position to face and reflect on the present. Furthermore, we must learn from the attempts made to understand the faith by Christians who are able to face up intensely to their times and to appeal to the gospel with clarity and courage. These men and women try to see clearly amid the changes of history and, in many cases, try to oppose the interests of the powerful. I am thinking here of the witness given by many sixteenth-century missionaries who did not forget the demands of the kingdom of life when they were faced with cruel exploitation and death being inflicted on the Amerindians. Among those missionaries, Bartolomé de Las Casas was perhaps the one who saw most deeply into the situation and best articulated a theological reflection based on it. He was, however, only *primus inter pares*, for he had many companions who shared his commitment and his hope. The witness of all those persons should feed the life of the Christian community today, for it is one tributary of the great ecclesial tradition within which every sound theology is located.

Although theology is a language for communicating God, in every place it must display the inflections given it by those who formulate it and those to whom it is directed. Every language has a number of dialects. The language of Jesus the Nazarene (like that of Peter, his disciple, to whom they said: "Your accent betrays you": Matt. 26:73) undoubtedly showed him to be a native of Galilee and seemed odd to the inhabitants of Jerusalem. Our theological language is subject to the same rule; it takes its coloring from our peoples, cultures, and racial groupings, and yet we use it in an attempt to proclaim the universality of God's love. This accent may not be to the liking of those who until now have regarded themselves the proprietors of theology and are not conscious of their own accent (to which, of course, they have every right) when they speak of God.

This dialogue between faith and culture in Latin America is accompanied by another, which is different in character but highly important and derives its tone from the first. I am referring to the encounter in recent years of theologies springing from human contexts unlike our own. I mentioned earlier the dialogue between the theologies of the Third World, in which the theologies emerging from minorities in different countries all participate on an equal footing. But this further dialogue does not stop at the borders of the Third World. There have also been very profitable meetings with representatives of types of theological thinking that originate in Europe and North America. Then there is the encounter with the feminist perspective in theology and with the new and challenging contribution this is making.[25] My impression is that the deeper importance of this dialogue is to be found, not in the coming together of theologians, but in the communication established among Christian communities and their respective historical, social, and cultural contexts, for these communities are the real subjects who are actively engaged in these discourses of faith.

In my view, the fact that any understanding of the faith has its roots in the particularity of a given situation should not cause us to neglect the comparison of what we are doing with efforts being made at the level of the universal church. Particularity does not mean isolation. It is true, of course, that each type of theological thinking cannot, and ought not, be applied mechanically to situations different from that in which it arose; whence the foolishness of attempts to do just that with liberation theology, as if it resembled a pharmaceutical prescription. But it is no less true that any theology is discourse about a universal message. For this reason, and to the extent that it springs from an experience that is both deeply human and deeply Christian, every theology also has a universal significance; or, to put it more accurately, every theology is a question and challenge for believers living other human situations.

Authentic universality does not consist in speaking precisely the same language but rather in achieving a full understanding within the setting of each language. The book of the Acts of the Apostles tells us that the reason for the astonishment felt by the speakers of different languages who were gathered in Jerusalem on Pentecost was not that the apostles all spoke in a unique tongue but that "we hear, all of us in *our own native language*" (Acts 2:6-8). The goal, then, is not uniformity but a profound unity, a communion or *koinōnia*. One element in this Christian *koinōnia* (which extends far beyond mere intellectual dialogue) is the understanding that the various forms of theology exist within a profound ecclesial communion and give a richly diversified expression to the truth proclaimed by the Only Son.

FRIENDS OF LIFE

Christians are witnesses of the risen Christ. It is this testimony that calls us together in a permanent way as the church and at the same time is the very heart of the church's mission. The realization that life and not death has the final say about history is the source of the joy of believers, who experience thereby God's unmerited love for them. To evangelize is to communicate this joy; it is to transmit, individually and as a community, the good news of God's love that has transformed our lives.

Theology is at the service of this proclamation of the reign of love and justice. Nothing human falls outside the purview of the reign, which is present in history and is transforming it, while also leading it beyond itself. Liberation theology made this perspective its starting point as it attempted to show the meaning of the proclamation of the gospel for the history of Latin America. This is indeed the most important point in this type of theological thinking—namely, that its major concern is with the proclamation of the gospel to the peoples of Latin America. This concern gave birth to it and continues to nourish its efforts.

The major achievement of the Latin American church from 1968 to 1988 was that it renewed with unwonted energy its mission of evangelization and, ultimately, of liberation. It is in this context that we must understand what the preferential option for the poor means. As a result, throughout Latin America (including sectors that used to regard themselves as estranged from the church) and on the international stage, the church has acquired a presence it never had before. Various factors have played a part in producing this result (which is in fact an ongoing process); one of them is liberation theology, which has in large measure articulated the way in which the Latin American Christian community now proclaims its message.

The witness given by Christians has, of course, inevitably elicited resistance and painful hostility. One thing is nonetheless certain: the commitment made by a church that is conscious of the necessity of proclaiming and building a peace based on justice for all, but especially for those who today suffer more from despoliation and mistreatment, has left its mark on the history of Latin America during these years. The Latin American church has made this commitment in many forms throughout the length and breadth of the region, and it has even begun to make its voice heard outside its own borders. Echoing the gospel itself, the Second Vatican Council called on the entire church to make such a commitment. It is the special characteristic of the Christian community that it goes out into the world to "make disciples of all nations" (Matt. 28:20) and is therefore never satisfied with successes already obtained. It must continually go out of itself and look forward in expectation of the Lord's coming.

To Liberate = To Give Life

The historical process in which Latin America has been involved, and the experiences of many Christians in this process, led liberation theology to speak of salvation in Christ in terms of liberation. This approach meant listening to the "muted cry [that] wells up from millions of human beings, pleading with their pastors for a liberation that is nowhere to be found in their case" (Medellín, "Poverty," 2). Puebla added that this cry "might well have seemed muted back then" but today it is "loud and clear, increasing in volume and intensity, and at times full of menace" (no. 89). In speaking thus, the two episcopal conferences were displaying a manifest fidelity to the message of the God who acts in history to save a people by liberating it from every kind of servitude. Continuing in the line of Medellín and Puebla, Pope John Paul II addressed these strong and sensitive words to the bishops of Brazil: "The poor of this country, whose pastors you are, and the poor of this continent are the first to feel the urgent need of this *gospel of* radical and integral *liberation.* To conceal it would be to cheat them and let them down" (letter of April 1986; emphasis added).

The combination of these two factors—the message that is at the heart of biblical revelation, and the profound longing of the Latin American peoples—led us to speak of liberation in Christ and to make this the essential content of evangelization. Something similar has been happening in other sectors of the human race and in the Christian churches present in their midst. There is a longing for liberation that wells up from the inmost hearts of the poor and oppressed of this world and opens them to receive the saving love of God. This longing is a sign of the active presence of the Spirit. The various theologies of liberation to which I have referred are meeting the challenge and giving expression to the experience and its potentialities.

From the outset, liberation was seen as something comprehensive, an integral reality from which nothing is excluded, because only such an idea of it explains the work of him in whom all the promises are fulfilled (see 2 Cor. 1 :20). For that reason I distinguished three levels or dimensions of liberation in Christ, and Puebla made the distinction its own (nos. 321–29). First, there is liberation from social situations of oppression and marginalization that force many (and indeed all in one or another way) to live in conditions contrary to God's will for their life. But it is not enough that we be liberated from oppressive socio-economic structures; also needed is a personal transformation by which we live with profound inner freedom in the face of every kind of servitude, and this is the second dimension or level of liberation.

Finally, there is liberation from sin, which attacks the deepest root of all servitude; for sin is the breaking of friendship with God and with other human beings, and therefore cannot be eradicated except by the unmerited redemptive love of the Lord whom we receive by faith and in communion with one another. Theological analysis (and not social or philosophical analysis) leads to the position that only liberation from sin gets to the very source of social injustice and other forms of human oppression and reconciles us with God and our fellow human beings.

This idea of total liberation was inspired by that of integral development that Paul VI set down in *Populorum Progressio* (no. 21). With the help of this concept the pope showed how it is possible, without confusing the various levels, to affirm the deeper unity of a process leading from less human to more human conditions. Among the "more human" conditions he listed "finally and above all: faith, a gift of God accepted by human good will, and unity in the charity of Christ, who calls us all to share as

offspring in the life of the living God, the Father of all human beings."[26]
The pope was obviously speaking of human possibilities in a broad sense,
not disregarding the gratuitousness of faith and love.

There is no slightest tinge of immanentism in this approach to integral
liberation. But if any expression I have used may have given the impression
that there is, I want to say here as forcefully as I can that any interpretation
along those lines is incompatible with my position. Moreover, my repeated
emphasis (in my writings) on the gratuitousness of God's love as the first
and last word in biblical revelation is reliable evidence for this claim. The
saving, all-embracing love of God is what leads me to speak of history as
profoundly one (in saying this, I am not forgetting the distinctions also to
be found within history). What I want to say when I speak of history has
been expressed with all desirable exactness by the Peruvian bishops:

> If we mean by the "history of salvation" not only those actions that
> are properly divine—creation, incarnation, redemption—but the
> actions of human beings as they respond to divine initiatives (either
> accepting them or rejecting them), then there is in fact only one
> history, for the uncertain endeavors of human beings, whether they
> like it or not, whether they even know it or not, have their place in
> the divine plan [*Documento sobre teología de la liberación,* October
> 1984].

History is, after all, the field where human beings attain to fulfillment as
persons and in which, in the final analysis, they freely say yes or no to God's
saving will.[27]

Liberation theology is thus intended as a theology of salvation. Salvation
is God's unmerited action in history, which God leads beyond itself. It is
God's gift of definitive life to God's children, given in a history in which
we must build fellowship. Filiation and fellowship are both a grace and a
task to be carried out; these two aspects must be distinguished without
being separated, just as, in accordance with the faith of the church as
definitively settled at the Council of Chalcedon, we distinguish in Christ a
divine condition and a human condition, but we do not separate the two.

This christological truth enables us to determine what gives unity and
what creates duality in the process of liberation—that is, in the saving work
that God calls us to share. Puebla makes the distinction in carefully worded
language at the end of its lengthy section on the three dimensions or levels
of liberation:

> We are liberated by our participation in the new life brought to us by
> Jesus Christ, and by communion with him in the mystery of his death
> and resurrection. But this is true only on condition that we live out
> this mystery on the three planes described above, without focusing
> exclusively on any one of them. Only in this way will we avoid reducing

the mystery to the verticalism of a disembodied spiritual union with God, or to the merely existential personalism of individual or small-group ties, or to one or another form of social, economic, or political horizontalism [no. 329].

The very complexity of the concept of liberation prevents us from reducing it to only one of its aspects.

In this view of the matter, a key point—not always assigned its proper value—is consideration of the "second level," that of human liberation. I myself have always emphasized its necessity in my writings. This emphasis reflected an effort to avoid the narrow approach taken to liberation when only two levels, the political and the religious, are distinguished. The political and the religious are certainly basic aspects of liberation, but exclusive attention to them often led to a simple juxtaposition of them, thus impoverishing both, or else to an identification of the two, thus perverting the meaning of both. From the theological standpoint, emphasis on the mediation of aspects of the human that are not reducible to the socio-political made it easier to think of the unity of all the aspects without confusing them; it also made it possible to speak of God's saving action as all-embracing and unmerited, without reducing it to a purely human set of activities, as well as to interrelate the political and the religious dimensions while also incorporating the needed ethical perspective. Inertia, however, caused some to interpret the three dimensions distinguished by liberation theology and later by Puebla in the more common, but theologically different, perspective: the relationship between only two of the levels or dimensions.

In his Apostolic Exhortation *Evangelii Nuntiandi* Paul VI made this very careful statement:

We must . . . say the following about the liberation that evangelization proclaims and endeavors to bring about:

a) It cannot be limited purely and simply to the economic, social, and cultural spheres but must concern the whole person in all dimensions, including the relationship to an "absolute" and even to *the* Absolute, which is God.

b) It is based, therefore, on *a conception of human nature*, an anthropology, which can never be sacrificed to the requirements of some strategy or other, or to practice, or to short-term effectiveness.[28]

As a matter of fact, in the measure that we acquire a more complete vision of the process of liberation, its humblest level—the second—helps us understand better the process in the light of faith.

All that has been said shows that liberation, understood as an integral whole (as it is in liberation theology and in the Medellín documents), is the central theme of evangelization. It is at the heart of the Lord's saving work and of the kingdom of life; it is what the God of the kingdom seeks.

On the Way of Poverty and Martyrdom

It is general knowledge that, inspired by John XXIII, Cardinal Lercaro and other fathers of the Vatican Council wanted to make the evangelization of the poor the main focus of their discussions. A passage of the Constitution on the Church (*Lumen Gentium*), a document that bears witness to this desire, says that the church, like its founder, lives "in poverty and oppression" (no. 8). And one of the richest documents issued by the council says that the church, like its Lord, must walk the "way of poverty" (decree *Ad Gentes*, on the Missionary Activity of the Church, 5).

Living as it does in a part of the world marked by massive poverty and by the premature and unjust death of multitudes, the Latin American church made its own the outlook of Pope John and pleaded at Medellín that "the church in Latin America should be manifested, in an increasingly clear manner, as truly *poor, missionary, and paschal*, separate from all temporal power and courageously committed to the liberation of each and every person" ("Youth," 14, emphasis added).

Evangelizing means proclaiming, by word and action, that Christ has set us free, but evangelization is always an ecclesial task. The church must be a sign of the kingdom within human history. Medellín saw that the sign must take the form of being poor, missionary, and paschal. Puebla thought that what Medellín wanted was beginning to come about: "Bit by bit the church has been dissociating itself from those who hold economic or political power, freeing itself from various forms of dependence, and divesting itself of privileges" (no. 623).[29]

John XXIII, whom we can never forget, called the church "the church of the poor," and John Paul II has forcefully repeated the phrase on various occasions. The church is to be a poor church at the service of all, but paying special attention to the lowly of this world. The base-level ecclesial communities, which Paul VI greeted as "a real hope for the church" (*Evangelii Nuntiandi* 58) and which Puebla described as "an important ecclesial event that is peculiarly ours" (no. 629), are a manifestation of the presence of the church of the poor in Latin America. These communities are a major source of vitality within the larger Christian community and have brought the gospel closer to the poor and the poor closer to the gospel—and not only the poor but, through them, all who are touched by the church's action, including those outside its boundaries.

This entrance into the world of the poor has had numerous consequences for the mission of the Latin American church. Among others, it has made it possible to discern new dimensions in the part to be played by the poor themselves in the work of evangelization and in meeting the challenges that this raises. This has been a foundational experience that has nourished reflection within the framework of liberation theology and to which Puebla referred in an often cited passage:

Commitment to the poor and oppressed and the rise of grassroots communities have helped the church to discover the evangelizing potential of the poor. For the poor challenge the church at all times, summoning it to conversion; and many of the poor incarnate in their lives the evangelical values of solidarity, service, simplicity, and openness to accepting the gift of God [no. 1147].

On the other hand, if we view the church as the people of God—that is, as the sum total of Christians—we must acknowledge that the effort to see the Lord's features in the faces of the Latin American poor (see Puebla, 31–40) has also brought difficulties within the church itself. Some have felt their interests adversely affected by the challenges the bishops have issued, and they have tried to draw a curtain of silence around these alerts. Others have gone further: from their positions of power they have openly violated the human rights defended in the documents of the church and have struck hard at Christians who were trying to express their solidarity with the poor and oppressed. These latter cases have led bishops (in Paraguay, Brazil, and Chile, for example) to adopt means not often used in our day, such as the excommunication of those who claimed to be Christians but disrespected the most basic demands of the gospel message.

Others have claimed to be in solidarity with the poor and oppressed but have acted impetuously, not respecting their slower pace or making them uneasy, and have therefore often met with rejection.

The various forms of de facto opposition are typical in periods of difficulty and change. At such times it becomes even more urgent to try to strengthen the unity that is the church's fundamental vocation. Such is the commandment and prayer of the Lord: that we may be one as the Father and the Son are one with each other and in us, in a unity that we must live out while not withdrawing from a world in which the forces of evil tend to divide us (see John 17). This communion—common union—is at once a gift of God and a task set for us.

The growing solidarity of the Latin American church with the poor and oppressed has at times raised concerns about the religious outlook at work in this movement. Is this commitment causing the church to lose its identity? The matter is important because the preservation of identity by each partner in a dialogue is undoubtedly an indispensable condition for the authenticity of dialogue itself. The church's raison d'être is to be found in the mission that Christ gave it: the mission of preaching the gospel. Only if the church maintains this identity can it engage in a dialogue that is fruitful for salvation.

Today, perhaps more than at other periods, certain tendencies within the church make it necessary to strengthen our ecclesial identity in fidelity to the Lord and in the determination to serve those to whom we preach the word. But a proper involvement in the world of the poor by no means detracts from the church's mission; rather in such involvement the church finds its full identity as a sign of the reign of God to which all human beings are called but in which the lowly and the "unimportant" have a privileged place. Solidarity with the poor does not weaken the church's identity but strengthens it. Paul VI gave memorable expression to this truth in his address at the close of the council, when he answered criticisms of its alleged excessive humanism.[30]

It is true, however, that we must pay a high price for being an authentic church of the poor. I am referring not to the cost entailed in the manner of life and action proper to the church, but to that inflicted by the hostile reactions that the church meets in its work. In present-day Latin America this means frequent attacks on the church and its representatives and, more concretely, the determination to hamper their mission, undermine their reputation, violate their personal freedom, deny them the right to live in their own country, and make attempts against their physical integrity, even to the point of assassination. The experience of the cross marks the daily life of many Christians in Latin America.

The murder of Archbishop Oscar Romero was undoubtedly a milestone in the life of the Latin American church. This great bishop risked his life in his Sunday homilies (the same was true of Bishop Angelelli in Argentina) and in interventions that responded to First World pressures by continually calling for a peace founded on justice. He received several death threats. The murder of six priests in El Salvador during the preceding years was already a warning close to home. A month before his own death he said with reference to those in power in his country: "Let them not use violence to silence those of us who are making this demand; let them not continue killing those of us who are trying to bring about a just distribution of power and wealth in our country." Calmly and courageously he continued: "I speak in the first person because this week I received a warning that I am on the list of those to be eliminated next week. But it is certain that no one can kill the voice of justice."

He died—they killed him—for bearing witness to the God of life and to his predilection for the poor and the oppressed. It was because he believed in this God that he uttered an anguished, demanding cry to the Salvadoran army: "In the name of God and of this suffering people whose wailing mounts daily to heaven, I ask and beseech you, I order you: stop the repression!" The next evening his blood sealed the covenant he had made with God, with his people, and with his church. Martyrdom (in the broad sense of the term) is the final accomplishment of life; in this case, it was a concrete gesture toward the poor and thereby an utterly free encounter with the Lord.

Those who have given and are now giving their lives for the gospel demonstrate the consistency that the gospel demands. The Apostle St. James (1:8 and 4:8) warns us against the danger of being "double-minded" (*dipsychos*)—that is, of speaking in one way and acting in another. What brought Jesus to his death, and is bringing his present-day followers to their death, is precisely the coherence of message and commitment. It has traditionally been said that the church is enriched by the blood of the martyrs; the present vitality, amid distress, of the people of God in Latin America is due in great part to the same experience.

The testimony given by martyrdom shows clearly how ignoble are the maneuverings of the powerful, their accusations, and their fears, and how far removed from the gospel they are. The men and women—and there are many of them today in Latin America—who bear witness to their faith in the resurrection of the Lord are proof that they who sow death will depart empty-handed and that only they who defend life have their hands filled with history.

CONCLUSION

In speaking of liberation theology I have been referring to a vast movement now to be found in various parts of the world. The longing for liberation from every form of servitude (which John Paul II has once again called "something noble and legitimate": *Sollicitudo Rei Socialis*, 46), as well as the active presence of the gospel in Christians who share this longing, have given rise to a quest and a praxis; these in turn are the soil in which is rooted an understanding of the faith at the service of the church's mission of evangelization.

Twenty years after the beginning of liberation theology in Latin America and, more importantly, twenty years after the decisive event of Medellín, new challenges face us. This is the best reason for deepening our fidelity to the God of life, to the church that is called to be a sign of the reign of God, and to the oppressed who are struggling for their liberation. In his letter to the bishops of Brazil (April 1986) John Paul II said:

Liberation theology is not only timely but useful and necessary. It should be seen as a new stage, closely connected with earlier ones, in the theological reflection that began with the apostolic tradition and has continued in the great fathers and doctors, the ordinary and extraordinary exercise of the church's teaching office, and, more recently, the rich patrimony of the church's social teaching as set forth in documents from *Rerum Novarum* to *Laborem Exercens*.

Liberation theology is in fact "a new stage" and, as such, strives to be in continuity with the teaching of the church. This theology, in my understanding of it, does indeed seek to be "closely connected" with the church's teaching. In my opinion, its power and importance are due to a *freshness* or newness that derives from attention to the historical vicissitudes of our peoples, for these are authentic signs of the times through which the Lord continually speaks to us. At the same time, its power and importance are due to the *continuity* that leads it to sink its roots deep in scripture, tradition,

and the magisterium. These factors play a determining role in the continuing evolution of a theology that aims at being "a reflection on praxis in
the light of faith." I have been discussing this evolution in the preceding
pages, and it is within it that I locate myself.

In connection with the fifth centenary of the coming of the gospel to
these lands, John Paul II has spoken of the need for "a new evangelization."
The expression has far-reaching implications. The preaching of the reign
of God is always something new, just as the commandment of love which
Christ left us is continually new (see John 13:34). But there are many other
reasons for speaking of a renewed evangelization in Latin America. The
cumulative experience and reflections of the last few decades can serve as
a springboard capable of giving a major impetus to this task.

One of the great achievements of these years has been the vital presence
of the gospel in our midst. The change begun at Medellín and ratified at
Puebla gave many a new vision of the church in Latin America. Despite
our tremendous problems and the especially painful conditions in which
the vast majority of Latin Americans live, it can be asserted that the Christian community in Latin America is experiencing a fruitful and vital period,
a period that is certainly not any easy one to deal with but that is heavy
with promise. It is therefore cause for concern, and sometimes for anguish,
to see the resistances and hostilities of some among us to the most fruitful
trends in pastoral practice and in theology.

The challenges we face in Latin America are, of course, very great, and
the changes needed are radical, even within the church. That is why Puebla
several times called for the conversion of all Christians and of the church
as a whole in face of the poverty prevalent throughout the region (see part
4, chapter 1, "A Preferential Option for the Poor"). We must nevertheless
face our new situations with faith and love; according to the Bible, fear is
the opposite of both. In the Gospels the words "Have no fear" are a
response to a "man of little faith" (Matt. 14:26–31). St. John, for his part,
tells us that where there is love there is no fear (1 John 4:18).

I am not saying that we should urge imprudence and thoughtlessness,
but only that we should be convinced that the Spirit will lead us to the
whole truth (see John 16:13). His presence is visible in the new face of the
Christian community in Latin America: the face of a church that is poor,
missionary, and paschal. We would betray and sin against the Spirit if we
were to lose what has been gained in these years by Latin American Christians and non-Christians.

John XXIII has left a standard in this area, one that cannot be bettered.
In a passage that reflects his strong sense of the God who "makes all things
new" (Rev. 21:5) and his deep spirit of hope, the pope said with crystal
clarity:

> Today more than ever, certainly more than in previous centuries, we
> are called to serve humankind as such, and not merely Catholics; to

defend above all and everywhere the rights of the human person, and not merely those of the Catholic Church. Today's world, the needs made plain in the last fifty years, and a deeper understanding of doctrine have brought us to a new situation, as I said in my opening speech to the Council. It is not that the Gospel has changed: it is that we have begun to understand it better. Those who have lived as long as I have were faced with new tasks in the social order at the start of the century; those who, like me, were twenty years in the East and eight in France, were enabled to compare different cultures and traditions, and know that the moment has come to discern the signs of the times, to seize the opportunity and to expand the view.[31]

To expand our view—beyond our little world, our ideas and discussions, our interests, our hard times, and—why not say it?—beyond our reasons and legitimate rights. The church in Latin America must combine its forces and not wear itself out in discussions from which it derives little strength. In this way it will be able to "seize the opportunity" for a new evangelization to be carried on in solidarity with all, beginning with the poorest and least important in our midst. To this end we must hear the Lord speaking to us in the signs of the times; they call for interpretation but more than anything else, they call for a commitment to others that will make us friends of him who is "the friend of wisdom" (Wisd. 11:26).

Allow me to end with a personal story. Some years ago, a journalist asked whether I would write *A Theology of Liberation* today as I had two decades earlier. In answer I said that though the years passed by, the book remained the same, whereas I was alive and therefore changing and moving forward thanks to experiences, to observations made on the book, and to lectures and discussions. When he persisted, I asked whether in a love letter to his wife today he would use the same language he used twenty years ago; he said he would not, but he acknowledged that his love perdured. My book is a love letter to God, to the church, and to the people to which I belong. Love remains alive, but it grows deeper and changes its manner of expression.

—translated from the Spanish by Matthew O'Connell

NOTES

1. My lecture entitled "A Theology of Liberation," which had been delivered to a national meeting of lay persons, religious, and priests, was published first in Lima and then, a few months later, in Montevideo (MIEC, Pax Romana, 1969). It was expanded and delivered again at a meeting of Sodepax (Cartigny, Switzerland, 1969). It appears in English in Alfred Hennelly, ed., *Liberation Theology: A Documentary History* (Orbis, 1990), pp. 62–76.

2. I have endeavored to meet this obligation by reassessing my original insights

in various forums. I have done so in books—*Beber en su propio pozo* (1983; English translation, *We Drink From Our Own Wells,* Orbis, 1984); *Hablar de Dios desde el sufrimiento del inocente* (1986; English translation, *On Job: God-Talk and the Suffering of the Innocent,* Orbis, 1987); *El Dios de la Vida* (1988)—and in numerous interviews for newspapers and periodicals. I have also taken account of recent discussions in my book, *La verdad los hará libres* (1986; English translation, *The Truth Shall Make You Free* [Orbis, 1990]).

3. I have in mind especially the two Instructions of the Congregation for the Doctrine of the Faith—*Libertatis Nuntius,* 1984, translated in *Origins,* 14 (1984-85) 193-204, and *Libertatis Conscientia,* 1986, translated in *Origins,* 15 (1985-86) 713-28—and the important letter of John Paul II to the bishops of Brazil (April 1986), translated in *Origins,* 16 (1986-87) 12-15. All are reprinted in Hennelly, op. cit.

4. See M. H. Ellis, *Toward a Jewish Theology of Liberation* (Orbis, 1987).

5. I have added to the body of the book a few notes that aim at revising and completing, as far as possible, aspects discussed in this Introduction. The section "Faith and Social Conflict," in chapter 12, is a reformulation of the section "Christian Fellowship and Class Struggle" found at the same point in the first edition.

6. I sought to highlight this connection by dedicating *A Theology of Liberation* to two dear friends: José María Arguedas, a Peruvian writer on Indian culture, and Henrique Pereira Neto, a black priest in Brazil. That same intention was in my mind when I wrote the opening lines of the original introduction: "This book is an attempt at reflection, based on the gospel and the experiences of men and *women* committed to the process of liberation, in the oppressed and exploited land of Latin America."

7. Some aspects of this world have been discussed at length in my *We Drink From Our Own Wells* (Orbis, 1984).

8. At the beginning of a year dedicated to calling attention to the plight of the black population, the Brazilian bishops wrote as follows: "The Campaign of Fellowship 1988 is one more summons to the preferential option for the poor for which the gospel calls. The black community is suffering the consequences of its past enslavement. But awareness of this also makes us aware of other social sectors in Brazil that are not given sufficient attention by the liberating fellowship of Christians and by Brazilians generally in their solidarity with one another" (*Ouvi o clamor desto povo. Texto base,* 1987).

9. On this subject, see the encyclical *Sollicitudo Rei Socialis,* 20-22.

10. On the subject of Marxist analysis, *Octogesima Adveniens* of Paul VI (1971) and the letter of Father Arrupe (December 1980) provide important distinctions and guidelines for this work of discernment.

11. I have dealt at length with these themes in "Teología y ciencias sociales," *Páginas,* 63-64 (September 1984), and in *The Truth Shall Make You Free,* pp. 53-84.

12. For example, in the encyclical *Redemptoris Mater* (March 1987), 37, and in his address at Ars, France (May 1987).

13. Final Report 11, in *Origins,* 15 (1985-86) 450.

14. See, e.g., *On Job; The Truth Shall Make You Free,* pp. 141-73; and *El Dios de la Vida.*

15. "Cartaal Consejode Indias" (1531), in *Obras escogidas* (Madrid: BAE, 1958), p. 44.

16. See *We Drink From Our Own Wells,* pp. 124-26.

17. "Towards an Asian Theology of Liberation: Some Religio-Cultural Guide-

lines," in *Asia's Struggle for Full Humanity,* V. Fabella, ed. (Orbis, 1980), pp. 75-95.

18. See the Final Statement of the Fifth EATWOT Conference (New Delhi, August 1981) in *Irruption of the Third World,* V. Fabella and S. Torres, eds. (Orbis, 1983), p. 201: "It is well known that liberation (*mukti*) has been a perennial quest of the world religions. Although the emphasis has been on internal and spiritual liberation, their search also includes dimensions with social relevance: the stress on freedom from greed as well as from overattachment to material or mental possessions and to one's private self. Voluntary poverty, so central to Asiatic religious ideals, and the simplicity of lifestyle it implies, are powerful antidotes to capitalist consumerism and to the worship of mammon."

19. J. Cone, *The Spirituals and the Blues: An Interpretation* (New York: Seabury, 1972).

20. All this is clear for Latin America, but it is also valid for other perspectives adopted in the area of liberation theology, as South African theologian Allan Boesak wisely says in his *Farewell to Innocence* (Orbis, 1977), p. 7: "While we acknowledge that all expressions of liberation theology are not identical, we must protest very strongly against the total division (and contrast) some make between Black Theology in South Africa and Black Theology in the United States; between Black Theology and African theology; between Black Theology and the Latin American theology of liberation. As a matter of principle, we have therefore treated all these different expressions within the framework where they belong: the framework of the theology of liberation."

21. As the Peruvian bishops said in dealing with this subject, "for Christians the supreme norms of truth in ethical and religious matters are to be found in revelation as interpreted by those who have legitimate authority to do so. Every theology must be based on revelation as contained in the deposit of faith. With that as its starting point it can reflect on anything and everything, including praxis, which is always subordinate to revelation" (*Documento sobre teología de la liberación* [October 1984], 44).

22. See *The Truth Shall Make You Free,* pp. 100–105.

23. See *We Drink From Our Own Wells,* pp. 45–51.

24. These are questions I have asked in my book *On Job.* (Ayacucho, a city in Peru that has been buffeted by poverty and violence, is a Quechuan name meaning "the corner of the dead.")

25. On undertakings in this area in Latin America, see *El rostro femenino de la teología* (San José, Costa Rica: DEI, 1986; English translation, Elsa Tamez, ed., *Through Her Eyes: Women's Theology from Latin America* [Orbis, 1989]), which is a collection of the position papers read by various women theologians at the "Reunión Latinoamericana de Teología de la Liberación desde la perspectiva de la mujer" (Buenos Aires, 1985).

26. Translated in J. Gremillion, ed., *The Gospel of Peace and Justice: Catholic Social Teaching Since Pope John* (Orbis, 1976), p. 393.

27. On this point, see my *The Truth Shall Make You Free,* pp. 116-27.

28. *The Pope Speaks,* 21 (1976) 19.

29. Still echoing Medellín, Puebla would say at a later point: "We opt for . . . a church that is a sacrament of communion . . . a servant church . . . a missionary church . . . that commits itself to the liberation of the whole human being and all human beings" (13014).

30. Address of December 7, 1965: "It might be said that all this and everything

else we might say about the human values of the Council have diverted the attention of the Church in Council to the trend of modern culture, centered on humanity. We would say rather not diverted but *directed*. ... If we remember, venerable brothers, and all of you, our children, gathered here, how in everyone we can and must recognize the countenance of Christ (Matt. 25:40), the Son of Man, especially when tears and sorrows make it plain to see, and if we can and must recognize in Christ's countenance the countenance of our heavenly Father—'He who sees me,' Our Lord said 'sees also the Father' (John 14:9)—then our humanism becomes Christianity, our Christianity becomes centered on God. To put it differently, a knowledge of the human person is, of necessity, a prerequisite for a knowledge of God" (in *Catholic Mind* 64, no. 1202 [April 1966] 62-63).

31. Words dictated to Cardinal Cigognani on May 24, 1963, shortly before the pope's death. The passage is cited in Peter Hebblethwaite, *Pope John XXIII: Shepherd of the Modern World* (Garden City, N.Y.: Doubleday, 1985), pp. 498-99 (emphasis added).

PART II

INTERPRETATIONS, DISPUTED QUESTIONS

2

The Birth of Liberation Theology

PENNY LERNOUX

The first time I read Gustavo Gutiérrez's *A Theology of Liberation* was during Christmas 1977, just after the birth of my daughter. And I have always associated the book with birth and hope—the birth of the infant Jesus and the arrival of my own child, after many years of hoping; and the growth of a new faith among the Latin American poor in which the central vision is the hope of the resurrection, not defeat by death on the cross.

All birth is wondrous, but the emergence of such faith seems to me nothing less than miraculous. Latin American Catholicism, as I remember it in the early 1960s, was a narrow, stifling religion that encouraged fatalism. Rituals were somber, joyless; effigies spoke only of suffering and death—statues with multiple wounds, paintings of a profusely bleeding Christ, a weeping virgin Mary. If there was light, the Latin Americans did not perceive it. The poor believed it was God's will that they be downtrodden, for so they had been taught for centuries. "I'm a nothing"—a phrase heard frequently among the poor—summarized the widespread feeling of cultural and religious inferiority.

Consequently, when the Latin American bishops at their hemisphere meeting in Medellín in 1968 announced a preferential option for the poor, many were amazed and incredulous. Even before the Second Vatican Council in the early 1960s, changes had been occurring in some Latin American churches, notably those of Brazil, Chile, and Peru, but they were limited primarily to the middle classes. Similarly, Vatican II did not impact Latin America at the time of the council because it was seen as a European and hence middle-class event. Nevertheless, seeds had been planted among a small but influential group of Latin American bishops, such as Brazil's Dom Helder Câmara; the Chilean bishop, Manuel Larraín; and Cardinal Juan Landázuri Ricketts, the archbishop of Lima, as well as among young Latin American theologians studying in Europe, including Gutiérrez.

Vatican II produced numerous and far-reaching reforms, but perhaps the most important for future developments in Latin America was the redefinition of the church as a community of believers—the "people of God." The expression conveyed the biblical image of the Hebrew people in exodus, and for the church of Vatican II it symbolized a community on the move in search of a deeper understanding of faith. When translated into Spanish and Portuguese, however, "people of God" took on an even deeper meaning, for it became *Pueblo* or *Povo de Dios*—and *pueblo* has always been understood as the masses, the poor.

It was from this particular social location—*el pueblo*—that Gutiérrez and other Latin American theologians developed their original vision: a theology grounded in the reality of poverty. And it was this vision that prevailed at the Medellín Conference, particularly in the documents on justice and peace, which Gutiérrez helped write as an official *peritus* at the meeting.[1]

Like all others, theologians are a product of their environment. Most of them work in intellectual centers removed from the strivings and hardships of ordinary persons, and this is reflected in the sometimes esoteric quality of their writings. The first generation of liberation theologians was trained in such environments, primarily in Germany, France, and Belgium, but on their return to Latin America they found the real world in the slums and rural villages. So they put away their books in French and German, and began to learn a new theology based on the experience of the impoverished masses. This was no academic exercise but an awakening that came from actually living with the poor—being exposed to the hunger, smells, noises, and sickness that comprise the daily struggle for survival in an overcrowded Third World slum.

Gutiérrez, for example, began to compare the reality of the poor neighborhood where he lived in Lima with what he had learned in middle-class Europe, and found that the two worlds were as remote as different planets. His analysis of the causes of poverty and injustice in Latin America would have added little to the debate—the statistics of misery were well known—had he written as a social scientist, but Gutiérrez was a priest who felt passionately about the suffering he experienced in Lima's slums. He therefore focused on the religious dimensions of the issue, producing a new understanding of faith, truth, and grace from the perspective of the Latin American poor.

Looking at Peru's history, which was typical of Latin America's tragedy, he rejected the trickle-down theory of development that the United States had tried to sell the Latin Americans through the Alliance for Progress. It had not worked and would not work, Gutiérrez concluded, because the majority would continue in bondage to the rich. The only answer was economic and political liberation from a neo-colonial relationship with the United States and Europe and from internal structures of oppression. The basis for his analysis of liberation was not Marxist revolution but the exodus and Christ's good news to the poor of freedom and oppression. Therein lay its originality, for in the framework of Catholic Latin America the God of the exodus and the Christ of the poor were much more radical than the unintelligible dialectics of Marxist intellectuals.

Gutiérrez also reinterpreted classic doctrines of sin to include the sins of societies as, for example, the U.S. behavior toward Latin America and that of the Peruvian oligarchy toward the country's campesinos. It was not enough to seek liberation from personal sin, he argued, for faith also meant a commitment to work for social justice. Conversion demanded society's transformation, not just a change of heart.

The call to change unjust structures was clearly political, but then the Latin American church had always been political. Originally it had been the proselytizing arm of the Spanish empire, the Inquisition being its CIA. It took Spain's part in the wars of independence and afterward allied itself with the most reactionary elements among the Latin American elites. Gutiérrez wanted the church to change sides; neutrality was impossible, he said, because of the church's historical influence in Latin America. Silence was also a political statement in support of the status quo.

Although it was not yet known as liberation theology, Gutiérrez's ideas received official sanction from the bishops' meeting at Medellín. Three years later his classic work, *A Theology of Liberation*, appeared, giving the new theology a name and winning worldwide attention as one of the most influential works of the period.

If there is a single message in Gutiérrez's book it is that God has historically been on the side of the poor. And it was this message that the impoverished masses gleaned from the bishops' declarations at Medellín — at first disbelieving, only gradually comprehending that poverty and repression were not foreordained by God but the result of man-made structures that could be changed.

In a culture imbued with Catholicism, such a message was political dynamite. Most poor Latin Americans had never heard of Marx or Lenin; many do not know the name of the president of their country. But most believe in God, and many families have a Bible, even if they cannot read it.

Many soon learned to do so through church-sponsored literacy classes, using the Bible as a primer and the adult literacy techniques of the Brazilian educational philosopher Paulo Freire, which teach the poor to understand their reality and the reasons for their oppression. In contrast to traditional rote catechism classes, the Bible readings emphasize the themes developed by liberation theology, showing the people that God has repeatedly taken the side of the humble and powerless.

Such education led to the creation of Christian base communities, in which small groups (20 to 30 families) of impoverished peasants or slum dwellers meet regularly, particularly in areas with a shortage of priests, to reflect on what it means to be a poor Christian in Latin America. In many parts of Latin America the communities have developed into local versions of the early New England town hall meetings. For the first time in their lives, persons are able to express themselves freely and without fear, and to take common action to alleviate their suffering—for example, through the construction of a health clinic or a road.

By the mid-1970s, when base communities had spread throughout Latin America, it had become clear to the upper classes and the military that they were a threat to their entrenched privileges. At the time, most of Latin America was under the boot of military dictatorships, and these regimes were determined to wipe out all dissent. They were able to destroy political parties, labor unions, a free press, and other opposition, but they failed to stop the growth of the base communities, because the institutional church gave them its protection. Hundreds of priests and nuns, and even some bishops, were threatened, arrested, tortured, murdered, or exiled, yet the church stood firm. Because of the church's institutional power—most dictators were Catholics, as well as 90 percent of the population—the military regimes did not close the churches, and the churches, particularly the base communities, became surrogates for democracy.

The experience of the 1970s, when tens of thousands of persons were assassinated or "disappeared" and when the poor became even poorer, indelibly marked the Latin American church. The Medellín documents had shown intellectual and pastoral vision, but only in the 1970s did the institution really become a church of the poor, through its suffering with and on behalf of the victims of repression. In such countries as Brazil the church's call for democracy in secular society was echoed in the church itself, which became more pluralistic, open, and dedicated to the priorities of the poor, such as agrarian reform and a more equal distribution of national wealth. At the start of the base community movement the Brazilian bishops had seen the communities as a means of converting the poor, but by the end of the 1970s the poor had converted the Brazilian church.

That conversion has given the church unprecedented influence in Brazil. For example, in the 1960s two-thirds of the Catholic university students polled in Rio de Janeiro called themselves "atheist" because the church "is on the side of an order that is unjust and antipeople." By 1978 three-quarters of the students declared themselves "believers" because the church had become the voice of the voiceless. Slum dwellers expressed similar feelings. "In 1978, seeing that the church was helping the people, I began to participate again," said a lapsed Catholic who is active in a popular movement. "It wasn't that I stayed away from the church for all those years, but rather the church that stayed away from the people."[2]

Although Brazil's church is more advanced than others in the region in its institutional commitment to a "people of God," bishops in other countries have also worked toward that vision, sometimes at the cost of their lives, as shown by the martyrdom of El Salvador's Archbishop Oscar Romero and Argentina's Bishop Enrique Angelelli, both assassinated by right-wing death squads. Indicative of such commitment was the regional meeting of bishops in Puebla, Mexico, in 1979, which not only reaffirmed Medellín but went beyond it by singling out the base communities as a model for the future and by making a more realistic assessment of the many obstacles that stand in the way of political and economic change.

Religious who work with the poor in Latin America often observe that they will not live to see the fruit of the seeds they are planting, for change in Latin America, Archbishop Câmara once noted, is measured in centuries. Twenty years of work having produced approximately 300,000 base communities—not much perhaps for the effort and blood expended—yet as pointed out by the Swiss Catholic writer Walbert Bühlmann, the miracle is that a seed should have been planted at all.[3]

Although the base communities are small in number relative to the total population, political scientists argue that the religious empowerment brought about by the communities is among the most significant political developments in Latin America in recent decades. The communities are primarily concerned with prayer, but because of their reflective reading of the Bible, and the application of such readings to their own reality, they have developed a new faith in themselves. The communal solidarity fostered by the communities and the living out of faith in daily life have had a multiplier effect on many slum neighborhoods and rural villages, where community members have been instrumental in the formation of other organizations, such as amateur drama groups, women's clubs, labor unions, and peasant federations. For the first time in the region's history, intermediate groups of poor persons have emerged to seek reforms at the local, regional, and national level. Unlike mass organizations manipulated by traditional politicians and populists, these groups are genuinely representative of and responsive to the poor.[4]

Indicative of the potential of such groups is the experience of Salvador, a sprawling slum in the sterile desert surrounding Lima. Salvador was founded in 1971 after the military government forced residents from the overcrowded inner city slums to what are euphemistically known as "young towns"—that is, outlying slums. The left-of-center regime was not a typical Latin American dictatorship, however, for it broke the stranglehold of the Peruvian oligarchy through a sweeping agrarian reform and labor reforms that enabled workers a share in the profits and ownership of industries. The regime also promoted grassroots organizations that became the seeds of self-government in the "young towns" and elsewhere. Although many of the reforms were halted after a takeover by more traditional generals in the second phase of the military government, the Peruvian church continued to carry the banner for social justice. Strongly influenced by Gutiérrez's ideas, it took the lead among the Latin American churches in upholding the preferential option for the poor in the years immediately following Medellín. In the first episcopal assembly after Medellín, for example, the bishops announced that the Peruvian church would look for ways and means of living out evangelical poverty, in order to become the "sacrament of union of the people with God and of the people among themselves." All social reforms, they said, should promote the idea of "elevating the way of being a human person" and of "announcing the liberation of the oppressed." To attain that goal, they proposed to encourage conscientization among the poor and to help them create new social structures that would fulfill the needs and aspirations of the people.[5]

Consequently, church persons were present from the time of Salvador's founding, including a group of teachers led by Salvador's current mayor, Michel Azcueta, a soft-spoken Spaniard who has worked for more than two decades with the Peruvian poor. The slum's first school, "Fe y Alegría," was constructed with church help, and socially concerned priests, nuns, and lay persons played a key role in the population's growing conscientization and in the promotion of base communities. "The church realized from the beginning that it had to become involved and accompany the people on their journey," said a teacher working with the Teresian Institute, one of several church groups active in the area.[6]

Early on, the people adopted a slogan: "Because we have nothing, we will make everything." They did so in the face of overwhelming odds, including widespread poverty and unemployment as well as the sterile site itself. Today the "young town" of 400,000 boasts several schools, in addition to popular libraries, a weekly newspaper, a radio station, four churches, and the beginnings of an industrial park. Many of the older homes have brick and cement walls instead of the flimsy reed mats used in the original construction. Even the poorest sections are shaded by trees in spite of the scarcity of water in the surrounding desert. The women, who lug cans of water from a distant well, first use the water for cooking, then recycle it for washing. Whatever remains of the dirty liquid is thrown on the saplings, which miraculously thrive.

The people's accomplishments reflect Salvador's block-by-block organization in which communal work is shared—for example, through neighborhood soup kitchens or Sunday morning building activities, such as the repair of a roof. Each neighborhood elects representatives to Salvador's local government, which holds regular assemblies to discuss problems of concern to the people, such as running water and road construction. Paralleling this civic structure is a network of base communities whose elected lay leaders set pastoral priorities. Like Salvador's schools, which encourage self-reliance and democracy, the communities are charged with preparing their children for First Communion and other important rites.

Building together has deepened the people's faith commitment; it has also made Salvador one of the most politically effective neighborhoods in Lima. For example, Salvador has had electricity since 1975, but the nearby slum of Tablada, which is older than Salvador, obtained electricity only in 1983. Some of the most active lay leaders, such as Azcueta, have become involved in local politics through election to municipal office or have taken an important role in the development of labor unions. Such slum movements serve as a counterweight to the right-wing military and their allies in the upper classes as well as to the viciousness of the *Sendero Luminoso* guerrillas.

While the movement's main contribution is political, it is politics with a difference because, as Azcueta observed, religious values challenge the system. "I think one begins to change," he said, "when one goes back to the Gospels and discovers a small but very important difference. When one says that it is necessary to help the poor, I think everybody accepts that. But often we hide the causes of poverty—it's easy to say that someone is poor because he is lazy or a drunkard or squanders his money. But when one decides to serve the exploited, that's when it becomes clear that poverty just doesn't happen and that there are reasons for it. That's when a political commitment arises, but it's a commitment that originates in faith itself."[7]

As in Brazil, where the commitment to the poor converted the church, the experience of the Peruvian church in places like Salvador has had a profound effect on the institution. "The church of Peru has been revitalized because of its social commitment," said Bishop José Dammert Bellido. "Many Christians, lay persons as well as priests, have discovered a richness of the Gospels that perhaps before had been ignored because of merely spiritualist or ritualistic actions." For that, said Dammert, the church owes a debt of gratitude to Gustavo Gutiérrez, who "was the first Peruvian to make a contribution to Catholic theology. Before, we had some good imitators of European theological formulas, but it is now recognized that Gutiérrez contributed to something native." And it is the native—"the eruption of the poor onto the world scene," as another Peruvian bishop put it—that has proved both a gift and challenge to First World Christianity.[8]

Phillip Berryman, a popular American religious writer, points out that liberation theology was the herald of a large movement "of the excluded—women, nonwhites, the poor—onto the stage of history."[9] Just as women are asserting a new role in First World societies, Third World peoples seek their own cultural and political identification. The imperial powers, the United States and the Soviet Union, face a cultural explosion that promises to fragment spheres of influence, making the imposition of a single political, economic, or religious model more difficult. But that is also true of a centralized Roman order. Despite attempts to restore the old ways, such efforts are doomed, not only by the changes brought about by Vatican II but also by the demographic shift in Catholicism. With 907 million members, Catholicism now ranks as the world's largest religion. At home in every continent, it is culturally and ethnically more diverse than at any other time in its history. But if it were given a face, its color would not be white: more than half the Catholic population lives in the Third World. By the end of the century the figure will rise to 70 percent, with Latin America accounting for the largest number. Such a far-reaching change has occurred only once before in Christianity, wrote the late Jesuit theologian Karl Rahner—in the first century, when the primitive church, under the Apostle Paul, opened itself to the diverse cultures of the ancient world.[10]

Gutiérrez's gift was to announce this conversion and to give us a glimpse of the spirituality and community found among God's chosen—the poor. The experience of such poverty and the struggle with and for the Latin American poor "is our well," he says of the liberation theologians.[11] It is also a well for us to drink from in the First World—so rich in material goods but so barren in the humanity and solidarity that characterize daily life in the slums and villages of the Third World. Yet seeds have also begun to sprout here and there in the United States, just as they did in Latin America after Medellín. In such promise lies the fulfillment of the "people of God."

NOTES

1. *Medellín Conclusiones* (Bogotá: Secretariado general del CELAM, 1973).

2. Tarcisco Beal, "Brazil's New Church: Revolution and Reaction" (unpublished paper), n.d.; Scott Mainwaring, "Brazil: The Catholic Church and the Popular Movement in Nova Iguacu, 1974–1985," in *Religion and Political Conflict in Latin America* (Chapel Hill: University of North Carolina Press, 1986), pp. 124–55; author's interviews, São Paulo, Nov. 1984.

3. Walbert Bühlmann, *The Church of the Future* (Maryknoll, N.Y.: Orbis, 1986), pp. 26, 89–100.

4. On the political significance of religious empowerment by the base communities, see, for example, Daniel Levine, "Religion and Politics: Drawing Lines, Understanding Change," *Latin American Research Review*, 20/1 (1985) 185–200; Maria Helena Moreira Alves, "Grassroots Organizations, Trade Unions, and the Church," *IDOC Bulletin*, (Rome), 16/4 (Aug. 1985); Jane Kramer, "Letter from the Elysian Fields," *The New Yorker*, March 2, 1987; *Religion and Political Conflict in Latin America*, ibid.; José Marins and Teolide M. Trevisan, *Comunidades Eclesiales de Base* (Bogotá: Ediciones Paulinas, 1975); *Uma Igreja que Nasce do Povo* (summarizing the results of the first national meeting of base communities in Brazil) (Petrópolis: Vozes, 1975); Paul Singer and Vinicius Caldeira Brant, *O Povo em Movimento* (Petrópolis: Vozes, 1982); Frei Betto, *O Que e Comunidade Eclesial de Base* (São Paulo: Editora Brasiliense, 1981); idem, *CEBS, Rumo á Nova Sociedade* (São Paulo: Ediçioes Paulinas, 1983); Domingos Barbé, *Fé e Ação* (São Paulo: Ediçoes Loyola, 1980); and the Rev. Joseph G. Healey, "Comunidades Cristianas de Base," *Latin American/North American Church Concerns*, Monograph no. 1, Institute for Pastoral and Social Ministry, n.d.

5. Bishop Alban Quinn, "The Church and the Option for the Poor in Peru" (London: Catholic Institute for International Relations, 1982), p. 13.   6. *Vida Nueva* (Madrid), Nov. 7, 1987.

7. Ibid.

8. Interview by Mario Campos with Bishop José Dammert Bellido, *La República* (Lima), Sept. 9, 1984; Quinn, "The Church."

9. Phillip Berryman, *Liberation Theology* (New York: Pantheon, 1986), p. 215.

10. *Newsweek*, Dec. 9, 1985; *America*, June 13, 1987.

11. Robert McAfee Brown, "Drinking From Our Own Wells," *The Christian Century*, May 9, 1984.

3

The Originality of the Theology of Liberation

LEONARDO BOFF

The importance of Gustavo Gutiérrez transcends the borders of Latin America because what he has created possesses a universal theological significance. His achievement has been to have helped to create a new epistemological field within Christian thought. Creators of an epistemological break—that is, of a new possibility of interpreting reality—are rare. In modern Western philosophy such creators have included Descartes, Kant, Hegel, Marx, Heidegger. In theology there have been Thomas Aquinas, Luther, Bultmann, Rahner. Gustavo Gutiérrez has opened up a new and promising path for theological thinking; he has invented a new way of doing theology. The claim of the theology of liberation as a current within Christianity is to be a new way of thinking about God and everything connected with God. Liberation is not just one item on the theologians' list. It is a horizon against which everything is illuminated, a plane in which everything has a position and acquires new meaning. In other words, liberation is not just an entry in an encyclopedia alongside other entries. It is a perspective from which all the other terms are understood, analyzed, and explained. This basic claim of the theology of liberation was recognized by the papal magisterium in April 1987 in a letter to the bishops of Brazil, which contains the explicit statement that "the theology of liberation should constitute a new stage . . . in theological reflection."[1]

In 1971, when he gave literary form to his intuitions about liberation theology, Gutiérrez wrote, quite deliberately:

The theology of liberation offers us not so much a new theme for reflection as a *new way* to do theology. Theology as critical reflection on historical praxis is a liberating theology, a theology of the liberating

transformation of the history of humankind and also therefore that
part of humankind—gathered into *ecclesia*—which openly confesses
Christ. This is a theology which does not stop with reflecting on the
world but rather tries to be part of the process through which the
world is transformed.[2]

This is the new element introduced by Gutiérrez, a new task for Christian
reflection: to examine critically, in the light of faith and revelation, historical
action, to understand theology as one moment in a much larger process of
the transformation of the world and its relationships.

THE CREATION OF A NEW EPISTEMOLOGICAL FIELD

In history Christians have provided themselves with the theology they
needed and were able to produce. So, in the first centuries, they constructed
a sapiential theology: confronting the word of God with life, they were able
to draw lessons of wisdom and spirituality which sustained their existence
and helped them to understand the challenges of culture. Later, when the
demands of society were for rationality, Christianity developed a theology
that was a form of rational and systematic knowledge. Now there was not
just faith and life, but faith and critical and systematic reason. It is a permanent requirement of faith that Christ and the pursuit of the kingdom
should be in the deepest sense human and therefore rational. Theology as
rational knowledge deals with this permanent requirement. But it also takes
up the challenge of the social process, which gives reason a central place.
In this encounter between faith and reason, theology takes on the role of
an organized form of knowledge, as critical and as systematic as possible.

In the present period Christians are associating themselves with the
desire for social transformation, as embodied particularly in the aspirations
of the oppressed. Human history is above all else "an opening to the
future . . . a task, a political occupation, through which we orient and open
ourselves to the gift which gives history its transcendent meaning: the full
and definitive encounter with the Lord and with other humans."[3]

In this context living and reflecting on faith means doing a theology of
history, of human action, of social events, of politics, and of transformation.
And if this transformation is produced from the position of and in the
interests of the oppressed (who are the great majority of Christians) and
by the oppressed themselves (and their allies), this theology will be a theology of liberation. The theology of liberation will therefore be the theory
of a particular form of action. In Gustavo Gutiérrez's words: "Theological
reflection would then necessarily be a criticism of society and the Church
insofar as they are called and addressed by the Word of God; it would be
a critical theory, worked out in the light of the Word accepted in faith and
inspired by a practical purpose—and therefore indissolubly linked to historical praxis."[4]

To have identified this challenge, to have formulated its conscious and critical expression, this is Gustavo Gutiérrez's achievement. In doing so he has inaugurated forever a new way of doing theology, from the transforming action, from within the action, as a critique of and in support of this action for liberation. Now that this epistemological field has been opened, believing reason can put up its buildings and design its landscape. With this new grammar of interpretation and action, it incorporates other, older, forms of doing theology. This is another achievement of Gustavo Gutiérrez: he has succeeded in giving due weight to, and consciously and creatively incorporating, the other ways of doing theology, theology as wisdom and theology as rational knowledge. Not only that, but he has also shown that theology as critical reflection on historical action presupposes and needs the other two, because they represent permanent functions of any Christian thought. Nonetheless he forces them into a fundamental redefinition. Now wisdom and rational knowledge take their starting point and context from historical action. The relationships between faith and life, on the one hand, and faith and science must now be placed within the context of the relationship between faith and society or faith and social injustice, which gives rise to the practice of liberation.[5]

This presentation of theological method will enable us to see the importance of theology in a Latin American perspective. In Latin America the need for social change is strongly felt: the oppressed—in their great majority, a religious and Christian throng—are crying out for liberation. Their faith can be a factor in historical liberation, and reflection on this action gives rise to the theology of the liberation—that which has been achieved and that which is still to be won. Perhaps the theology of liberation could only have emerged in Latin America, because only there could one find the cultural, ideological, ecclesial, and popular preconditions for such an occurrence. It required a huge faith, lived out by oppressed peoples, most of them Christian, who no longer accept oppression, because of their faith, because of faith in the biblical God, the God of Jesus Christ. All this was present in Latin America. Gustavo Gutiérrez learned this situation through his own commitment and formulated the requirements of a theology of liberation. Let us see how he articulates this new way of doing theology.

WHO HAS THE FIRST WORD?

Theology lives on something greater than itself. It is not the original datum. It is a result. It is the result of an attempt to express a primary and fundamental reality, spirituality. A point that repeatedly returns with emphasis in Gutiérrez's writings is the reference to spirituality. It is in spirituality that the true root of the theology of liberation is to be found. In Gustavo Gutiérrez spirituality has little to do with inwardness or individualism; nor is it based on the Greek concept of spirit. Spirituality is connected to spirit in the biblical sense. Spirit is the principle of life, of change, of the bursting in of the new. Spirituality implies walking according to the spirit in the spirit; that is, it is a form of action before it is a world-view.[6] Before talking *about* God it is important to talk *to* God. Prior to the talking that is the specific activity of theology is the being silent that belongs to contemplation and action. This is precisely what Gustavo Gutiérrez rightly emphasizes.[7]

First comes the silence of contemplation. We are absorbed by the gra-tuitousness of God and by God's saving and liberating plan. But this silence is not the silence of closed eyes that we find in some ancient and modern mystics but the mysticism of eyes open on the world, the mysticism of ears attentive to the cry of the oppressed and the demands of God that come from history and innocent suffering.

The second silence is that of action. This involves the hands rather than the lips. In action, in solidarity for liberation, we have to do with a political act. The relationship is not primarily prayer-action, but mysticism—politics, contemplation, and the desire to change society. Today's historical imper-ative moves in this direction: How, starting from faith and the subversive memory of Jesus, can Christians help in the immense process of bringing to birth a new society in which the oppressions suffered by the poor will be overcome? Rather than talking about God, what is important is to act in the light of God, to be an implementor of God's historical design, in which the oppressed undoubtedly have a central role. This silence, focused in contemplation and action, precedes any responsible speaking about God. "Theologizing done without the mediation of contemplation and practice does not meet the requirements of the God of the Bible."[8]

This God of the Bible sets one other prior condition for any Christian theology: listening to the cry of the oppressed. God is the God of the cry of the victim of injustice. God hears the cry. A theology deaf to the poor weeping for their innocent suffering is also dumb before God and before society. A theology which is dumb before the oppression of the majority finds it hard to escape charges of cynicism and triviality. This situation poses the central question of the theology of liberation:

> How are we to talk about a God who is revealed as love in a situation characterized by poverty and oppression? How are we to proclaim the God of life to men and women who die prematurely and unjustly? How are we to acknowledge that God makes us a free gift of love and justice when we have before us the suffering of the innocent? What words are we to use in telling those who are not even regarded as persons that they are the daughters and sons of God?[9]

Gustavo Gutiérrez's book, *On Job: God-Talk and the Suffering of the Innocent*, has already become a classic. It does not speculate. It gives a commentary on the book of Job in a way which shows today's question to be the question of yesterday and of all times: Lord, why? God, how long?

"The suffering of the innocent and the questions it leads them to ask are indeed key problems for theology—that is, for discourse about God. The theology of liberation tries to meet the challenge."[10]

After contemplation, after the silence of action and of listening to the cry of the victims of injustice, there can be speech. Theology is thus a second stage, derived from the first stage, which is contemplation and action as a response to the oppression of the poor.[11]

FROM WHAT PERSPECTIVE SHOULD WE DO THEOLOGY?

There are many perspectives from which theology has been done in the past and is done today. When I say "perspective," "horizon," or "viewpoint," I mean a set of vital social interests that is the motor of theological thinking. Under what conditions is theological work done? In First World conditions, where there are universities and abundant means of production? For whom is theology done? To whom is it addressed? Modern progressive theology has as its audience persons who have been educated and who have absorbed a considerable critical mass, a distinctive feature of the modern period. Their big question is how to combine faith and science, the church and democracy; how to justify religion in the face of the critiques of the masters of suspicion (Marx, Nietzsche, and Freud). The situation of the theological community in the Third World is different. Here the main features are desperate poverty and abundant faith. The masses are abandoned and semi-illiterate, and the theologians have few institutional spaces to do theology; for the most part they are tied by pastoral responsibilities in poor communities. The central question is how to combine faith with social oppression. How should the ecclesial community interact with the political community? The audience is not the critical and secularized man or woman, but the oppressed, the victims of social injustice.

This last question determines the social and epistemological locus from which Latin American theology finds meaning and is able to formulate an utterance that will have religious and political relevance. There is no theology of liberation that does not presuppose, in advance of all its work, this epistemological break. It has to take up its social and historical position; it has to reflect on faith at the heart of the suffering of an oppressed people, in contact with their hopes and starting from their struggles for liberation. This is the perspective of the theology of liberation. Gustavo Gutiérrez successfully developed this perspective in a text of extraordinary theological power, "Theology from the Underside of History" (1979).[12] Theology is done from the perspective of history's absentees, from the position of Las Casas's "scourged Christs of the Indies."[13] This theology makes its own the interests of the wretched of the earth; with its theological production it seeks to reinforce their cause, legitimize their struggles, and give their lives political weight. Faith confronted with the historical oppression of the great masses of our peoples can only result in a theology of liberation. This is the permanent dignity and evangelical mark of the theology of liberation; it has taken as the audience for its message the same persons who were the first audience for the gospel of Jesus. And it will always be a worthy aim to become one with the hopes and struggles of the least of this world in order to help them escape from their marginality into human and Christian communion.

A theology that makes its own the interests of the poor and their way of looking at the world, history, the church, and revelation will inevitably be a theology that provokes conflicts. It will clash first with theologies for which the poor are a subject, but not the perspective from which all theology is developed; these theologies feel themselves challenged as to their evangelical character, because of their ability (or lack of it) to evangelize the vast impoverished masses and in their function as sources of legitimacy for a society that creates poor persons and turns its back on them. It will also be a theology assimilated with difficulty by the ecclesiastical institution, whose historical interests have been and continue to be largely bound up with the dominant classes. The theology of liberation makes a vigorous appeal for conversion; this appeal is not always understood, and is quickly slandered as infidelity to the church and an obsessive desire to criticize institutional practices. Finally, the theology of liberation, because of its option for the poor, is misunderstood, distorted, and sometimes slandered and persecuted by the dominant powers in society because they see their interests opposed, delegitimized, and resisted. The theology of liberation presents itself, objectively, whether the theologian speaks or is silent, as a prophetic theology. And very often its members suffer the fate of the prophets.

In short, the theology of liberation, like any other theology, talks about God, the blessed Trinity, Christ, the Spirit, grace, sin, the church—about all the topics of theology; but that is not where its specificity and originality lie—it talks about all these topics from the perspective of the oppressed person who longs for liberation. Reading history from the position of the poor is the dominant (though not the only) perspective of the Bible. This methodological option gives the theology of liberation a strong biblical coloring and places it within the same field of activity as the message and activity of Jesus, who made the poor the arbiters of his messianic status.

HISTORICAL ACTION AS THE MATTER OF THEOLOGY

I remarked earlier that for Gutiérrez theology is fundamentally critical reflection on action. Let us try to understand how historical action is matter for theological reflection. This question is delicate, because it is the target of the main criticisms of the theology of liberation. These criticisms derive from a lack of attention to the specific perspective of the theology of liberation, and often from pure ignorance of the texts.

The very first task is to establish a minimal understanding of historical action. For the Christian the fundamental form of action is love. Whoever has love, as St. Paul sees it, has everything (1 Cor. 13:8): love is the nourishment and the fullness of faith, the gift of one's self to the other and, inseparably, to others. This is the foundation of the *praxis* of Christians, of their active presence in history.[14]

If God is love (1 John 4:8), all love has God dwelling within it. Love in itself is, by its nature, theologically significant. Whoever practices love is already within the sphere of salvation. This explains the identification that the New Testament itself makes of love of neighbor and love of God. It is the same movement, going in the direction of the other and also of the great Other. The challenge to us today in Latin America is not this perspective, which is classic in Christian thought. The challenge is macrolove — that is, love lived in the wider relationship of society, love that goes beyond the limits of the heart and reaches the structures of society. Love understood in this larger dimension means the ability to turn relationships of oppression into relationships of collaboration. It is out of love that we make an option for the poor against their unjust poverty, not to glorify poverty but to challenge it from within and to attempt, with the poor, to escape from it in the direction of justice, not of wealth.[15] This love is political and is translated by politics — that is, by the organization of critical consciousness, by giving structure to popular action in terms of a strategy and a project for society.

The theological question that now arises is: How far is the action of the oppressed in search of liberation directed toward the kingdom of God or, better, how far does it already imply the presence of seeds of the kingdom? In what way does it embody social grace? God is present in those who are the historical sacrament of the Son, in those who suffer, are naked and hungry, but not just in their persons, rather, fundamentally, in their struggles for justice, participation, and life. It is theology's task to carry out this interpretation with its arsenal of categories, drawn from revelation, from the church's tradition, from the reflection of theologians, and the life and witness of the faithful. As I said earlier, the theology of liberation does not remove the need for, or replace, theology as wisdom or theology as rational knowledge, which codifies our understanding of God and God's mystery in history. It requires and presupposes this work. In the light of the question asked by the oppressed, liberation theology is rediscovering the face of God as the God of life, enriching the understanding of Jesus as liberator, deepening the vision of the Spirit as consoler and strengthener of the poor (*consolator pauperum*), reinterpreting the mystery of the blessed Trinity as the communion and perichoresis of the divine three, which forms the perfect community. To make historical action the matter of theology means being able to see at the heart of that action the incarnation or rejection of the kingdom, of fidelity or infidelity to God. Only those who are secularized or who lack a mystical perspective could regard this interpretation as a politicization of faith. In other words, historical action is also the bearer of

God and the kingdom or the rejection of them (but always related to God and the kingdom). Consequently, historical action is also an object for theological consideration.

Finally, ever since the incarnation of the Son and the presence of the Spirit as a person within history, God is in history, or rather, God has become history. From now on, history will never again be just secular; for a Christian it is pregnant with God, and so must be interpreted by theological reflection. Nothing that occurs in history can leave the Christian indifferent, especially the history of Jesus' weakest brothers and sisters, the poor (cf. Matt. 25:40). To reflect theologically on action implies reflection on the kingdom in the world, on the presence of the risen Lord, who may still remain crucified in those whom history crucifies, as we wait in hope for the new heaven and the new earth.

This reflection will always be prophetic. It denounces forms of behavior that are opposed to God's plan, in society and in the church, just as it proclaims signs that appear of the kingdom present in history, particularly in the poor.[16]

This theological concern was already present in 1964 when a meeting of Latin American theologians took place in Petrópolis (Rio de Janeiro) in which Gustavo Gutiérrez took part. At the meeting he proposed as an important task for theology in Latin America "to carry out an analysis of forms of behavior from the religious point of view, from the point of view of salvation, to analyze what are the underlying options of the various different types of persons."[17] Action, then, had a central place, interpreted in terms of the specific perspective of faith. But it was not just the forms of historical action of different social groups; in connection with them it was necessary to analyze as well the forms of action of the church to see how far it was carrying out its mission in the context of Latin America, visited by oppression and an urgent need of liberation.[18] Already present were the basic intuitions that later emerged in an explicitly formulated theology of liberation.

THEOLOGY AS CRITICAL REFLECTION

The last question raised above leads me to consider theology as critical reflection. By definition, theology — as rational, codified knowledge — entails critical reflection. But this criticism is not exhausted by theology's internal investigations. It extends to the presuppositions of theological activity, carried on within society and the church within its framework of socio-cultural, geopolitical, and community concerns.[19] Not to take account of such preconditions is naive and can mystify theological discourse. For theology to be critical therefore means that it has a capacity to analyze the forms of action of church and society in the light of faith and from the point of view of the oppressed. Without such analysis there is no guarantee of the *liberating* character of this action.

There are various forms of action, whether in society or within the church. The first task is to analyze forms of social action from the perspective of the poor. Here theology discovers that the predominant forms of action in society are not directed to serving the interests of the majority of the population, but those of the power elites. These forms of action highlight the system that oppresses the majority and therefore, in the light of faith, are wrong and, in the light of the aspirations of the poor, unjust and antipopular. In the context of this criticism of forms of social action, Gutiérrez has incorporated into his work the most valid and best-founded contributions of the critical and dialectical tradition of revolutionary and Marxist thought. He uses Marxism, not for its own sake, but as an instrument of clarification to unmask mechanisms of oppression and destroy illusions absorbed by the poor about the possibility of finding solutions to their problems within the capitalist system. The criticism also evaluates the effects of forms of action. There are ameliorative and reformist forms of action that bring about no more than an improvement within the system without touching its fundamental interests and privileges. These forms of action deceive the oppressed by perpetuating their relationships of dependency on the dominant classes. The whole of Gutiérrez's work is shot through with this criticism, which is an important aspect of his theological discourse.

At the same time, theology as a critical reflection on action has the task of identifying and acting in concert with liberative forms of action initiated by the oppressed themselves and their allies. These are forms of action that propose a real overthrow of the system of domination and make possible forms of freedom not previously tried. Theologically, they open the way for historical incarnations of the kingdom (always limited and subject to theological criticism), which lead forward toward eschatology.

Theology's second task is to analyze the church's forms of action, whether those of the church as a whole (of the church as the people of God) or those of the various segments within the church (of the bishops, the ecclesial communities, and the laity). Here it is necessary to discover what functional relationship the church's forms of action (theoretical and active) maintain with the forces in society, whether with dominant or subordinate classes. It cannot be denied that the church is divided by social conflict; its support is sought from all sides. It can, in important segments of its membership, work with the interests of that order which, for the majority of the population, represents social and moral disorder; so too, significant sectors of the church, and even whole bishops' conferences, can work in the interests of the oppressed and with them form the historical and social bloc of those who seek liberation and an alternative society. In both cases there is a difference in pastoral strategies and corresponding theological justifications. It is the task of theology to exercise discernment among these forms of church action. And not only that: it is the task of the theological ministry to reinforce those forms of action that proceed in the direction of the liberation of the oppressed and are initiated by the oppressed, for this purpose reflects the *ipsissima intentio Jesu* (Jesus' fundamentalism) and is inherent in biblical religion. A theology that does not help to produce life, justice, more human relationships, and greater happiness cannot call itself Christian or be an heir to the apostolic tradition, which preserves forever the liberating memory of Jesus and his Spirit.

THE MAIN LINES OF GUSTAVO GUTIERREZ'S THEOLOGY

Gutiérrez is a man of the silence of prayer and popular action. But when he speaks, we always have a spiritual experience, such is the depth of his feeling and his extraordinary spirit of discernment. His great work is still *A Theology of Liberation*. Because it is a foundational work, it is always worth going back to read again; and every time new and relevant perspectives appear. This book presents the main lines of the theology of liberation. Today Gutiérrez's book has new relevance, as the Vatican administration, in collaboration with conservative groups in national and continental bishops' conferences (in Latin America, with CELAM in particular), is attempting to make the whole church return to the situation before Vatican II, introducing new theological foundations to support a clerical vision of the church: separation between church and world, new emphasis on the relationship between supernatural and natural, separation between the sacred and the profane, redemption and liberation, clergy and laity, stress on the church as mystery as against the church as people of God. The encyclical *Sollicitudo Rei Socialis*, equating development with liberation (par. 46), without realizing that liberation seeks to be an alternative to development, forces us to reread with interest chapter 2 of *A Theology of Liberation*, which deals precisely with the relationship and opposition between liberation and development. The fundamental importance of this book lies both in its method and in its content.

First, it demonstrates the transition from a modern progressive theology, characteristic of the First World, to a theology of liberation, typical of Latin America and regions that live under global exploitation. It indicates the moves by the official church which supported a whole pastoral approach directed toward liberation; it analyzes the crisis of the alternative models of Christendom and neo-Christendom, and the superiority of the liberation model. Secondly, it outlines the socio-political features of the process of liberation and the place of Christians and the churches within it. Finally it sets out the main elements of a theology of liberation: a theological anthropology and cosmology (faith and the new human being, the encounter with God in history), basic features of a christology of liberation, of a liberative ecclesiology and of the fundamental relationships between faith and politics. It ends by outlining a spirituality of liberation: poverty, solidarity, and protest.

Gustavo's style is always dense, concerned with correct formulation and the most serious information in the field, whether it be theology or social analysis. Through it all runs, like a conducting wire, the perspective of the poor—of the oppressed classes and humiliated races. In his writings can be heard the cry of the oppressed, which has gone up from Latin America for the last five hundred years.

Three other works of the same type by Gutiérrez deserve special emphasis. They all deal with spirituality: *We Drink From Our Own Wells* (1984); *On Job: God-Talk and the Suffering of the Innocent* (1987); and *El Dios de la Vida* (1982). Why spirituality? Because Gutiérrez is profoundly convinced that the roots of the theology of liberation are to be found, as described above, in a firm and decisive encounter with the Lord in the great throngs of the oppressed. The process of liberation involves a deep conflict. Clarity of aim is not enough; there is a need for a mysticism of resistance and renewed hope to keep on returning to the path in the face of the defeats of the oppressed. It is through spirituality that we have access to the oppressed and faithful people. As long as this spirituality exists, there will always be a commitment of solidarity with the weakest and, arising from that activity, theological reflection on liberation.

Lastly, there is another volume of diverse contextual essays: *The Power of the Poor in History* (1983). This includes one of Gutiérrez's most profound and innovative essays, "Theology from the Underside of History." In it he sketches the opposition between progressive theology, practiced on the social base of bourgeois democracies, and the theology of liberation, coming from the oppressed and the victims of capitalist models of development. He also explains why we Latin Americans talk about liberation and Europeans talk about freedom, a freedom paid for by others' sacrificing their freedoms. This very penetrating essay demonstrates the degree of autonomy and critical force attained by Latin American liberation theology.

Gutiérrez's work, seen in its totality, represents a genuine fundamental theology. It lays down the premises and axioms for a new discourse on faith. He has not had the time or opportunity to develop themes at length, to produce a complete system. Nor is that the way of the theology of liberation. It reflects specific forms of action; this emphasis on action for liberation requires a way of thinking that is free and always adequate to the needs of the moment, leaving for other circumstances a more distanced view of problems and, correspondingly, a greater possibility of systematization.

CONCLUSION: A MARTYR'S LIFE

It is not just the theology Gutiérrez produces that is important. His theology is linked at a deep level to theological existence itself. Classic and modern theology was developed in the academic world, at a distance from real events in society and the church. As a result it is a theology that includes very little of the conflicts of history or the cry of the millions of innocents who suffer. In Gutiérrez we cannot separate personal and community life from theology. He is an activist before he is a professor, committed to the fate of the oppressed. His own lifestyle is poor: he shares the hardships of the area he belongs to and out of which he develops his theological reflection. This reflection is not the product of his speculation. It is the product of the community of life and work with which he lives and whose destiny he shares. In his own flesh he experiences the oppression of illness and in his own skin the weight of discrimination against native peoples and those of mixed race. This personal existence is material for theological reflection. In the midst of immense historical and social challenges he has been able to confront personal challenges: the hostility of his own brothers in the faith and persecution by sectors of the church in his own country, Peru, and by the doctrinal authorities of the Vatican. On all these occasions he has shown himself to be a man of faith, attached to the sacrament of the church, in and through all its contradictions and structural sins, conferring credibility on the church that takes a genuine option for the poor and their liberation. Theology turns into martyrdom. Theology and martyrdom point to sanctity, lived in a new mode, appropriate to the new mode of being the church and to the new model of society developing in germ in the action of the poor. But of this there must be silence, for God alone is the faithful and true witness of the paths of divine love in the lives of individuals.

—translated from the Portuguese by Francis McDonagh

NOTES

1. Letter of John Paul II to the bishops of Brazil on the mission of the church and the theology of liberation, April 9, 1986; English translation, *Message to the Church in Brazil* (Church in the World Series, New York: Catholic Relief Services; London: CIIR, 1987).

2. *A Theology of Liberation* (Maryknoll, N.Y.: Orbis, 1973; London: SCM Press, 1974), p. 15.

3. *A Theology of Liberation* (15th anniversary ed., Maryknoll, N.Y.: Orbis, 1988), p. 8.

4. Ibid., p. 9.

5. Ibid. (1973), pp. 13–14.

6. *We Drink From Our Own Wells* (Maryknoll, N.Y.: Orbis; London: SCM Press, 1984), pp. 54ff.

7. *On Job: God-Talk and the Suffering of the Innocent* (Maryknoll, N.Y.: Orbis, 1987), p. xiii.

8. Ibid., p. xiii; cf. *El Dios de la Vida* (Lima: CEP, 1982), pp. 63–88.

9. *On Job*, p. xiv.

10. Ibid., p. xv.

11. *A Theology of Liberation* (1973), p. 11; *We Drink From Our Own Wells*, pp. 35–36.

12. *The Power of the Poor in History* (Maryknoll, N.Y.: Orbis; London: SCM Press, 1983), pp. 169–221.

13. Ibid., pp. 193, 197.

14. *A Theology of Liberation* (1973), p. 7.

15. Ibid., pp. 299–302.

16. See the whole of chap. 10 of *A Theology of Liberation* (1973), pp. 189–212.

17. See the texts in R. Oliveiros, *Liberación y teología. Génesis y crecimiento de una reflexión 1966–1977* (Lima, 1977), p. 56.

18. Oliveiros, *Liberación*, pp. 56, 57.

19. *A Theology of Liberation* (1973), p. 11.

4

Seven Samurai and How They Looked Again: Theology, Social Analysis, and *Religión Popular* in Latin America

HARVEY COX

Twenty years ago an unlikely combination of actors surveyed Latin America and saw a specter haunting the land. The specter was *religión popular* and the odd coalition that descried its threatening visage was made up of seven fierce warriors who normally viewed each other with considerable suspicion. It included (1) pre-Vatican II Roman Catholic integralists intent on holding the line; (2) post-Vatican II liturgical and theological reformers intent on changing it; (3) Protestant missionaries from North America and the local clergy they had trained; (4) Pentecostal preachers, nearly all of them Latin Americans; (5) liberal developmentalists from agencies such as IMF, AID, and the World Bank; (6) Marxist activists; and (7) liberation theologians. These seven samurai agreed on virtually nothing else. But they could—and did—join hands in common opposition to popular religion. They could—and did—form a united front against unauthorized cults of the Virgin, "patronales," and raucous fiestas, against the use of holy water to cast spells, against pre-Christian healing rites and scapulars designed to ward off evil. The specter, it appears, bore many faces, but its presence was so menacing and so manifold that this heterogenous cohort of ghost busters set aside other differences to track it down.

Of course the different members of the alliance opposed popular religion for their own quite different reasons:

(1) *Integralists* saw in the local cults remnants of pagan piety and the subversive syntheses of official saints with pre-Columbian deities. Undis-

couraged by four hundred years of spotty successes, they were still pursuing the "cut and burn" policy initiated by the Franciscans at the time of the Conquista.

(2) *Post-Vatican II reformers* longed to gather congregations around the altar (newly moved out from the wall), which now became the table of the family of God. They did not look kindly on worshipers saying beads during Mass or siphoning off energies in individual devotions at side chapels. Christians were to become (in Vatican II terms) a "people of God," and popular religion—the reformers thought—worked against this goal.

(3) *Protestant missionaries and local evangelical leaders* saw popular religion as yet another example of the debased Roman Catholicism that had been disparaged since the Black Legend first appeared in the sixteenth century: superstition and magic blended with popery and ignorance. For them, to embrace Protestant faith obviously required eschewing all that.

(4) *Pentecostal preachers*—mostly Latin Americans themselves—railed against devil worship, and the drunkenness and lusty excess that often accompany fiestas and patronales. In their opposition to popular religion they seem—if anything—more zealous than their other Protestant colleagues.

(5) *Liberal developmentalists* saw popular religion as an unfortunate obstacle to the introduction of modern agriculture, education, and especially health care, for *curanderos* were often key leaders in popular religion.

(6) *Marxists*—rarely masters of nuance in making judgments about religion—dismissed popular religion along with all religion as one more opiate of the masses. Like other rural idiocies it would evaporate once capitalism was abolished.

(7) *Liberation Theologians*—most of them at least—tended to see popular religion as a fundamentally alienated expression of religiosity, a form of false consciousness that prevented Christians from responding to a gospel that called them to become aware of their role as subjects and agents of the historical project of building the kingdom of god.

Thus the seven samurai harbored their own peculiar *causae belli*, but for each the struggle against the perversions of popular piety was one they took up with enthusiasm.

This grim catalog of reasons why so many different actors showed so little sympathetic interest in what has accurately been called "the religion of the poor" seems remarkable given the "preferential option for the poor" some of the same parties trumpeted so widely at the same time. Yet, in retrospect, what now seems equally remarkable is that during the same period the "high" forms of scholarly and academic theology displayed equally minimal interest in the religion of ordinary persons. Protestant theologians were busy refining historico-critical methods and reappropriating the theologies of the Reformation, most of which were not sympathetic to popular piety. Catholics were absorbing the impact of Vatican II and reveling in their newfound freedom to engage in critical biblical studies.

With the possible exception of a few French Catholics who were still interested in "spirituality," and of an even smaller handful of "liberal" Protestants who continued to be intrigued by "religious experience," most of
theology simply ignored religion, popular or otherwise.

This benign neglect of the phenomenon of religion by most theologies
was even more evident with reference to the non-Christian religious
traditions. One can hardly locate a memorable paragraph in Gilson or
Maritain about the other religions of the world. The same lapse is true of
Barth, Bultmann, and Bonhoeffer. Hendrik Kramer, the only neo-orthodox
theologian who addressed himself to the issue, argued, in effect, when it
comes to world religions, the less said the better.

But by the late 1960s this picture was changing. The Vatican had established secretariats for dialogue with Jews, Protestants, and non-Christian
religions. In his last book published just before he died, Paul Tillich
declared that the vexing question of the relationship between Christianity
and the non-Christian faiths of the world now loomed as *the* most important
theological issue, one he had scarcely addressed at all in his fifty years of
scholarly theological production. By the early 1970s other Protestant theologians followed suit, and "theology of the religions" became a central
preoccupation. Even so, it has taken years for theologians to recognize that
in order to deal with this issue they must move beyond old comparativist
methods (which had focused largely on the scriptures of other faiths) and
learn something from more recently developed approaches to religious
studies, including the need to study both "high and low," both official and
popular versions, of world religions.

This brings us to the threshold of the 1990s where, due in no small
measure to the vast influence of the theology of Gustavo Gutiérrez and his
co-workers, the entire situation vis-à-vis attitudes both of activist parties
and of academic theologians toward *religión popular* has shifted dramatically. What I wish to do now is to chart briefly how parallel changes
occurred in each of the seven samurai, focusing especially on liberation
theologians. In doing so I want to suggest why this change signals a possible
quickening of the sometimes limping conversation between theologians and
those who study religion from the perspective of psychology, anthropology,
and sociology. After that I wish to hazard some tentative hunches about
what all this might mean for the more general question of the "theological
problem of religion."

CHANGES: THE FIRST SIX SAMURAI

How did the seven samurai come to look at the ever-present reality of
popular religion in Latin America in a new way? In each one the change
came about both because of internal developments within the party itself
and also because of changes in the functioning of popular religion itself.

1. *Pre-Vatican II integralists* continue to play some role in the Catholic

Church, but their influence is waning. Admittedly, Pope John Paul II has appointed conservative bishops nearly every time a vacancy has occurred in Latin America. But the men he appoints cannot usefully be described with the old-fashioned term "integralist." Rather, they represent the school of thought within Catholic ecclesiology that holds that the reforms of Vatican II have gone too far, and that the time has come for retrenchment and consolidation. The most articulate spokesman of this line is of course Cardinal Joseph Ratzinger, prefect of the Sacred Congregation for the Doctrine of the Faith, who declares repeatedly that the most pressing need in the Catholic Church today is for what he calls *recentrage*. He uses this French term to refer to a tendency he welcomes, in particular within the French church, to look more to Rome and to deal sternly with the various forms of democratization and decentralization that have crept in since the 1960s.

When it comes to popular religion Cardinal Ratzinger is hardly an exclusivist or integralist. During a visit to Canada a few years back, he responded to a question about the prospects of Christianity with characteristic comprehensiveness by dividing the battlefield—as a previous dweller by the Tiber once did—into three parts. In the First World, he declared, consumerism and moral decay are the main challenges to the church. In the Second World—countries with communist governments—he found a growing disillusionment with Leninist ideology and a hunger for faith. He was most enthusiastic, however, about the Third World, including Latin America, where he suggested that "the natural piety and deep religiousness of the people present a genuine opening for christianization." This telling remark of the prefect parallels the position taken by Cardinal López Trujillo, the president of CELAM (the Latin American Bishops' Conference), who frequently declares that in time of rapid social change and jarring cultural dislocation the simple piety of ordinary persons should not be disturbed since it is what enables them to survive the traumas of history. This idea represents a conservative, in fact "functionalist," view of the role of religion, which differs from integralism in that virtually any faith that performs this role can be viewed with sympathy.

2. *Post-Vatican II reformers* who once swept through the churches of Latin America removing statues of saints, relics, and the accumulated detritus of previous waves of popular devotion, have now begun to take a second look at *religión popular*. The conviction is emerging among them that much of the enthusiasm for liturgical renewal that sprang from Vatican II had a certain elitist cast and that for liturgy to become the "work of the people" it has to incorporate elements of the local folk heritage. A good example of this rethought strategy can be seen in the history of the cathedral in Cuernevaca, Mexico. There, Bishop Don Sergio Mendez Arceo (now retired), first zealously removed all the saints' images and the traditional trappings from the church. But then, sensitive to popular tastes, he initiated the famous Mariachi Mass, using the instruments not so much of folk cul-

ture but of the regional music tradition of his people. A form of popular devotion was thus readmitted.

3. *Protestantism* of the "mainline" variety has not officially altered its abiding suspicion of popular religion. But this form of Protestantism appears to be one of decreasing vitality in Europe. On one wing its youngest leaders are drawn toward liberation theology and therefore toward a form of cooperation with Catholics, which their grandfathers—most of whom were converted from folk Catholicism—would have rejected. A decade ago the North American sponsors of the Baptist Seminary in Mexico reacted with deep dismay when the local leaders of the school began including Roman Catholics not only in the student body but on the faculty as well. On the other level, mainline Protestantism is beginning to merge with pentecostalism. Indeed, it is often difficult for a visitor to a Protestant congregation in Latin America to detect its denominational affiliation. All these developments suggest that the Protestantism introduced by missionaries in the nineteenth century will probably not continue to nurture its animus against popular religion as ardently in the future.

4. *Pentecostal* changes in attitudes have also taken place but more as a result of the actual structure of pentecostal worship than as the fruit of theological analysis. With the exception of Afro-Brazilian spiritism, pentecostalism represents the most thoroughly indigenized expression of non-Roman Catholic religion in Latin America. Nearly all its preachers and leaders are themselves Latin Americans (this in contrast to Catholicism, which still relies on a high proportion of foreign-born priests and religious). This, along with the highly decentralized organization of pentecostalism, means that hierarchical forms of social control are less workable, so the censoring out of the folk elements that persons bring with them to worship is more difficult. Also pentecostalists encourage the use of indigenous musical instruments and melodies, and this inevitably allows elements of popular religion to sift in. Finally, the explicitly emotional tone of pentecostal worship and the "speaking in tongues" phenomenon permits images from what might be called the "cultural unconscious" to come to expression. Pentecostal leaders still vigorously discourage their members from taking part in most popular rituals and fiestas, but there is considerable evidence that at another level pentecostal spirituality may be preserving elements of folk piety that might otherwise have been eradicated by urbanization and other types of social change.

5. Among *developmentalists* who are interested in stimulating changes in societies, especially in matters such as food production, health care, and education, again the attitudes toward religion have begun to change. Though they once saw popular religion as the primary obstacle to any form of change, developmentalists now tend to be much less sweeping and judgmental in their assessment of religious practices and institutions. The general shift in attention among developmental theorists away from more technological fixes and toward questions of culture has brought this concern

into an even sharper focus, and developmentalists now try to cooperate with religious movements in the areas in which they are working. Some even look at them not as obstacles to innovation but as the main source of values and hopes by which persons may be motivated to make any changes at all.

6. One of the most dramatic changes has come in the *Marxist evaluation* of the significance of religion. Confronted with a continent where the only promising revolutionary activity seemed to be coming from Christian sectors, Latin American Marxists and their colleagues elsewhere were eventually forced to reassess some of the standard Marxist analyses of the role of religion in society. The most visible example of their new attitude toward religion is the one demonstrated by none other than Fidel Castro himself in his widely read book *Fidel and Religion* (Simon & Schuster, 1987) in which the *comandante* not only does not condemn religion out of hand, but in fact insists that for large numbers of persons faith may provide the principal motivation for their participation in revolution. When the leader of the communist country, who has the longest claim to longevity in office, thus speaks, many listen:

Basing themselves on their faith, believers can take a revolutionary stand and . . . there need not be any contradiction between their being believers and revolutionaries. As I see it, that phrase [that religion is the opiate of the people] cannot be, nor is it, a dogma or an absolute truth; it is a truth in specific historical conditions. Moreover, I believe that this conclusion is perfectly in keeping with dialectics and Marxism.

I believe that, from the political point of view, religion is not, in itself, an opiate or a miraculous remedy. It may become an opiate or a wonderful cure if it is used or applied to defend oppressors and exploiters or the oppressed and the exploited, depending on the approach adopted toward the political, social, or material problems of the human beings who, aside from theology or religious belief, are born and must live in this world.

From a strictly political point of view—and I think I know something about politics—I believe that it is possible for Christians . . . to work together with Marxist Communists to transform the world . . . even though, in the case of the Christians, their starting point is a religious concept.

At the more theoretical level, Latin American Marxists who were once dazzled by Lenin's rather idiosyncratic views about metaphysical materialism, have now begun to study religion more from the perspective of the Italian theoretician, Antonio Gramsci. As they do, they make their judgments more on a political rather than on a metaphysical basis. Consequently their attitude toward all forms of religion tends to be much more nuanced.

LIBERATION THEOLOGY

In the case of the seventh samurai, liberation theology, the story is both more complex and more immediately significant for the larger issue of "the theology of religion." The fact is that even at its inception there was an active discussion in the liberation theology movement about the significance of *religión popular.* Liberation theologians after all did not appear out of nowhere. Many had been trained in some form of pre-Vatican II integralism. Most were understandably intoxicated by the reformist currents of the council. Some were touched by various expressions of Protestant theology. All, as Latin American intellectuals, had had to come to terms with one or another type of Marxism. They were men of their time and of their region, and as one follows their early debate about *religión popular* and notes the course it has taken more recently, two things become evident. First, the positions various of the theologians took were deeply influenced by their theological and even confessional commitments, and secondly, the present, more positive, appreciation of popular religions emerged as a result of ideas that were there from the beginning. Both these observations can be confirmed by a brief examination of some texts from an earlier stage of the discussion.

In 1976 José Míguez Bonino published a widely discussed article entitled "La Piedad Popular in América Latina" in the journal *Cristianismo y Sociedad* (no. 47, Buenos Aires, 1976, pp. 31–38). Relying on the earlier work of Aldo Büntig and on the declarations of the Medellín Conference of Latin American Bishops (CELAM) Míguez Bonino drew a very grim picture of popular religion. Referring to a report by the director of the CELAM Instituto Pastoral, Míguez Bonino quoted as follows: "The religiosity of poverty does not work to change life. It is well known that such Catholicism strengthens a dualistic vision of reality and, therefore, a religious attitude alien to the tasks of this world." In Latin America, he insisted, such popular Catholicism reinforces the social system with all its injustices, contradictions, and forms of oppression.

But Míguez Bonino was hardly alone. A paragraph from the international catechesis weekly published in Medellín in 1968 makes—if anything—a more severe judgment:

> The manifestations of popular religiosity—even if they sometimes show positive aspects—are, in the rapid evolution of society, the expression of alienated groups—that is, of groups that live in a depersonalized, conformist, and noncritical manner and do not make efforts to change society.

This document, reflecting as it did the enthusiasm of the post-Vatican II era, did not withhold its indictment of the church for allowing such popular piety to continue. "This kind of religiosity is maintained and encouraged," the report said, "by the prevailing structures of which the church is a part. . . . The expansion of this type of religiosity slows down changes in the structures of society."

Five major elements appear in the harsh post-Vatican II liberationist critique of popular religion. The first pointed to its alleged *fatalism*: it encourages persons to accept the situation in which they find themselves as the will of God or as according to the order of creation. The second criticism, directed especially at pentecostal forms of popular piety, focused on *individualism*, on the attempt to "save my own individual soul" at the expense of corporate or cooperative action in society. The third had to do with what might be called *substitute satisfaction*, finding spurious solutions to genuine human dilemmas: lighting a candle before a saint's picture when a child is sick instead of summoning whatever health care is available. A fourth critique had to do with the *blessing of intergroup and interclass harmony* through an emphasis on love and reconciliation—a "false universalism." It was often noted that this universalism is gladly seized upon by those in power to maintain the status quo. Fifth, there was the critique (mainly of developmentalists) that immersion in the popular religious mindscape *prevented persons from "integrating,"* from participating in the development of the wider society.

Reading these critiques in historical perspective, it becomes evident, however, that both Bonino's widely read article and the Medellín catechetical material were written to attack other positions. Thus Bonino sounded an alarm about romanticism, and warned those who look for liberative potential in popular religion that it can never be found in a pure state. Folk religious expressions exist *within history,* he argued, and therefore in a context of class conflict and oppression. The Medellín paper echoed the same caution, adding that such movements are always to some extent misshaped by the distortions introduced by ruling elites in order to make use of religion to perpetuate the prevailing system of privilege. But both Bonino and the authors of the Medellín document realized that popular religion could not simply be ignored. It was present everywhere and had a special appeal for precisely the persons whom liberation theology was supposed to liberate. What was the answer?

Replies to the challenge of popular religion often followed theological positions in a remarkably predictable way. A Methodist, Bonino suggested that the only solution was that of conversion—*metanoia.* In order to encourage such a conversion, he said, popular religious movements needed to be brought to a point of crisis. The poor and marginated who participate in them had to be made to see the contradiction between the picture of the world religious movements project and the actual world in which they had to live. Out of the resulting breakdown would come a transformation not just of the person, Bonino hoped, but of the *tradition itself.* Its rudiments could be then redirected toward the proper historical task of human beings.

Míguez Bonino does not delineate more specifically what these rudiments might be, but his prescription drawn from the lexicon of Wesleyan theology is an understandable one: like individuals, religious traditions must also be brought to the mourner's bench, to a point of crisis, in order for a genuine conversion to occur. The resurrection comes only after the cross.

Similar prescriptions were advanced by many Catholic writers at the time, especially Juan Luis Segundo. Perhaps some of them were more influenced by protestantizing theological currents than they themselves were aware.

Still, neither Bonino's voice nor the Medellín instruction were the only sentiments being articulated. At about the same time Míguez Bonino's article was published, Juan Carlos Scannone, who like Míguez Bonino wrote from Buenos Aires, took a quite different position about what the appropriate attitude of liberation theologians toward popular religion should be. Scannone believed the Second Vatican Council had brought to Latin America two different forms of postconciliar theology. One was shaped by the European liberal enlightenment and its more rational way of thinking. Scannone criticized this stream for viewing popular religion with a thoroughgoing "hermeneutic of suspicion." It signaled a deep distrust of what he called the "sapiential wisdom" of ordinary persons, a wisdom embedded in their religious beliefs and ritual practices.

The other stream of postconciliar theology that Scannone noted was the one he himself represented. It is a theology that allows popular culture to provide what used to be called *locus theologicus* or *Sitz im Leben,* what Scannone calls the "hermeneutical locale." He argued that only this second theological approach could in the long run make a genuine contribution to the authentic liberation of Latin American peoples. "Without denying its ambiguities," Scannone wrote, "it [popular religion] is an expression of authentic Christian faith inherited from the past and received from the preaching of the first missionaries. It should continue to be evangelized but in terms of its own proper cultural values."

The heart of Scannone's argument lay in what Alisdair MacIntyre has since called the "tradition specificity" of any mode of reasoning. Scannone rejected outright the notion that universalistic and scientific modes of discourse were the only valid ones and argued forcibly that there are *different* traditions of reason. He further argued that incarnate in the religious practices of the Latin American peoples, there is a deeply symbolic mode of reasoning, which not only needs to be preserved in Latin America but has an invaluable contribution to make to other parts of the world. Scannone's point coheres well with the ideas advanced more recently by C. S. Song (*Theology from the Womb of Asia,* Orbis, 1986) about theologizing in the context of local symbolic codes.

Scannone's main argument with Bonino and the other liberation theologians who looked with suspicion on popular religion is posed by his most basic question: Who is the real subject of liberation theology? Granted that theologians make such theology explicit and critical, and that they reflect on it, who is the *original subject* of this discourse? Furthermore, who is the genuine addressee? Is the addressee of theology all persons of faith or is it mainly elites—religious or nonreligious—who have been conscientized into the process of social change and historical responsibility?

Scannone views the "hermeneutic of suspicion" with suspicion. He suspects that it is informed by a scientistic bias that prevents it from fathoming the full potential of popular religion. He calls for a radical incarnation of the theological enterprise into the "culture-specific" religion of a particular people. He asked for a hermeneutic of appreciation, one that would be open to the significance of symbolic modes of thinking and would recognize that mythic thought is not merely a stage to be outgrown but a permanent component in any thinking that is essentially human. Scannone's approach to popular religion, it seems, is just as "Catholic" as Bonino's is "Methodist."

In the past twenty years it can be said with a considerable degree of accuracy that the old argument between Bonino and Scannone has moved more in Scannone's than in Bonino's direction. Such influential figures as Gustavo Gutiérrez have published significant works on the necessity for drawing on the spiritual resources and traditions of the people for the project of liberation. Gutiérrez's book *We Drink From Our Own Wells* is a particularly good example of this thesis. Nevertheless the argument is not over. Other theologians, such as Jon Sobrino, when they adumbrate a spirituality of liberation, rely heavily on a reinterpreted version of the classic European Catholic tradition itself. Sobrino for example refers hardly at all to popular religious devotions and movements in his work, *The Spirituality of Liberation.* Leonardo Boff, for all his difficulty with the Vatican and his radical criticisms of Catholic ecclesial forms, makes few references to popular religious movements in his writing. Still, a consensus seems to be appearing that those who do not take the religions of the poor with utter seriousness have fallen somewhat short of a genuine preferential option for the poor.

THE "THEOLOGY OF RELIGIONS"

What does all of this mean for the "theology of religion"? In the work that lies ahead on this vital subject, it seems clear that a deepened conversation between theologians and social scientists is required. In order to do their work theologians need to become students of religions not just in their classical scriptural expressions but in their *actual local* manifestations. Theologians, Marxists, and others have been forced to take another look at *religión popular* in part because, empirically, it has not conformed to the mental images they held of it. The revolutionary Christians of Central America and the Christian advocates of democracy in Brazil often came from the sector of *religión popular*. This suggests that the discussion, among theologians and others, about religion must move outside the abstract level on which it has often been lodged. It must also focus on highly particular expressions of popular religion. Only then can informed theological judgments and evaluations be legitimately made.

There can be no doubt that the religions of marginated and oppressed peoples frequently serve an absolutely indispensable positive function. Such religious expressions preserve a *mythic past,* which then can become a source of what Metz calls the *subversive memory* that can bring a critical perspective to the present world around them. Popular religion also nurtures the *values* and *moral practices* that hold together a culture under siege and without which a people collapses into anomie. As has been pointed out frequently, popular religions also to some extent *protect cultural minorities* from the intrusive domination of cultural and religious majorities, and in some measure inoculate them against the narcotizing effect that hegemonic religions (of elites) exert on those on whom they are imposed. Finally it has been pointed out that popular religions nourish a *Prinzip Hoffnung* (Ernst Bloch); they project the *hope for a better time,* a future redemption, a utopian realm. Without such hope any people becomes cynical and defeated. These are all persuasive reasons that are advanced to suggest why harsh judgments about popular religions are often inappropriate. In short, it is held, popular religion serves a genuine function and should not be tampered with until that function is clearly understood.

Theology, however, is an *evaluative* discipline and must eventually make judgments. It asks questions not only about the *functionality* of religious beliefs but about their truth and their value for life as God intends it. Theology has various ways of asking these questions but at least these ways — albeit "traditional specific" — are *explicit.* Theologians have much to learn from the empirical specificity of students of religious phenomena. But perhaps theology's value-explicitness should evoke from social scientists on the other hand a more candid clarification of the values and commitments that underlie their work. We can no longer accept the premise that social science is merely descriptive, while theology is normative. Both are both normative and descriptive, and their specializations must be seen to lie elsewhere.

A Christian theology of popular religion will be informed by an explicit and value-conscious anthropology. Therefore Christian theologians will probe specific expressions of popular religion with some of the following questions:

What is the *nature* of the mythic past preserved in ritual and legend? Does it sacralize oppressive patterns of rank and gender discrimination? Does it stigmatize certain groups within the society in a degrading way? Is it, to use a theological category, "idolatry"?

What about the values it perpetuates? *Which values* are they? How does one judge *among* values especially at a time when the word "values" itself has become a cliché? The mere "preservation" of values is surely not an ethically positive function. Which values should be nurtured? Which subverted?

In protecting minority groups against cultural domination, do popular religions sometimes erect an obstacle to that minimal degree of recognition and coping with the dominant culture needed to ward off extinction or lethal marginalization? What is the optimal form of human community and how can it be attained?

Finally what about transcendent hope? *How* transcendent is it? Is it so otherworldly as to undercut constructive action within the society? Is it individualistic rather than corporate? How does the kingdom of God impinge on the kingdoms of this world?

There are many questions to be asked from a theological perspective of any popular religious movement. This is how a positive and appreciative engagement must take place. After all, Christian theology itself projects a mythic past, a set of prescribed values, a circumference that delineates who is in and who is out, and a hope for the coming of a reign of peace and justice. Christianity is not completely asymmetrical to other religious movements in these regards. But in its prophetic mode Christianity is also highly critical of the dehumanizing and oppressive components of religious practices and institutions. Both Judaism and Christianity emerged initially as religious protest movements against a dominant sacral system. Both began as "liberation theologies." Still if this theological engagement is to be specific rather than merely general, if it is to be concrete rather than abstract, some of the tools of observation and modes of analysis that have heretofore been the monopoly of social scientists will need to become part of the tool box of theologians as well.

We may be entering a new and fruitful place of the sometimes troubled relationship between theology and the social scientific study of religion, one in which the latter can help the former to be more concrete, while theology can challenge social science to be more explicit about its value commitments.

If there is anything to be learned from the story of the seven samurai it is that history is open and that no theological or ideological judgments are final. Things change and persons change, even religiously. So in the matter of what "popular religion" is and what it might contribute to the liberation of women and men in the future, it is always useful to take another look.

5

Religion and Society: Sacred Canopy vs. Prophetic Critique

ROSEMARY RADFORD RUETHER

Fifteen years ago, when Gustavo Gutiérrez's *A Theology of Liberation* was published in English, North Americans were in the throes of many social conflicts. American racism had been decisively challenged by the black civil rights movement, and other racial minorities, such as Amerindians, were making their voices heard. Women were challenging the patterns of patriarchy in society and in the churches. American foreign policy was being exposed as neocolonialist, and the United States was on the brink of ignominious defeat in Southeast Asia. Its claim to represent "democracy" against totalitarian communism was being questioned.

In the last fifteen years, particularly under the presidency of Ronald Reagan, there has been a concerted effort to reestablish the hegemony of the unself-critical pro-Americanisms that were being challenged in the 1960s. This has included an effort to delegitimate liberation theology in Latin America, and black and feminist theologies in North America. The Reagan administration recognized the political power of liberation theologies. It sought to vilify liberation theology by labeling it as simply a front for Marxism and to categorize the Sandinista government as "persecutors" of the true Christians—for example, Cardinal Obando y Bravo. It also sought to promote the wealthy right-wing evangelist as the normative expression of churchmanship in America.

We can evaluate this struggle between liberation theology and the Reaganite right-wing evangelism by putting this in a broader context. In the biblical and Christian tradition, there are two opposed ways of seeing the relationship of religion (and God) to society. One way I call "the sacred canopy," the other the "prophetic critique."

72

"Sacred canopy theology" assumes that the dominant social order is founded by God. Its social relationships are given by God as the order of creation. The king-ruler was seen as the divinely appointed representative of God on earth. To obey the king-ruler was to obey God. The social hierarchy of man over women, ruling class over subject classes, the election of a privileged nation to rule other nations as God's people – all this is seen as "natural," divinely given, and expressions of God's will.

The theology of prophetic critique, by contrast, locates God and the spokespersons for God on the side of those victimized or despised by the social and political elites. The word of God comes as a critique of these elites, calling them to reform their ways in order to be faithful to divine justice or else threatening them with a revolutionary intervention of God in history that will overthrow their power and bring in a new world, where justice and peace will be established. Prophetic critique also questions the way in which religion has become a tool of unjust social privilege, focusing on private and cultic ways of reconciliation with God, to the exclusion of God's agenda of justice.

In the 1960s and 1970s there arose a number of theological movements in the Third World, first of all in Latin America, and then in Africa and Asia, and also movements among disadvantaged groups in North America, blacks and women among others, who have challenged the dominant type of theology and religiosity as "sacred canopy piety." They have shown the way in which established theology and religiosity ignore the poor and the oppressed, and unconsciously make it appear that white ruling class males of the Western colonialist world are the normative human beings.

Black theology has shown how dominant theology is racist, both in its obliviousness to black suffering and in its assumption that the problems of the white elite culture are the normative problems of theology and ethics. Feminist theology has shown the way in which Christian theology has validated patriarchy as the "order of creation" and made male power over female subjugation seem both God's will and the metaphor for the rule of God over humanity and creation.

Latin American liberation theology has been about the challenging of two types of "sacred canopy theology"; the theology of colonial Christendom, which directly sacralized the ruling class as representatives of God, and neocolonialist theology, which does this indirectly by separating the sacred and the secular, and seeking to confine the purview of religion to private, nonpolitical matters. For liberation theology, the gospel is, first and foremost, "good news to the poor," whereas establishment theology creates a religion of "bad news" to the poor. God is present in history through Christ to create new social and political, as well as personal, relationships between human beings that will make for justice and effective love on earth. If Christians are to be a part of Christ's work on earth as the church, they must be about a struggle against unjust poverty and the creation of new social systems that equitably distribute the resources of the world.

Reaganite theology is basically about the reestablishment of "sacred canopy religion" as normative, and the vilification of any type of liberation theology as politics falsely garbed as religion. Reaganism thus continues the claims of privatized theology that true religion is purely individual and spiritual, and has nothing to do with politics, although this claim itself becomes, all too clearly, a political one. Underneath the split between private and public, religious and political, lies in actuality the conflicts between two types of understanding of religious faith, one that sacralizes the social status quo and another that challenges it.

I suggest that there are two main poles of Reaganite "sacred canopy theology": the family and the nation. On the one side, Reaganite theology seeks to reassert patriarchy as order of creation. Male headship is seen as the natural order for the family and for the whole of society. The Equal Rights Amendment was to be defeated because it challenged this divinely established order of male headship. It is assumed that if women get out of their place and seek equality with men, the whole fabric of society will come unhinged. Juvenile delinquency and homosexuality are but two of the social evils that are seen as flowing directly from the destabilizing of patriarchal hierarchy in the family.

Implicitly it is also assumed in the Reagan ideology that the hierarchy of wealth in America is just and represents the merits of the righteous. Reagan and his friends are rich because they deserve to be rich. The poor are poor because they are lazy and want to live on welfare. If one helps the poor with social welfare, this just encourages their laziness. If they have to face the consequences of their laziness in starvation, they will get down to work. Wealth and prosperity are signs of divine favor, and so the wealth of Reagan and his associates are proof that they are doing God's will.

Reaganite theology has, as its second pole, religious nationalism. America is God's new Israel, God's elect nation. America is uniquely righteous and divinely favored. Its actions in the world are God's actions. Those whom America favors, God favors. Those whom America rebukes, God rebukes. Its military might is the expression of the righteous might of God. By contrast, communists, both in Asia and Eastern Europe, and in the Third World, and Arabs, are seen as enemies of God. To bomb Libyans and to arm counterrevolutionaries against Nicaraguan peasants is nothing less than God's righteous wrath against evildoers.

Reagan's world is divided into two camps, which are ultimately theological camps: the righteous empire, America, and the evil empire, communist Russia. All other divisions in the world are simply subdivisions of that fundamental dualism between the righteous America and the evil Russia. Reagan's God is a war God, a God of the holy war of America against its evil enemies, who are fronts for the great evil one, Satan.

Reagan's theology is basically optimistic, for divine favor and grace upon the righteous are assured. It is not necessary to bother one's mind with laboring details about particular countries and their histories, for all is determined in advance. This assurance of grace and divine favor lends itself even to an optimistic apocalypticism, in which nuclear war can be contemplated cheerfully on the expectation that it will be the final outburst of divine wrath against evildoers and the final establishment of the righteous on earth.

The Reagan revolution in religion has lent itself to a new emphasis on the corporate church as the counterpart to the business corporation. The millionaire evangelist becomes the living proof of divine favor upon those who "get right" with God. The Reagan administration has been characterized by more scandals of public corruption than any other administration in recent American history. Not accidentally, the new corporate church and millionaire evangelist have also been plagued by continual revelations of scandal. But it is characteristic of Reaganite theology that the sins of these evangelists are seen primarily as sexual. Their racism, sexism, and militarism, their readiness to bless South African apartheid, and racial and economic injustice in America, are not seen as scandalous. This is just religious business as usual.

Liberation theology unmasks this kind of religiosity as blasphemy, its god as an idol. It shows us that the real struggle of faith today, as in ancient times, is not the conflict between theism and atheism, but between the true God and the idols. The idols clothe war and injustice, violence and oppression, in religious mantles and claim that these come forth from the hand of God. The true God of biblical faith speaks through prophets and prophetesses who break through the lies of idolatrous religiosity. We are called to conversion to God by being called to conversion to the poor.

How does one know the difference between true faith and the religion of the idols? By their fruits you know them. Those who truly believe in God distance themselves from social privilege. They live simply and work to bind up the wounds of the victims. The worshipers of the idols grow fat and bless the bombs and systems of violence. Their sins are many, and the least of them are one-night stands in motels with willing secretaries.

The theology of Gustavo Gutiérrez has allowed us to name authentic prophetic faith and unmask the idols for our times. Gutiérrez has been the key founder, not simply of a new "school" of theology, but of the renewal of Christian self-understanding in the context of the conflict between rich and poor nations. The preferential option for the poor has been the heart of his theological message. This call to solidarity with the poorest and most oppressed of the earth searches the conscience of the leaders of the church, who too often have allied themselves with the elites of society.

The challenge of Gutiérrez's theology is a church that starts at the base, identified with the poorest, rather than with those in power. The revolution it seeks is not one that would simply upend the pyramid, creating a new class of oppressors from the leaders of a revolutionary party. The church is called to witness to a society where justice and love are really and practically incarnate. This may never happen perfectly or finally, but the Christian must seek continually for new and better approximations of the just and loving society. Liberation can never be identified simply with ideologies or theologies about liberation. Nor can it be assumed to be the assured possession of any particular social system. Prophetic critique must be based on continual discernment of the realities of the times. Reading the "signs of the times" means asking about what is actually happening, not just discussing theoretical constructs that substitute themselves for reality.

A church that opts for the poor is one that must learn anew what it means to be baptized into the death and resurrection of Christ. For this church, the cross has ceased to be a golden and jeweled decoration on a church wall, and has become the living reality that Christians bear in their bodies. The option for the poor calls down upon the church the wrath of those powers and principalities that uphold the privileges of the rich. To opt for the poor is to risk suffering and death. The cry *presente*, by which the Latin American church remembers its martyrs, is the concrete, living expression of the presence of the risen Lord. In this living presence of the martyrs, one discovers once again what resurrection and the commitment to continue the witness of Christ really mean.

The churches and theological faculties of the First World would like to have it both ways. We would like to entertain Third World theologians, like Gustavo Gutiérrez, as "stars" in a new "field" of theology. We wish to bring them to give invitational lectures and prove thereby that we are au courant. But liberation theologians have sought to avoid becoming simply a new intellectual elite. As Gustavo Gutiérrez has repeatedly said, "the subject of liberation theology is not theology, but liberation." The criteria of its truth lies in praxis. The critical question is not whether one has the correct words, but rather how one commits one's life.

"What side are you on" is the challenge of Gutiérrez to those who profess to be Christian among the churches of the powerful and affluent. The future of Roman Catholicism in the world today rests very much on how it responds to that revolutionary challenge from a Third World Christianity, personified in Gutiérrez. Will the Catholic Church choose to stand for a new future for all humanity, through solidarity with the poor, or will it fall back on its traditional alliances with the ruling classes? The ambivalent response of church leaders to Gustavo Gutiérrez and their theological role signifies their ambivalence in the face of that call to commitment.

6

Dependency Theory, Marxist Analysis, and Liberation Theology

ARTHUR F. McGOVERN, SJ

Over the past twenty years no theological movement has stimulated more writing or engendered more controversy than has liberation theology. Liberation theology has drawn attention dramatically to the plight of the world's poor nations and it has challenged the church to question its political alignments and its very presentation of the Christian message. While liberation theology seeks first of all to articulate the meaning of faith for a particular context, most of the criticism has centered on its political implications, especially on its use of Marxist analysis. It was this use of Marxist analysis that first drew my attention to liberation theology.

This present essay constitutes an "interim" investigation of the use of Marxist analysis and dependency theory by Gustavo Gutiérrez and other liberation theologians. It will become part of a more comprehensive book on liberation theology and its critics, following some more extensive studies in Latin America. In this interim study I should like to consider first the role that dependency theory has played in liberation theology: its main theses, how it developed, what liberation theologians have said about dependency, and some issues about its use. The second part of the essay will deal with Marxist analysis: what it involves, what liberation theologians have said about its use, how in fact they have made use of it, and finally some comments about its use.

The social sciences have played an essential role from the outset in liberation theology. Clodovis Boff and José Míguez Bonino both assert that the social sciences form a "constitutive part" of liberation theology, the first of three essential "mediations" according to Boff.[1] Other socio-scientific theories figure in the analyses used by liberation theologians, but

77

dependency and Marxist analyses have played very prominent roles in considering the major problems faced by Latin America.

This last point—major problems—merits special emphasis. Liberation theology operates at two very different, though interrelated, levels. In practice, most of the social analysis used by base communities and Christian programs of popular education focus on very specific problems: agricultural development, violations of human rights, health care, land reform, and so on. In most instances this type of analysis relies very little (and often not at all) on Marxist analysis or dependency theory.

Liberation theologians have, however, addressed issues about the root causes of problems in Latin America, and at this level dependency theory and Marxist analysis do come into play. We will see, in the course of the article, various reasons given by liberation theologians for accepting these methods of analysis as "useful tools." But one initial point stands out: most liberation theologians view Latin America's situation as one of "dependent capitalism." They judge this combination, dependency on an exploitative world capitalist system, as the major source of Latin America's problems. One could, then, present a unified view of liberation macroanalysis focused on a common target: dependent capitalism. One could also group the forms of analyses used by liberation theologians under the common heading of "dialectical" methods (methods that view conflict rather than functionalist striving for equilibrium as necessary for understanding Latin American reality). But liberation theologians distinguish between the uses of dependency theory and Marxist analysis, and their uses raise quite different issues, as we shall see. Hence I have treated them separately, while acknowledging from the outset their convergence on a common problem.

DEPENDENCY THEORY

I begin with dependency theory because it played an instrumental role in the very articulation of a theology of liberation. The new theology rejected "developmental" policies and called explicitly for "liberation" from dependency. I will discuss how liberation theologians used dependency theory in their initial formulations of liberation theology, but I need first to recall briefly some key points about dependency theory itself.[2]

Prior to the development of dependency theory, conventional economic wisdom proposed a "modernization" model for underdeveloped countries like those in Latin America. Latin America, according to this model of analysis, faced the same problems that Europe had faced before its industrial revolution: scarcity of capital, undeveloped technology, and a lack of entrepreneurs seeking to make profits through more efficient production. To achieve development, underdeveloped nations must break out of traditional mores, adopt a profit incentive, and discover newer ways to become productive. Advanced countries, from this perspective, could play an important role in supplying some of the missing components needed to "prime the pump" of development. Foreign companies (multinationals) could help by bringing in needed capital, new technology and managerial know-how.

In the first decades after World War II, Latin America sought to pattern its development according to this model. But one aspect of conventional wisdom soon came under attack by Raúl Prebisch and the United Nations Economic Commission on Latin America (ECLA). They challenged especially the conventional view that international trade was mutually beneficial for all trading powers. ECLA studies indicated that Latin American countries suffered from short-term instability caused by fluctuating prices and from long-term deterioration in terms of trade. This resulted, ECLA argued, from Latin America's reliance on export of primary goods (bananas, coffee, minerals, etc.) to provide income to finance the buying of imported industrial goods. Far from being mutually beneficial, Latin America continued to run a deficient balance of payments. The "center" nations profited; the "peripheral" nations suffered. Prebisch and ECLA still retained much of the modernist model for development, but they introduced a framework of analysis that would become an essential part of all dependency theory: the division of the capitalist world into dominant "center" nations and subordinate "peripheral" nations such as those of Latin America.

The dependency theorists of the 1960s (Cardoso, Frank, Dos Santos) focused on the influence of foreign trade and investment on Latin America. Using Prebisch's "core-periphery" framework the new analysts sought to show that weaknesses in Latin American economy resulted in large measure from policies controlled by the "center," from the United States and Europe. Dos Santos defined dependency as "a situation in which a certain group of countries have their economies conditioned by the development and expansion of another country's economy."[3] The relationship between countries becomes dependent when the dominant center countries alone have a power of self-starting and expansion, whereas the dependent, peripheral nations can only act in reaction to the dominant countries' policies and development. In this relationship, the dominant countries impose their dominant technology, commerce, and values on the dependent countries who find themselves easily exploited and subject to loss of revenues produced in their own countries.

This dependency theory took different forms. The strongest form, enunciated by André Gunder Frank, argued that capitalist countries in the North created and have maintained underdevelopment in Latin America. According to this position, development in the North and underdevelopment in the South represented "two sides of the same coin." Europe and the United States financed their own development by exploiting poor nations and draining off profits (surplus value) from them. They thus keep Latin America (and other Third World countries) from developing, by drawing off the capital needed for development, and imposing their own technology and controls. A more nuanced form of dependency analysis, proposed by Fernando Henrique Cardoso, gave far more attention to internal factors. It accepted the detrimental influence of foreign investors as an important factor, but tried also to show the social and political forces within Latin America that shaped its economy and socio-political systems.

Early works in liberation theology show the close connection between the concept of liberation and the fact of dependency. Gutiérrez proposed the concept of liberation to the bishops at Medellín (1968), precisely as a needed alternative to the failed policies of development. He spelled out his arguments in the early pages of *A Theology of Liberation*. Developmental policies, Gutiérrez judges, had obviously failed in Latin America. Not only did poverty and oppression continue but the gap between the poor countries of the world and the rich had widened. More importantly it was becoming increasingly clear that the continuing misery in Latin America was in great part *caused* by the dependency that developmental policies encouraged. Latin Americans were realizing that their own development would come about only through a struggle to break the domination of rich countries and their own native oligarchies. True development would come only through the struggle for liberation.[4]

Other liberation theologians echoed the same convictions. Hugo Assmann stated that the major contribution of the social sciences to liberation theology came from their critiques of developmentalism, critiques that pointed to dependence as the central problem. "Underlying liberation theology is the historical experience of the actual nature of *under*-development, as a form of dependence."[5] Marxism exercised an influence, Assmann continued, but the major influence was a new awareness that Latin Americans are "not merely underdeveloped peoples . . . but peoples 'kept in a state of underdevelopment.' "[6] José Míguez Bonino concurred: "Northern development is built on Third World underdevelopment."[7] Leonardo Boff spoke in similar terms: "The affluence and advanced scientific and technological development of the Northern hemisphere . . . has meant the impoverishment and marginalization of the dependent, underdeveloped nations."[8] Each of them spoke not only of the fact of dependence but used André Gunder Frank's formula that blamed Latin American underdevelopment on Northern development. A closer look, however, at the thought of Gustavo Gutiérrez and Leonardo Boff will indicate some important qualifications in the use of dependency theory.

Even in *A Theology of Liberation* Gutiérrez noted some important qualifications made by Fernando Henrique Cardoso about dependency theory. Latin American countries are constitutively dependent on rich nations, but Gutiérrez adds, "we are not dealing with a purely external factor."[9] He cites Cardoso's warning that "one can have recourse to the idea of dependence as a way of 'explaining' internal processes of the dependent societies by a purely 'external' variable."[10] Gutiérrez makes a similar point in his *The Power of the Poor in History*. "External dependency and internal domination are the marks of the social structures of Latin America." Although the early theories of dependency were beneficial, they sometimes failed by focusing too much on the conflict between nations (center versus periphery) and not enough on internal factors requiring class analysis.[11]

Gutiérrez added still further qualifications in a 1984 essay, "Teología y ciencias sociales." He stressed the provisional and transitory nature of all social science studies. To say these disciplines are scientific "does not mean that their conclusions are definitive and beyond discussion." Liberation theology, says Gutiérrez, needs to be attentive to the many variations of dependency theory and to criticisms made of it; it should avoid generalizations and be enriched by other types of analysis. He considers Cardoso the most important figure in dependency analysis and he notes also that Cardoso considers his theoretical attitude as situated at the "opposite ends" (*antipodas*) from Marx.[12]

Leonardo Boff, in *Liberating Grace*, affirmed the fact of dependency and used the strong formula of André Gunder Frank: "Development and underdevelopment are two sides of the same coin."[13] But he also voiced serious reservations about its use: "It is only a theory, not an established truth. It is one stage in an ongoing investigation and has its own intrinsic limitations. It offers a good diagnosis of the structure of underdevelopment, but it does not do much to offer any viable way out."[14] Expanding on this last point, Boff expresses skepticism about the revolutionary type of breakaway advocated by Frank. "More moderate advocates of the theory of dependency showed a greater historical sense" and recognized the need for work for change within the system.[15] Citing José Comblin, Boff says that one cannot choose both complete autonomy *and* development. Compromise is necessary. If development is the goal, says Boff, one has to work within the international system.

We have from liberation theologians, then, statements that seem to "blame" foreign countries and their companies for Latin America's problems, and more nuanced statements that affirm dependency but treat its causes and resolution as more complex. By distinguishing between the fact of dependency and the causes of its creation and continuance, we can better assess how much and in what way dependency causes or contributes to underdevelopment in Latin America. The points that follow constitute a necessarily brief and tentative assessment of this issue.

The Fact of Dependency. One important dependency analyst, Fernando Henrique Cardoso, claims that he never intended to create a special "theory" of dependency. He sought rather to challenge and correct existing models of development by investigating more fully what Latin Americans had experienced and discussed for years—the fact of dependency.[16] Indeed historians wrote about Latin American dependency well before dependency theory came onto the scene. Thus, for example, a history of Latin America written in the 1950s subtitled one of its chapters "Latin America's Decided Dependence on Foreign Trade and Foreign Capital." Moreover it described the Latin American situation in language that anticipated dependency theory as well. "Latin America became a weak outlying segment of the great industrial economies of the West."[17]

A more recent study, aimed explicitly at assessing dependency theory, questions the tenability of several theses proposed by some dependency theorists, for example that dependency necessarily impedes economic growth in poorer countries or necessarily results in authoritarian political rule. But the same author argues that at least two theses from dependency theory are "easily defensible": (1) "Because of their dependence on the developed 'core' countries, the peripheral countries are experiencing a growing loss of national control over their economic, political, social, and cultural life"; and (2) "The current economic growth in less developed countries is unevenly distributed among sectors of the society. . . . Because income distribution is badly skewed, the poorest half of most societies is left relatively untouched by economic growth."[18]

Reports by the International Monetary Fund and the World Bank—hardly suspect sources—give contemporary evidence of the dependence of Latin American countries on the United States and other First World nations. When the United States and its allies experienced recession in the early 1980s, the economies of every Latin American nation suffered even greater losses. An IMF report noted that growth rates in Latin American countries, which had averaged 5 to 7 percent annually from 1967 to 1980, fell dramatically to 2.3 percent in 1983. The reasons given by IMF are consistently *external*: "a major factor" in the problems faced by developing countries has been "the recession in industrial countries." Weakness of foreign exchange earnings and indebtedness made developing countries "particularly vulnerable" to interest rate increases in 1980. The weakness of economic activity in the industrial world had a "substantial adverse effect" on the terms of trade in countries not involved in oil developing. "Faced with an abrupt change of external finance, many developing countries had *no option* but to cut back sharply their current account deficits."[19] A World Bank report reflected this same causal relationship. Restrictive monetary policies used by the United States to control inflation had a "profoundly adverse effect" on the rates of growth of many developing countries. "Enormous pressures" have been exerted on the positions of countries in Latin America.[20]

Dependency affects not just a country's economy, but the poor in that country especially (as argued in the second "easily defensible" thesis noted earlier). Even in times of growth, income distribution in Latin America has remained extremely skewed. Of all countries listed by the World Bank in its *World Development Report 1987* Brazil shows the worst record in the world for disparity of income distribution. The lowest 20 percent of the population in Brazil receives only 2 percent of the national income; the top 10 percent account for over 50 percent of the income.[21] The poor suffer most, however, when the economy declines. Another World Bank study (1986) asserts that the poorest sectors of society in Latin America were hit hardest by the 1980 recession. The rural poor in Mexico, for example, suffered a 31.3 percent wage decline.[22]

The Causes of Dependency. The fact of dependency and its sharply negative consequences in recent years do not, however, explain how such dependency developed or how much dependency causes underdevelopment. The strong form of dependency theory articulated by A. G. Frank, and supported by some statements of liberation theologians, focuses on external forces primarily. This strong form tends to read the history of Latin America as successive epochs of domination and exploitation by foreign powers: by Spain and Portugal from 1500 to 1800, by England and other European nations in the nineteenth and early twentieth centuries, and then by the United States in more recent decades. But such an explanation, if neatly simple in theory, overlooks some important causal factors. In contrast, the type of analysis done by Cardoso studies internal and external factors and avoids targeting any single factor as a primary cause.

Most historians would certainly hold Spain and Portugal accountable for Latin America's original dependency and for creating severe impediments to development. The conquistadores subjugated the native peoples, forcing them to labor in fields and mines. The Amerindians became and remain "oppressed" peoples. The Spanish and Portuguese made vast fortunes from the gold and silver resources of Latin America. And, as some Marxist analysts have noted, this wealth often passed from Spain and Portugal into the hands of the English and Dutch, helping to finance the industrial revolution. Thus one reading of Latin American history would emphasize these factors of plunder and exploitation.

The same colonial heritage, however, points to other factors that help to explain why Latin America failed to follow the path of industrial development — and agricultural development — that occurred in Northern Europe and the United States. The Spanish brought with them a disdain for manual work, and Spanish mercantilist policies prevented Latin America from producing manufactured goods for itself and from open trading with other nations. In striking contrast to the United States, where four of every five white Americans owned their own land or trade prior to the civil war, property ownership in Latin America was concentrated in the hands of a few and the vast majority were left propertyless. In the United States, free enterprise developed and agricultural industrial development met domestic needs (though it did so by ruthlessly excluding Amerindians and enslaving blacks). Latin America, though subordinating these groups in rigid class structures, at least included them in society. But concentration of ownership and failure to invest profits into new domestic markets crippled Latin America's efforts to build a productive economy. The concentration of land ownership begun in colonial times continues into the present with 1.3 percent of landowners in Latin America controlling 71.6 percent of all land under cultivation.[23] This structure of concentrated ownership deprived the great masses of the population access to their own land and trades. One could characterize this legacy in Marxist terms as lack of control over the means of production; but one could also describe it in terms of the absence of any real experience of free enterprise.

As for the Spanish conquerors' disdain for manual-industrial work, even the liberationist philosopher Enrique Dussel acknowledges its devastating consequences:

> Spain chose the easy way: exploiting the American mines with the Indians rather than taking the narrow road that England chose, namely, the hard work of an industrious people. The Spanish lack of economic vision was catastrophic for Spain and also for the Latin American countries. Spain could easily have had coal and steel in Europe, but this would have signified an austere, simple, daily industrial effort. Spain preferred to mine only gold and silver, which in the short run produced ephemeral splendor, but in the long run produced economic catastrophe from which Spain as well as Latin America has never recovered.[24]

With the coming of independence in Latin America (the 1820s), British and other foreign investors did move in and accounted for much of the commercial-industrial development that did emerge. But here again one can attribute blame as much to the failure of Latin American elites who lacked the capital and motivation to build up an industrial economy, and who remained content to gain wealth from massive *latifundios* devoted primarily to supplying crops for export to Europe and the United States (e.g., bananas, coffee, sugar).

Latin Americans have good reasons for resentment against the United States and transnational influence. Often in the past U.S. companies literally dominated the economies of some Latin American countries—for example, United Fruit in Guatemala and U.S. copper companies in Chile. Often these companies have taken out millions in profits and done so with exorbitant profit rates. When Chile nationalized U.S. copper companies in 1971, the Allende government claimed that the companies had taken out of Chile wealth estimated at $10.8 billion dollars over a sixty-year period. Chile refused compensation on the grounds that the copper companies had already been compensated by exorbitant profit rates. Kennecott, Allende claimed, had an average annual profit rate of 52.8 percent from its Chilean operations from 1955 to 1970; Anaconda averaged 21.5 percent in profits from Chile during the same period, as opposed to 3.6 percent from their investments elsewhere.[25]

Political interventions by the United States have also blatantly violated the autonomy of Latin American countries, with interventions in most cases aimed at overthrowing democratically elected governments (Guatemala in 1954, Brazil in 1964, the Dominican Republic in 1965, Chile in 1970–1973, and Nicaragua in the 1980s).

One can easily overstate, however, the causal relationship between U.S. and foreign investment and the problems of underdevelopment in Latin America. Complete withdrawal of U.S. business and political influence would not solve the problems created centuries before by concentrated local ownership and consequent failures in internal development. Statistics showing that transnationals take out more in profit than they invest do not of themselves prove that underdevelopment has been caused by "draining off of surplus value," for the transnationals do at least create new wealth. Chile might not have developed a copper industry, at least not at the same level of productivity, without the capital and technology invested in it from without. One can still criticize, however, the fairness of the terms involved in transnational investment. Thus although U.S. copper companies paid Chile more in taxes, after World War II, than it took out in profits, they also so aggravated Chileans by their profit rates, by not investing profits from Chilean copper in Chile itself, and by U.S. government restrictions on trade and control of copper prices, that the Chilean assembly called *unanimously* for nationalization in 1971.[26]

Dependency analysis does help to explain problems in Latin America, but Gutiérrez's cautions should also be heeded. Liberation theology does need to note variations within dependency theory and it needs to weigh legitimate criticisms against those dependency arguments that oversimplify causes and solutions.

MARXIST ANALYSIS

Dependency theory has its critics, but it does not begin to generate the militant opposition (or support) that one connects with Marxism. The reason for this is clear. Dependency theory may prompt various strategies of response, some reformist and some more radical, but it has not led to the creation of political parties and popular movements committed to a specific program of change. Marxist analysis, on the other hand, has become linked with concrete tactics, strategies, and goals, as well as realized embodiments of Marxist ideas in many countries of the world. Hence, though liberation theology has more explicit ties with dependency analysis, the strongest criticisms against it have focused on its use of Marxist analysis.

Marxist analysis includes various components. It involves first of all a method of studying societal changes in history (historical materialism). This method considers modes of production and economic structures as far more determinative in shaping history and society than the political figures or ideologies that historians had tended to focus upon. This method views the class struggles generated by divisions of labor and ownership as driving forces in history. It includes also a critique of religion (with religion seen as pacifying the poor and justifying the status quo) and of other dominant ideas or ideologies in a given society.

Related to this general view of history, Marx developed a more pointed and specific critique of the capitalist system. Marx believed that capitalism systematically alienated workers from their work, their products, from nature and from other humans. Capitalism exploited workers by paying wages that did not reflect the true contribution of workers, but were based on what they needed to subsist. The difference between what workers actually received in wages and the real value of their work constituted a "surplus value," which owners expropriated as profit. Concepts like alienation and exploitation provide Marxism with much of the moral power it generates, but Marx sought also to show "scientifically" how various contradictions within the capitalist system would create its downfall: overproduction and underconsumption, falling rates of profit, crises leading to mass unemployment and ultimately to workers' revolution and the overthrow of capitalism.

When capitalism did not collapse, new Marxist theories were developed to explain its continuance. The theory of capitalist "imperialism," made prominent by Lenin, argued that the creation of industrial and banking monopolies created greater price and market stability, whereas the development of colonies created new markets for investment as well as supplying cheap labor and raw materials. This analysis of imperialism concurs with dependency theory in their common perception of a capitalist center dominating poorer peripheral colonies. But Marxists and dependency theorists also disagree on numerous other points.[27]

In the early years of liberation theology especially, many Latin American theologians spoke positively about Marxist analysis as a "useful scientific tool" for understanding conditions in Latin America. Many critics of liberation theology focused on Gutiérrez's discussion of class struggle in his *A Theology of Liberation*. Even in these pages, however, Gutiérrez does not "call for" class struggle or view it as the "driving force of history" (as later Vatican critics implied), but only affirms that the church should recognize the "fact" of class struggle and should place itself on the side of the poor.[28] Throughout the rest of the book Gutiérrez has only a handful of short comments about the contributions of Marx and Marxist analysis. For example, he writes: "Marx created categories which allowed for the elaboration of a science of history."[29] Gutiérrez felt that Marxist analysis could be separated from Marxism's atheistic worldview. In making this separation he appealed to José Carlos Mariátegui, a Peruvian religious-minded Marxist, who viewed historical materialism as a flexible "method" of interpreting society not dependent on philosophical materialism. Gutiérrez referred also to Althusser's distinction between Marxism as a science and as an ideology.[30] His only other notes on Marxism in this first book dealt with its influence on modern theology (showing the need for transforming the world) and on the challenge of Marx's critique of religion.[31]

Gutiérrez speaks directly to the issue of Marxist analysis in his 1984 essay on the social sciences and theology. He stresses that the presence of elements of Marxist analysis does not mean identification of social science with Marxism. He notes the conflicts between Marxist analysis and dependency theory on many issues; he insists that liberation theology involves no use of Marxism that would deny human liberty; he agrees with warnings made by the magisterium about uncritical use of Marxism; and he asserts that there has never been any proposal in liberation theology to synthesize Marxism and Christianity.[32]

José Míguez Bonino wrote extensively about Marxism in the mid-1970s. One would hardly classify his own writings as Marxist, but he did speak of the "unsubstitutable relevance of Marxism" for Christians concerned about social change.[33] If Christians are serious about the commitment to the poor, Míguez Bonino asserted, they need some instrument for analyzing society, and Marxism offers "a scientific, verifiable, and efficacious way to articulate love historically."[34]

Hugo Assmann's early writings seemed the most Marxist. He noted that liberation theology confronts problems arising from dependence, exploitation, and imperialism. Assmann then adds: "For most of those who use this language, this implies the use of a sociological analysis derived from Marxism."[35]

The most militant statements in favor of Marxist analysis came from the Christians for Socialism groups in the early 1970s. They called not only for Marxist analysis but for the realization of a Marxist socialism: "In this matter, our Movements recognize the contribution of Marxism, insofar as the latter aims at a scientifically rational history, connected with a praxis that constructively transforms the project of a new and different society." "We accept Marxism as a theory and praxis that are indispensable if our Christian love is to take concrete form."[36]

If one concentrates on Christians for Socialism documents and the period of the early to mid-1970s, one can find a strong influence of Marxism. But such a focus gives a very incomplete picture of liberation theology overall. In a collection of essays, *Frontiers of Theology in Latin America*, none of the thirteen theologians affirms Marxist analysis as a necessary or integral tool for liberation theology.[37] One could read Jon Sobrino without knowing that Marxism constituted even an issue in liberation theology. Juan Luis Segundo uses Marx (critically) as only one source among many social theorists. José Comblin has written strong criticism of Marxist analysis and especially of Marxist socialism. He warns against ideologies that "appear" scientific but impose their own values and programs, and against philosophies that replace free human activity with some underlying "movement" shaping history.[38] Comblin speaks with even sharper critique of Marxist regimes, comparing the Soviet Union to Latin American military dictatorships, which seek control over all parts of society. "Consequently, in Marxist revolution there is no freedom for the people, only for the Party."[39]

Liberation theology remains, however, profoundly and rather uniformly "anticapitalist." Consequently, while references to Marxism have become more muted and nuanced and the framework of liberation analysis has broadened, some use of Marxist analysis remains precisely because it serves as the most prominent instrument of criticism against capitalism. Thus Leonardo and Clodovis Boff's comments about Marxism, in their *Introducing Liberation Theology*, probably represent positions held by the majority of liberation theologians. The Boffs state that liberation theology uses Marxism "purely as an instrument" and that it "maintains a decidedly critical stance" in relation to Marxism. Marxism can be a companion, but never *the* guide—a position reserved for Jesus Christ.[40]

Nearly all the references one finds in liberation theology, however, affirm only that Marxist analysis *can* be a useful scientific tool for understanding conditions in Latin America. But liberation theologians do not tell us much about *why* they find Marxist analysis useful, *how* they adapt it, and *what* specific works of Marxist analysis have proven helpful. Exploring these questions about "why, how, and what" use of Marxist analysis one finds in liberation theology proved insightful to me.

Why do liberation theologians find Marxist analysis useful? Some liberation theologians have said that the very pervasiveness of Marxist ideas in Latin American political and intellectual movements make some use almost inevitable. But this would not explain the generally positive assessment attributed to Marxist analysis. Others have stated that commitment to the poor means commitment to the "popular movements" that struggle with and for the poor, and that such movements use Marxism as a guide. This justification, however, raises a serious problem. Marxist ideas, as Lenin noted, do not arise spontaneously in the working class or the poor; revolutionary theory must be brought "from without." The historical record of Marxism does not lend great assurance that Marxist ideas represent the true desires or the needs of the poor.

When liberation theologians stress the usefulness of Marxist analysis as a scientific tool, the most fundamental reason, in my judgment, is that they believe that Marxism has correctly identified the basic root of Latin America's problems—the capitalist system. And Marxist analysis does offer a penetrating criticism of capitalism. But the usefulness of Marxism depends on its correctness in naming and analyzing capitalism as the central problem.

For many Americans and others the "scientific" claims made in behalf of the social sciences, and of Marxism in particular, seem greatly exaggerated. In the natural sciences we have methods of testing that lead to clearly verified results. Social sciences rarely produce conclusive results. Even in conventional economics, which uses the most quantifiable testing, economists differ sharply in their assessments of a given situation and often prove far wide of the mark in predicting outcomes. Americans lend more credence to positions that build upon extensive empirical data, but they recognize even then that the data used can be very selectively chosen to support a given position. They view Marxism as especially suspect in this regard. Its "scientific" record of predictability appears quite weak. In each new period over the past century and a half, Marxists have pointed to crises of overproduction that would "soon" bring the downfall of capitalism. Most of Marx's predictions about the increasing pauperization of the working class and about continual decreases in the middle class proved to be almost the reverse of what actually occurred in industrialized countries.

There exists a striking difference between the strong sense of scientific truth, which many Latin Americans associate with the social sciences (and Marxism), and the skepticism expressed by many in the North. The difference arises in great part from very different views about what scientific theory means. Phillip Berryman states this difference well:

A discussion of theory and practice reveals clear cultural differences between the intellectual milieux of North America (and often Western Europe as well) and Latin America. In our everyday usage "theory" is often contrasted pejoratively with "reality." We tend to take as normative the "scientific method" in which theory is the result of an empirical, self-correcting trial-and-error process.

Among Latin American intellectuals, on the other hand, "empirical" is most often a pejorative term, denoting superficial appearance rather than the deep reality of things. Theory is regarded as a tool for cutting through appearance to get at the heart of things. Many essays by Latin American social scientists, for example, seem to be focused largely on constructing a "theoretical framework." Concrete data often seem to take second place. What Latin Americans understand as "praxis" is poles apart from Yankee "practicality."[41]

How do liberation theologians use Marxist analysis? One line from Berryman's quote goes far in explaining both the "how" and the "what" in the liberation theology use of Marxism: "Theory is regarded as a tool for cutting through appearances to get at the heart of things" — and the very genius of Marx's mode of inquiry is precisely its dialectical method questioning "appearances" to get at the reality of things. For all the controversy over use of Marxist analysis in liberation theology, I have yet to find (at this stage of my investigation) *any* specifically Marxist studies of Latin America that serve as guides to liberation theology analysis. One finds in Gutiérrez and others many references to dependency theorists and the use of *ideas* from earlier Marxist writers (Mariátegui in Peru, Gramsci and Althusser from Europe, and of course Marx). But at this point I have not found in liberation writings any references to detailed contemporary works of analysis by Latin American Marxists. One does find, on the other hand, Marxist concepts and insights used as "heuristic" principles (the Boffs refer to methodological "pointers" in Marxism) to challenge prevailing, traditional ways of thinking.

This use can be illustrated with numerous examples. Liberation theologians place great stress on the idea of "praxis" borrowed from Marx. The idea of praxis emphasizes the need for "transforming the world"; it stresses also the need for changing unjust "structures." (On this point and the following ones as well, liberation theologians reacted against what they saw as a weakness in traditional Christian thought with its emphasis focused on personal, moral conversion.) The Marxist critique of religion seemed too often accurate in its description of prevailing Christianity as an ideology used to pacify the poor and justify the status quo. The concept of "ideology" and the method of studying the use of ideologies by dominant socio-political groups have been broadly and frequently used by liberation theologians. Many liberation theologians see their own position in reference to the poor as that of "organic intellectuals." They take this idea, along with the struggle to win "hegemony" in society, from the Italian Marxist Antonio Gramsci. Franz Hinkelammert's *The Ideological Weapons of Death* constitutes a prolonged reflection based on Marx's concept of the role of "fetishism" in capitalism. Otto Maduro's *Religion and Social Conflicts* offers a lengthy and modified use of Marx's sociology of religion to explain the involvement of religion in the conflicts that have occurred in Latin America.

Along the same lines, concepts of "exploitation," the theft of "surplus value," the dominant influence of "imperialism," and the moral critique of capitalist "profit-seeking" have all been used by liberation theologians. Again these indicate a "heuristic" use of Marxist concepts, but they do not constitute what many U.S. social scientists would view as the "scientific" — that is, empirical — side of Marxism (studies of overproduction, falling rates of profits, etc.). For all the criticism of Gutiérrez's use of the *concept* of "class struggle," I have yet to find in liberation theology any detailed class analysis, or even less any program directed against a certain class or classes in Latin America.

A longer study would be needed to assess the validity of Marxist charges. Certainly "exploitation" is obvious in Latin America. But its clearest expressions lie in concentrated landownership that predated the development of "capitalism" in Latin America. The predominance of "state ownership" of industries in many Latin American countries has also created a situation far different from the capitalism criticized by Marx. Sweeping and generalized critiques of capitalism often fail to distinguish what structures create injustices (for example, exclusive concentrated ownership) and what structures may prove healthy for Latin America (for example, widespread distribution of private property, including workers' cooperatives, as opposed to Marxist state control). The importance of free, independent political organizations needs also to be stressed.

A fuller study would also need to take up the issue of whether Marxist analysis can be "separated" from Marxist ideology and tactics. (I believe a separation can be made, but it requires a very cautious and critical discernment, for the still dominant "classic" Marxism does not make such a separation and builds its analysis on an atheistic, materialist philosophy.)

Liberation theology has undergone significant developments in recent years. Many of its critics still focus on statements by activists of the early

1970s. The great effort to build up base communities has given the poor themselves greater voice and active participation in determining their own praxis and goals. Many liberation theologians have already incorporated the cautions and self-criticisms noted by Gutiérrez in his 1984 essay on the use of the social sciences. Liberation theology has provided a much needed voice in Latin America, as Pope John Paul II, encouragingly affirmed in his letter to the bishops of Brazil: "We are convinced, we and you, that the theology of liberation is not only opportune, but useful and necessary."⁴²

NOTES

1. Clodovis Boff, *Theology and Praxis: Epistemological Foundations* (Maryknoll, N.Y.: Orbis, 1987), p. 30, and José Míguez Bonino, *Toward a Christian Political Ethics* (Philadelphia: Fortress, 1983), p. 45.
2. This summary of dependency theory and of its development is drawn from several studies. A word about each may be helpful. (1) Gabriel Palma, *Dependency Theory, A Critical Assessment* (London: Frances Pinter, 1981), first published in *World Development* (July-August 1978), is the best source I found, especially in relating dependency theory to Marxism. (2) Philip J. O'Brien, "A Critique of Latin American Theories of Dependency," in Ivar Oxaal, Tony Barnet, and David Booth, eds., *Beyond the Sociology of Development* (London: Routledge and Kegan Paul, 1975), gives a useful account of ECLA, and of A. G. Frank and Cardoso. (3) Ronald H. Chilcote has edited or co-edited several helpful studies dealing especially with the debate between Marxism and dependency. See his *Dependency and Marxism* (Boulder, Colo.: Westview, 1982); Chilcote and Dale L. Johnson, eds., *Theories of Development* (Beverly Hills: Sage, 1983); Chilcote and Joel C. Edelstein, eds., *Latin America: The Struggle with Dependency and Beyond* (New York: John Wiley, 1974). (4) James L. Dietz, "Dependency Theory: A Review Article," *Journal of Economic Issues,* 14/3 (September 1980), compares Frank and Cardoso. (5) Míguez Jorrin and John D. Martz, *Latin American Political Thought and Ideology* (Chapel Hill: University of North Carolina Press, 1970); chap. 14 deals especially with ECLA and the early dependency theorists in Brazil.
3. Theotonio Dos Santos's definition (brief form) from a work he co-edited, *La dependencia política-económica de América Latina* (1971) is cited by Michael J. Francis, "Dependency: Ideology, Fad, and Fact," in Michael Novak and Michael P. Jackson, eds., *Latin America: Dependency or Interdependence?* (Washington, D.C.: American Enterprise Institute, 1985), p. 89.
4. Gustavo Gutiérrez, *A Theology of Liberation* (Maryknoll, N.Y.: Orbis, 1973), pp. 26–27.
5. Hugo Assmann, *Theology for a Nomad Church* (Maryknoll, N.Y.: Orbis, 1976), p. 37.
6. Ibid., p. 49.
7. José Míguez Bonino, *Revolutionary Theology Comes of Age* (London: SPCK, 1975), p. 16.
8. Leonardo Boff, *Liberating Grace* (Maryknoll, N.Y.: Orbis, 1979), p. 29.
9. Gutiérrez, *A Theology of Liberation,* p. 85.
10. Ibid., p. 87.
11. Gutiérrez, *The Power of the Poor in History* (Maryknoll, N.Y.: Orbis, 1983;

the original articles written from 1974 to 1978), pp. 45, 78.

12. Gutiérrez, "Teología y ciencias sociales," appeared originally in *Christus* (Mexico City), October-November 1984; it will be published also in Gutiérrez, *The Truth Shall Make You Free* (Maryknoll, N.Y.: Orbis, 1990).

13. Leonardo Boff, *Liberating Grace*, p. 66.

14. Ibid.

15. Ibid., pp. 77–78.

16. F. H. Cardoso, "The Consumption of Dependency Theory in the United States," *Latin American Research Review*, 12/3 (1977) 8.

17. J. Fred Rippy, *Latin America, A Modern History* (Ann Arbor: University of Michigan Press, 1958), pp. 389–90.

18. Francis, "Dependency," pp. 92–95.

19. *International Monetary Fund Annual Report, 1984* (Washington, D.C.: IMF, 1984), pp. 9–11; quote, p. 31.

20. *The World Bank Annual Report, 1984* (Washington, D.C.: The World Bank, 1986), p. 32.

21. *World Development Report 1987* (New York: Oxford University Press, 1987), Table 26, pp. 252–53.

22. *Poverty in Latin America, The Impact of the Depression* (Washington, D.C.: The World Bank, 1986), pp. 16–17.

23. Michael P. Todaro, *Economic Development in the Third World* (New York: Longman, 1981, 2nd ed.), p. 260.

24. Enrique Dussel, *A History of the Church in Latin America* (Grand Rapids: Eerdmans, 1981), pp. 77–78.

25. From a summary of a speech given by Salvador Allende before the General Assembly of the United Nations, December 1972.

26. Theodore H. Moran, *Multinational Corporations and the Politics of Dependence, Copper in Chile* (Princeton: Princeton University Press, 1974), p. 55 on taxes paid by the copper companies; pp. 87–94 on trade restrictions and price-setting; pp. 102–15 on ways profits were used (and the mounting discontent in Chile).

27. On the differences and debates between Marxists and dependency theorists, see Chilcote, *Dependency and Marxism.*

28. Gutiérrez, *A Theology of Liberation*, pp. 272–79.

29. Ibid., p. 30.

30. Ibid., on Mariátegui, p. 90; on Althusser, p. 97, n. 40.

31. Ibid., pp. 9, 220.

32. Gutiérrez, "Teología y ciencias sociales."

33. José Míguez Bonino, *Christians and Marxists: The Mutual Challenge to Revolution* (Grand Rapids: Eerdmans, 1976), p. 19.

34. Ibid., p. 115.

35. Assmann, *Theology of a Nomad Church*, p. 116.

36. The Christians for Socialism statements cited by Bonaventure Kloppenburg, O.F.M., *The People's Church; A Defense of My Church* (Chicago: Franciscan Herald Press, 1978), pp. 72–73.

37. *Frontiers of Theology in Latin America*, Rosino Gibellini, ed. (Maryknoll, N.Y.: Orbis, 1979).

38. José Comblin, *The Church and the National Security State* (Maryknoll, N.Y.: Orbis, 1979), pp. 66, 140–42.

39. Ibid., p. 132, and quote, p. 220.

40. Leonardo Boff and Clodovis Boff, *Introducing Liberation Theology* (Maryknoll, N.Y.: Orbis, 1987), p. 28.

41. Phillip Berryman, *Liberation Theology* (New York: Pantheon, 1987), p. 85.

42. Pope John Paul II, to the Brazilian bishops, 1986, published in Alfred Hennelly, ed., *Liberation Theology: A Documentary History* (Maryknoll, N.Y.: Orbis, 1990).

7

Theology in the Struggle for History and Society

JOHANN BAPTIST METZ

The following reflections are dedicated to my friend Gustavo Gutiérrez. In his recent publications he has always stressed that liberation theology is not about a new social ethics for the church but about theology. It is this fundamental theological character of liberation theology that I wish to discuss here from various aspects that seem to me important.

I

Within the Catholic Church I find three principal concurrent theological models in operation. This does not cover everything but does single out three representative ideal types of theology. I mean neoscholastic theology, a transcendental-idealist theology, and a postidealist theology. Although they are very different, all three models fall within the scope of theology in the Catholic sense. They reflect the complexity and tensions of the present state of the church.

The neoscholastic view is still predominant in the church as a whole. Indeed, given recent developments in the church, which I see as reflecting and confirming neoconservative social trends, we may even speak of a "late summer" for this paradigm. Although in no way wishing to detract from the merits of neoscholasticism in the nineteenth and early twentieth centuries, we may describe this paradigm as mainly defensive and traditional, and unable to deal fruitfully with the challenge of modern Europe. Significantly, the principle work of nineteenth century neoscholasticism is called "theology of antiquity." This fixation on (scholastic) antiquity shows how Catholicism became spiritually and socially cut off in Europe, especially in Germany. Catholics barricaded themselves in a Catholic—and political—stronghold, a pale imitation of the great Christian stronghold—*corpus chris-*

tianum—of the Middle Ages. They adopted a strictly defensive position to the challenge of the modern world, in both social and political debates and interdenominational theological controversy. Church orthodoxy was more rigorous than radical; a defensive concern with security-minded pastoral theology—until Vatican II.

The transcendental-idealist view of theology stems from the most important and influential change in present Catholic theology. This is the attempt to use the church fathers and scholastics in a productive offensive confrontation with the challenges of modern Europe: the discovery of subjectivity as a crisis in classic metaphysics; the critico-productive confrontation with Kant, German idealism, and existentialism on the one hand, and the social processes of secularization and scientific civilization on the other. This theology found its ecclesiastical and social counterpart in new forms of church life. Taken as a whole, these can in fact be regarded as the impulse for the Vatican II Council.

Meanwhile theology was faced with crises and challenges that, in my view, could not adequately be dealt with by the two theological models so far described. Hence, I should like to mention a third theological model, which seeks to test and develop the church's theological legacy as it faces these crises and challenges. Somewhat at a loss, I call this model of Catholic theology "postidealist." It is recognizable in reflections on a new political theology in Europe and in the central thrust of liberation theology. This third theological model also has its roots in the last council. I should like to name three crises and challenges on which this theological model seeks to adopt a position:

1. Theology comes to the end of its historical and social innocence—that is, theology engaged in a dispute about its foundations in terms of ideological and social criticism. This amounts to an attempt by theology to establish a new relationship to history and society. Theological theories of world secularization and modernization have not yet fully clarified this relationship. And the problems cannot be solved simply by the usual division of labor between systematic theology and social ethics.

2. Theology comes to the end of a system that took no account of the individual situation or person—that is, theology concerned itself with the "irruption" of the poor, which does not permit the poor to vanish into an impersonal theory of poverty. Moreover the European version of postidealist theology has also been shaped by the "irruption" of the Auschwitz catastrophe. Nothing could show more plainly that the time for theological systems divorced from situation and person is over, because no one can possibly force this catastrophe into a "peopleless" system of meaning.

3. Theology comes to the end of cultural monocentrism—that is, theology relating to an ethnically and culturally polycentric world. Here a traditional Christian theology needs to overcome not only a great deal of social but also ethnic blindness. As well as the "option for the poor" it must adopt the "option for others in their otherness," for ethnic and cul-

tural characteristics are not just an ideological superstructure based on economic problems, as Marxist theory and Western praxis would like to suggest.

II

History and society are and remain the place for Christian language about God—that is, for Christian theology. The crisis that has long confronted theology may also be formulated as an epistemological problem, a problem of knowing the truth. Therefore, it is a question of the relationship between knowledge and interest. From the time of the Enlightenment, religion and theology have had to deal with the axiom that all knowledge is governed by interest. This axiom is the foundation of the Enlightenment's critique of religion and theology, on the part of Voltaire, for example; religion and theology are deciphered in terms of their social interest context, but without any application of social criticism. Social criticism, of course, is applied by Karl Marx. Even if theology did not lose its innocence through the Enlightenment's critique of religion, it certainly has since Marx.

The attempt to take this situation into account and remain a proper theology capable of speaking the truth distinguishes postidealist theology's first phase of development. This tries to create the awareness that theology and church are never simply politically innocent and therefore one of theology's fundamental tasks is to consider political implications. But this is still not the main problem in theology's crisis. How can theology admit the connection between knowledge and interest without either giving up or perverting the question of truth? Is the question of truth not reduced here to a mere question of relevance, along the lines of "true is what is in my interest or in the interest of a particular group of persons?" No, it is just that the question of truth now takes a different form, which may be formulated thus: Are there any interests capable of truth? Of course, interests can only be capable of truth when they are universal or universalizable— that is, when they relate without exception to all human beings or could be so related. For truth is either truth for everyone or not at all. In this sense postidealist theology speaks of universal or universalizable interest, based on biblical tradition itself. This is "hunger and thirst for justice" and indeed, justice for all, for the living and the dead, present and past sufferings.

Thus, the question of truth and the question of justice are interrelated: *verum et bonum (iustum) convertuntur.* Interest in undivided justice belongs to the premises of the search for truth. Thus knowledge of the truth and speaking about God acquire a practical foundation. In my view this is the basis of the rightly understood axiom of the "primacy of praxis," which is criticized in Rome's instruction on liberation theology. The only interest that is appropriate to theology, because it is a universal interest, is hunger and thirst for justice, undivided justice, justice for the living and the dead. Hence questions about God and about justice, the affirmation of God and the praxis of justice, can no longer be separated. In other words, the praxis of Christian faith always has an interest in universal justice, and is thus both mystical and political. This is emphasized in talk about the one and undivided following of Jesus, mystically and politically understood.

Therefore, Christian theology is not political *because* it has surrendered Christianity to an alien political ideology. It is political because it tries to preserve the dangerous memory of the messianic God, the God of the resurrection of the dead and judgment. Theology's political root in this remembrance is much more than mere political rhetoric.

Christian speech about God is not subject to the "primacy of praxis" because it blindly submits to some present political praxis, but because the biblical idea of God, which it represents, is in itself a practical idea. The stories of setting out and hope, stories of suffering and persecution, stories of resistance and resignation, are at the center of the Christian understanding of God. "Remembering" and "telling" are therefore not just for entertainment; they are basic forms of Christian language about God. Thus, postidealist theology will always try to explain dogmas of the faith formulated under the influence of classical Greek metaphysics in terms of dangerous and liberating ideas. It treats these unhistorical and impersonal doctrinal statements as shorthand and tries to relate them back to the biblical stories of exodus, conversion, resistance, and suffering, and the synoptic stories of Jesus and his disciples. The result is that "simple believers" are now no longer merely being "talked at"; they become the active subjects of the language of faith and theology, a language in which individual life histories and faith histories are linked together.

If I am right, in its base communities liberation theology is trying to relax the usual division of labor in the church and to overcome the model of the church as "minder." This usual division of labor may be summed up thus: the bishops teach, the priests look after, the theologians explain and defend teaching and educate the minders. And what about the people? They are the recipients of this teaching and minding. Such a division of labor sees the church thus as a minding church and theology has to go along with the system willy-nilly. On the other hand, liberation theology works to change this minding church *for* the people into a church *of* the people — that is, a church with a community whose members are growing in personal awareness. It points out that besides the magisterium, the church's teaching office, there is also the authority of the faithful, to which theology (and not just theology but also the magisterium) is bound to listen. This view is the legacy of Vatican II. Finally, the church constitution of this council stresses the personal and subjective view of the church, in particular by its use of the biblical phrase "people of God" to designate the church. Hence, the council, at least in principle, underlined the active role of the faithful in the articulation and development of faith.

III

In my country, Germany, after the Second World War, there was a lot of theological talk about the "historicity" of human beings. I have a suspicion that with this general blanket term we were trying to retreat and get away as quickly as possible from the particular history of our own country, which, especially because of Auschwitz, was a catastrophic history. However, for the Judeo-Christian religion unlike all other great religions of the world, history has a specific importance. Christianity is dominated by the vision of "God and history," "God in history." There are several reasons why this is not fully clear to us today. One reason is that Christianity and theology—at least among us in Europe at this stage of evolution and technology—is under the anonymous pressure of a historical weariness, a tendency to posthistory. The less human beings are their memory, the more they are their own experience. Everything appears to be technically reproducible, finally even the human producer. Secondly, I think in present-day theology, Christianity's indispensable Jewish legacy, which has a thoroughly historical way of thinking, is overshadowed by its Hellenistic Greek legacy, which is more inclined toward an ahistorical dualism and therefore constantly threatening to transform Christianity into gnosticism, in which history is without salvation and salvation outside history.

I think theological talk of "two histories," one natural and one supernatural, falls into this danger. This is another dualistic undermining of the important adventure of our historical lives. And it cancels our history's final horizon, its ending in the parousia, the "Lord's Second Coming." In fact, there is not world history and, "after it" or "above it," salvation history. The history of salvation, about which Christian theology speaks, is that same world history, shot through with a constantly threatened and disputed but unshakably promised hope: the hope of God's justice, which also includes the dead and their past sufferings, and forces the living to be interested in justice for all. Faith in the messianic God, God of the resurrection of the dead and judgment, God before whom not even the past is fixed (before whom past sufferings do not disappear into the impersonal abyss of an anonymous, eternally indifferent evolution). This faith is not opium to lull us in humanity's historical struggle; it is the guarantee and measure of the dignity of every human person.

It shares with Marxism the discovery of the world as history, historical project, in which human beings are to be the enactors of their own history, and this challenge should be taken seriously. But, this, of course, raises two important questions for a postidealist theology orientated toward history and society. First, there is the question of the status and value of past suffering in the process of history and, secondly, the question of individual guilt. Although it is central to postidealist theology, I pass over here the first (very important) problem, the problem known classically as that of theodicy—that is, the justification of God in the face of the world's pain. Certainly in this context Gustavo Gutiérrez's reflections of Job are especially important.

However, I shall concentrate briefly on the second question, about the status and dignity of individual moral guilt. Unlike Marxism, postidealist theology stresses that this guilt is not an assumed but an authentic phenomenon in the historical process of personal lives. It cannot be regarded as an expression of pure alienation, even though theology and its preaching of guilt and sin have all too often been alienating and oppressive. Denial of this guilt is an attack on freedom, because the dignity of freedom includes the capacity for guilt. And acceptance of guilt before God does not prevent human beings from having full responsibility for their own history. On the contrary: where moral guilt is denied as an original phenomenon—that is, denounced as false consciousness—mechanisms arise to make excuses for the sufferings and contradictions in life. We get self-defense strategies for allegedly guiltless individuals. The historical responsiblity of the person in history is irrationally halved, and the horror and dismay projected one-sidedly onto the historical opponent. Thus, the question of guilt and non-guilt, right and wrong, cannot be reduced to a purely political opposition between friend and foe.

If and insofar as Marxist praxis of class struggle is mistaken about the abyss of human guilt and thus implicitly denies human moral dignity, it cannot be taken as a fundamental principle in the historical process of salvation. If and insofar as Marxist historical and social analysis is based on this premise, it cannot be accepted by theology uncritically as it stands. Of course, this is also true of all historical and sociological theories, which see themselves as metatheories for religion and faith, for whom Christianity is a historico-culturally necessary but now superceded phase in the evolutionary history of humanity. Theology cannot justify itself with regard to these theories by producing an even more comprehensive "pure theory." It can only do so by returning to individual believers and their praxis of a single, undivided discipleship, which must take effect in historical and social life. Of course, this theological claim must question its ecclesiastical basis, and the question will be particularly demanding where the usual ecclesiastical division of labor is in force. In my view this is shown in the exchange between theology and basic community life in the so-called poor churches.

The individual development of the believer in poor Third World churches is threatened at the moment by a danger that I think liberation theology fails to take into sufficient account. This is the threat of what I will call here "secondary colonization," through the invasion of the Western cultural industry and its mass media, particularly television, which increasingly holds persons captive in an artifical world, alienating them from their original images, languages, and history. Does this "soft" terror of the culture industry have more dangerous effects in poor countries than in Europe? Does it not threaten to paralyze the process of liberation? Finally, is not the opium of the poor no longer religion but mass media culture, which reaches even the most miserable slums? This mass media culture makes the poor and exploited feel overloaded even before they have achieved any personal liberation: it robs them of their memory, even before they have become aware of their own history; it threatens their language even before they have acquired this language and become culturally literate. An important amount of liberation work is taking on this "new immaturity," not only in Latin America but also in Europe.

IV

To conclude, I should like to turn back to Europe. In the present intellectual culture of Europe, often described as "postmodern," the usage I have adopted here of "history" (in the singular!) and "society" has been very strongly criticized. It is regarded as a suspiciously totalizing way of talking, which threatens the individual. It is regarded as language destroying the colorful multiplicity of life and leading to the dictatorship of a monolithic praxis. The scapegoat is often biblical monotheism. It is regarded as the godfather of a predemocratic, antipower-sharing autocracy, the father of an obsolete patriarchalism, the forerunner of totalitarian ideologies of history—in short, as a mania for uniformity in religious garb. In contrast to this monotheism, mythical polytheism is praised because it is said to guarantee an innocent multiplicity of life. God is sacrificed to the gods. There is talk of new mythologies: a new enjoyment of myths is spreading in secularized Europe; a new cult of innocence, deeply unpolitical, with a voyeuristic attitude toward social and political crises, a life on a reduced scale, private nest-feathering and new-age fantasies as a new religion. In the postmodern manner, what is proposed is the abandonment of all universities, and single-minded reason in the name of a praxis-free, colorful multiplicity of life and its unreconciled histories.

There are European theologians who see a chance for Christianity in this polymythic atmosphere. There is no theologico-political perspective I recognize here. I see only a calling into question of the substance of the Judeo-Christian religion and the danger of atrophy to our political culture. I distrust the promise of exoneration from the obligation to make choices and the promise of liberation for the sake of greater individualization. This latter is linked to the postmodern dismissal of the idea of unity and with the esthetic-mythical birth of a new multiple way of thinking. Will not new power settle down in a world of unrelated and "hands-off" multiplicity? In the history of my German people was there not a dangerous suspension of the idea of unity and equality of all human beings? Were not the Jews, before being sent to the gas chambers, excluded metaphysically and legally from this unity? Thus, politically and culturally can we allow ourselves that innocence we esthetically propose? Can we allow ourselves it in the face of the world's misery? The "new thinking" in Europe works toward the suspension of morality, it fascinates by its presumption of a new innocence for humanity. Friedrich Nietzsche is regarded as the new prophet. But is this new thinking not ultimately an excuse-making strategy, against the individual and against history? A bit like this: the excuse for the individual in the face of historical and social catastrophes in the world is that the individual does not exist as an individual person capable of guilt. If capacity for guilt belongs to the dignity of freedom, then this "new thinking" in Europe actually withdraws from the history of freedom that it claims to be saving. Here what is needed is Christianity's power of social criticism and historical imagination.

This Christianity and its theology do not derive from a guilt-free poly-mythic "spiritual wealth," but from the gospel "poverty of spirit," which does not take comfort in myths far removed from history and praxis. This Christianity compels us, against the mythical ban of a posthistorical world, to speak again and again of humanity and solidarity, oppression and liberation, and to protest against injustices crying to heaven.

—translated from the German by Dinah Livingstone

8

Community and Identity

GREGORY BAUM

There are many ways of looking upon liberation theology. It is possible to understand it as a theological methodology. Gustavo Gutiérrez takes us through several distinct steps in his famous *A Theology of Liberation*. The starting point is solidarity with the oppressed. It is out of this solidarity that all subsequent questions are asked. Commitment and action here precede theological reflection. The first question asked is: Why this suffering? What is the cause of the increasing misery and powerlessness of the majority in Latin America? To reply to this question theology must enter into a dialogue with the social sciences. With many Latin American searchers, Gutiérrez found the theory of dependency a convincing explanation of the poverty in Latin America. In a generalized form this theory has since been used in many ecclesiastical documents.

The next question that arises is: Why have these structures of oppression had such a hold over the whole of Latin America? They were not only imposed by the powerful, they were also legitimated by the dominant culture and the religious tradition. What is required, therefore, is a critique of ideology. To what extent has the church, its organization, its teaching, and its piety, contributed to the stability of the structures of oppression?

After such an analysis some Christians turn their backs on religion altogether. But the Christians whose option for the poor has been a response to the gospel realize that the biblical tradition contains elements that promise liberation. The question they now have to answer is how they can formulate, after the critique of ideology, the liberating message of the scriptures. Christians realize that they cannot speak of Jesus Christ truthfully unless they first analyze the character of social sin in their place and then present Christian teaching as the message of liberation for that place. In this sense, liberation theology is always and inevitably contextual.

Juan Segundo has called this methodology the hermeneutical circle of liberation theology. The methodology is indeed circular because new historical experiences may reveal that the solidarity with victims must be extended to sectors of the population—for instance, women or racial minorities—that were previously overlooked. Calling the methodology a circle assures us that liberation theology never offers a once and for all theological theory but always comes back upon itself to examine whether its own critical proposals are truly liberating or whether they have unintended and at first unrecognized implications that legitimate new forms of oppression. Calling liberation theology a circular methodology brings to light its affinity with critical theory, which has been so influential in European and North American political theology.

In this article I wish to ask a question often posed by conservative thinkers but not only by them: What are the implications of preferential solidarity for community and identity? The secular left has left this question unattended. Solidarity with victims produces a conflictual perception of society: society is seen as divided between oppressor and oppressed. From this perspective, expressions that praise the unity and harmony of society appear as political ideologies that disguise the class conflict. Socialism has seen itself as an internationalism. It has opposed nationalism as an ideology that creates the illusion of social solidarity. Solidarity, socialists argue, must first of all be preferential—that is to say, there must be identification with the exploited sector.

In order to promote solidarity among workers and constitute them as a class, socialists have had little sympathy for the ethnic and religious heritages of these men and women. Workers were to define themselves simply in terms of their economic location. Attachment to ethnicity or religion was seen as divisive and an obstacle to class unity. In many countries workers faithful to their religion or their ethnic heritage were disappointed by the socialist movement because it seemed to rob them of the values that in their situation of powerlessness gave them a sense of personal dignity. Cornel West records that blacks in the United States were repeatedly put off by Marxism because the purely economic analysis of oppression proposed by socialists made insignificant the ethnicity through which blacks defined their own collective identity.[1]

Socialists in colonized nations have been well aware of this unresolved ambiguity. In nineteenth-century Eastern Europe, socialists in nations that had become part of the Russian, Austrian, or Ottoman empires were debating whether they should be internationalists and identify with the struggles of the entire working class in the empire or whether they should be nationalists, join the national independence struggle led by the bourgeoisie, and then, after national independence, pursue the struggle for socialism in their own country. In contemporary Quebec this continues to be an important debate.

Liberation movements tend to break up existing unities by unmasking them as structures of domination. The conflictual perception of society puts a question mark behind national identity. Preferential solidarity threatens to undo community. Is the family the small social cell built upon love that renders possible a just and harmonious society? Or is the family, as Marx and Engels believed, the matrix of oppression? Does the women's liberation movement leave any ground for bonding in the family?

One of the reasons why political conservatism and, in the 1930s, European fascism attracted so many ordinary followers, including workers and the marginalized, was that the socialist movement of economic liberation did not seem to protect the values these persons cherished, especially identity and community. At a recent conference on social democracy today, held at the University of Ottawa, democratic socialists from Europe and North America discussed the present success of neoconservative values in the societies of the West and concluded that the exclusive emphasis of the economic factor often made the political left overlook the fact that individuals were attached to community and their collective identity.[2] From these, even the poor derived their sense of dignity. This neglect on the part of the left allowed neoconservative politicians to mobilize the public around these values.

The reason that social thinkers and political scientists are so fascinated by liberation theology is that here they see a social theory of the left that gives those who struggle for justice a tremendous sense of identity and community. Liberation theology does not say to the people, you have nothing to lose but your chains. It assures them, on the contrary, that they have inherited a religious tradition that is the bearer of radical values. Liberation theology gives them an extraordinary sense of historical continuity, reaching back to the exodus community whom God delivered from oppression in the land of bondage. The identity and community that liberation theology communicates is of course that of the Christian church.

The question I wish to raise in this article is what liberation theology might say regarding community and identity of the wider society.

Sociologists tend to argue that a nation preserves its historical identity not simply through its political structure but also through a collective myth or a set of symbols that blesses and legitimates these structures and the values they express. The national myth allows persons to internalize the dominant values. This theory is upheld by many sociologists who do not regard themselves as functionalists. If this theory is true, the following question poses itself. Should a liberation struggle unmask and demystify the national ideology as an illusion of unity aimed at disguising class division? Or should those who struggle against oppression unmask a certain national self-understanding and in its stead propose an alternative interpretation of national identity and national purpose?

This question is so important that some liberation theologians have argued that it may not be useful at all to use the word "ideology" in a purely pejorative sense as legitimation of injustice. Radical social theories must not only reject the distorted values of the past but also bless and legitimate new values, partially derived from the past, that are to constitute the new society. The Canadian political theologian, Harold Wells, has recently drawn attention to the work of Paul Ricoeur and Juan Segundo to defend a wider definition of ideology, one that includes the negative and the positive sense.[3]

Reading the work of Latin American liberation theologians from a distance, I have the impression that they say very little about national identity. However, they do have a very strong sense of the historical unity of Latin America. They see the multitudes of Latin America, of all regions, subject to the identical forces of oppression, and thus they propose a social liberation project that involves the whole continent. Their contextual theology is Latin American. In the Puebla Document the bishops entitled their pastoral message "God's Saving Plan for Latin America."

Latin American liberation theology is not concerned with the nation, but it does communicate a sense of collective identity beyond the religious realm. It promotes a collective self-understanding of Latin America. The conflict sociology adopted by Latin American liberation theology is not used to explode all secular symbols of collective identity. The community promoted by liberation theology directly and immediately is the religious one. But beyond this, liberation theology offers an interpretation of Latin American history that provides a collective myth, an ideology—if the word is used in the wider sense—that reinforces the unity of Latin America and grounds the continental social project of liberation.

The secular left has been so suspicious of myth and symbols that its social theories offer only critiques of ideology and hardly ever spell out the set of symbols and values that ought to pervade the imagination of those who struggle. It will eventually be institutionalized and reritualized in the liberated society. Marxist theorists understand the role of myths in such a negative way that they do not even analyze the symbolic power exercised by their own movement. Even the critical theory of the Frankfurt school, which has criticized the economics of Marxist orthodoxy and recognized the political power of culture and myth, was quite unable to define a set of symbols that would insinuate the just society, legitimate socialist struggle, summon forth energy, and intensify the yearning for emancipation. Because the secular left was so uncomfortable with symbols of identity, its social theories easily gave the impression that while promising economic liberation, the socialist struggle would take away from citizens many of the values they treasured, especially community.

The religious left, by way of contrast, has a strong sense that the ever-necessary, ongoing critique of ideology must not be allowed to explode all symbols of unity and identity. It is precisely the task of liberation theology to criticize collective identities that legitimate oppression and to redefine them in accordance with collective stories that (1) bind persons together in the struggle for justice and (2) reveal the nature of the liberated society.

It is instructive to examine the famous debate involving sociologists and theologians over the "civil religion" of the United States of America. In an article written in 1967, Robert Bellah, a distinguished sociologist in the tradition of Emile Durkheim, argued that examining American political culture over two centuries, including the inaugural speeches of the presidents and other texts of the public liturgy, the social scientist discovers the existence of a myth relating to God and the destiny of America, a myth that deserves to be called religion, though a religion different from Christianity and Judaism.[4] It is the "civil religion" of the United States of America. Bellah's article was not without its ambiguity. In an explanatory note added later, Bellah explained more clearly that the civil religion he examined referred to a set of "transcendent values" by which Americans evaluate and judge the government's domestic and foreign policies.[5] He suggested that the student movement of the late 1960s represented an exercise of America's civil religion because the students supported the civil rights movement in the South and opposed the involvement in Vietnam in the name of traditional American values—democracy and freedom from colonial control.

Bellah's critics understood this civil religion in a variety of ways.[6] Some argued that Bellah's civil religion referred to the religious ethos of churchgoing persons, the sanctification of the American way of life, with little reference to the biblical message. Others feared that Bellah's theory fostered an exaggerated nationalism, a quasi-religious devotion to America as the first of many nations. Some Christian theologians argued that if the civil religion is made consistent with Christian self-understanding, then this civil religion may be the contextual form of Christianity in the United States. By contrast, other theologians denounced Bellah's civil religion as a form of idolatry leading America astray.

This celebrated debate clearly reveals that the national myth of the United States, whether it is called religion or not, exists in a variety of forms and is capable of being interpreted in several ways. The task of liberation theology is here to critique forms of the national myth that legitimate oppression and exploitation, and to reach out for a possible interpretation of the civil religion that would promote the cause of justice.[7] If, for the moment, we return to the strict (pejorative) definition of ideology, we may say that liberation theology, following its proper methodology, must reject the ideological collective self-definitions of America and in its stead search for a national myth with utopian possibilities.

Writing during the period of the student movement, Rosemary Ruether insisted that it was a fatal mistake of the American left to allow the symbols of nationhood to become representative of the right and to define itself by the rejection of the flag and other symbols of the republic.[8] What was demanded instead, she argued, was to replace the ideological meaning of the national symbols by a radical interpretation of America's mission, based on its struggle for independence and democracy.

These critical reflections on collective identities fit perfectly into the methodology of liberation theology. Solidarity with the oppressed—the starting point—calls for social analysis, including an ideological critique of the dominant culture. Such an investigation creates suspicion in regard to various collective identities. To what extent do these disguise the conditions of oppression? At the same time, collective identities play an essential part in the cooperative action of men and women building a stable society. This is an insight derived from the social sciences, from philosophy—and from scripture. Collective identities must therefore be negated dialectically: this means that the repudiation of their ideological meaning must be followed by a reconstruction of a collective self-understanding oriented toward emancipation.

In this context it may be useful to retain the strict (pejorative) definition of ideology, for this enables us to differentiate collective myths defined as ideologies from those constructed as utopias.

It is perhaps no accident that it was a Canadian political theologian who pleaded for a wider definition of ideology. He was probably afraid that a purely pejorative concept of ideology would make critical Canadians over-look the political importance of a national myth. Because Canada is an unlikely confederation of former British colonies, including one the British took from the French in 1759, Canadian society lacks symbols and stories that define its collective identity. It is this absence of ideology, understood here in the wider sense, that weakens Canada in its resistance to the grow-ing influence of the United States. The lack of a strong collective identity makes Canada vulnerable to increasing economic and political dependency on the United States. At this time, the Canadian government is negotiating a free trade agreement with the United States, an agreement that promises higher profit for the major corporations, yet that frightens workers and farmers who anticipate increasing unemployment and deterioration of the conditions of employment. Afraid of this free trade agreement are also Canadians, English and French-speaking, who treasure the Canadian social democratic tradition and Canada's greater sense of society's collective responsibility, expressed for instance in socialized medicine. Many of us fear that the cultural impact of this free trade agreement will weaken the Canadian socialist heritage. Canadian churches and church groups have joined the movement against free trade. In the Canadian situation, the interests of class and nation tend to coincide.[9]

Let me mention that left-wing secular political scientists do not agree in their analysis of Canadian capitalism. There are political economists who try to understand the Canadian economy by analyzing the structure of capital and the social relations it creates in this country. There are other political economists who argue that the Canadian economy is a dependent capitalism and for that reason can be understood only if this dependency on the center of the system is taken into account.[10] In the light of this second analysis, the interests of class and nation tend to coincide. It is worth noting that the recent Canadian church documents on the demands of economic justice in Canada have used this dependency theory to understand the plight of the Canadian economy and the marginalization of an ever-increasing sector of the population.[11]

Yet this "economic nationalism," supported by labor groups, farmers, and churches, has only a faint echo in the Canadian population. Why? Because of the weak sense of collective identity. Because of the absence of a national myth. The task of Canadian political theologians is not to institute a critique of the national ideology—for there is none—but rather to tell the stories of Canadian struggles for emancipation and the creation of a socialist tradition in English and in French Canada. Out of these efforts, joined by similarly oriented efforts of secular groups, may well emerge liberating symbols of national identity.

Although these theological reflections are contextual, they have universal implications. It may possibly be the task of liberation theology to help the secular left in various parts of the world to arrive at a positive evaluation of identity and community. Similarly it is often religious women in the woman's movement who reach for an emancipatory theory of marriage that negates inequality and yet affirms new forms of bonding in the service of love and of the community.

The Canadian collective identity raises other questions that deserve attention. Canada as a political entity has a weak sense of itself, but many regions in Canada have a fairly strong sense of their collective identity. This applies above all to the French-speaking community of Quebec, which understands itself as a people or a nation. English-speaking Canadians tend to look upon Quebec as an ethnic minority that, though entitled to its heritage, must fit itself into the political structure of confederation. Quebecers, on the other hand, see themselves not as a minority but as a people with the moral right to self-determination. Even Quebecers who favor remaining in the Canadian confederation see themselves as members of a nation: they understand Canada as a binational country. Many English-speaking Canadians oppose the binational understanding of Canada.

Let me mention in this context that church documents published by the Catholic Church and by the United Church, the largest Protestant church in Canada, have acknowledged the peoplehood of French Canadians and recognized their moral right to self-determination.[12]

Faced with these difficulties, the task of political theology in regard to collective identities is not only to distinguish between the ideological and utopian dimensions of the national myth but also to provide critical insight into the relationships of one collectivity to the other.

I wish to explore a startling idea taken from a long, as yet unpublished essay, written by an Iranian scholar, Modj Sadria, residing in Montreal, which tried to deal with the question of how the Orient should define its own collective self-identity. Let me lift this idea out of the essay's particular historical context. In general it can be said that it is politically dangerous for a collectivity to define itself out of its own tradition and only afterward, as a second step, turn to the other collectivity facing it. If a community creates its identity and produces its national myth by relying exclusively on its own experience, it will never be able to make room for the other as other. It will eventually look upon the other as stranger, as opponent, as rival, as enemy. To overcome this inner dynamic of hostility, a collectivity must define itself dialogically from the start. In constituting its own self-understanding it must simultaneously make room for the self-definition of the other. This respect for the other does not imply that one collectivity necessarily accepts the self-understanding another collectivity has of itself. No, it may indeed be necessary to reject this present self-understanding. What is always possible, however, is to imagine a possible self-understanding of the other collectivity that would facilitate dialogue and respect. There may, in fact, exist minority movements in the other collectivity that are critical of the present national myth, movements that actually strive for the reconstruction of that other collectivity and its culture so that respect and dialogue with a neighboring collectivity is possible. Persons involved in the definition of their own collectivity must simultaneously make room for the self-identity of the other collectivity and the easiest way to do this is to be in solidarity with minority movements among the other collectivity, which themselves strive for a dialogical self-definition.

If these reflections are valid, then we must humbly admit that the Christian churches have erred over the centuries. For the churches have always defined themselves nondialogically, in exclusive reliance on their own heritage, and for this reason they had to look upon other religious communities as stranger, opponent, revival, and eventually enemy. It was only the ecumenical movement of the twentieth century that taught the churches to define themselves anew, this time in dialogue with the ecumenical aspirations of the other communities.

If these reflections are valid, Canadians — by which I here mean mainly English-speaking Canadians — must try to define the collective identity of Canada by leaving room for the self-determination of Quebec and learn to do so by extending their solidarity to the movement in Quebec that also struggles for a dialogical self-definition.

Conversely, to avoid the political danger of projecting the other as opponent and enemy, Quebecers (whether or not they seek sovereignty) must also seek a collective self-understanding that makes room for an appropriate self-understanding of English Canada. The only way Quebecers can do this is to extend their solidarity with those groups in English Canada that are committed to social justice and a dialogical collective self-understanding.

Applying the same principle to Canada's presence vis-à-vis the United States, we recognize immediately that it is politically dangerous for the Canadian left to look at this powerful country simply as empire. There are of course many Canadians who like to think of Canada as junior partner in the American empire, just as many Canadians at the turn of the century wanted Canada to be junior partner in the British empire. But the Canadian left that strives for an economy beyond capitalist contradictions must avoid defining America as an enemy and instead make room in Canada's own self-symbolization for an appropriate collective identity of the United States. Again such a dialogical self-definition becomes possible if we extend our solidarity to those Americans who in their country wrestle against political and economic empire and envisage American culture based on social solidarity.

Nationalism has often been an ideology (in the wider sense) in the struggle for a people's self-determination against the remnants of the feudal order and, later, against crumbling colonial empires. Nationalism of this kind has been inspired by the quest for justice. The symbols of nationalism have tried to unite the social classes in a joint historical project to overcome national oppression. But nationalisms, however valid, have always been politically ambiguous because they tended to define national identities in a nondialogical way, making no room for an appropriate collective identity of ethnic minorities nor for a dialogically defined national identity of the other collectivity. A Zionist philosopher in Israel recently said: "When we were young, we thought we could pluck the raisins out of the poisonous cake of nationalism; now that we are old, we have discovered that even the raisins were poisonous."

In this paper I understand liberation theology as a critical social theory of the left that appreciates the values of identity and community. I regard this as an important service rendered by the religious left to the human struggle for emancipation.

In his remarkable book, *The Socialist Decision*, published in 1932, a few months prior to the victory of Nazism in Germany, Paul Tillich distinguishes two sets of political theories. The first, "the myths of origin," relates a society to the great moments of its history, especially its genesis, and the second, "the myths of destiny," relates a society to its evolution in the future. Myths of origin, be they religious or ethnic, are politically conservative; they hold up the past as a model and raise up barriers against outsiders. Myths of destiny, by contrast, look toward the unfolding of the rational possibilities in society. They dream of the future society defined in terms of equality and justice. Liberalism and socialism are myths of destiny. Socialism, Tillich argued, wants to overcome the unresolved contradictions of liberalism. Socialism wants to transcend the individualism and utilitarianism created through liberalism by constructing a society based on social solidarity. Yet, Tillich continues, socialism is as rationalistic as liberalism and hence has been unable to inspire values of community and identity. The contradictions of instrumental rationality cannot be overcome by a new application of the same instrumental rationality.

To inspire community and identity, socialism must be willing to turn to the myths of origin. This is a dangerous undertaking. Political philosophies guided by a myth of origin remain indifferent to rational definitions of human progress. Under certain critical circumstances, a myth of origin may even give rise to fascism. Still, if a myth of origin remains strictly subordinated to the principle of justice, it may be joined to a socialist project, and then it could teach the socialist movement how to create community and strengthen collective identity.

Tillich wrote his famous book when his own movement of religious socialism had hardly any political presence in Germany. Yet he appealed to communism and social democracy to abandon their scientific rationalism, to incorporate a myth of origin, strictly controlled by justice, in its social theory and by doing so find support beyond the working class in the entire lower sector of society, including farmers, crafts people, and village and small town populations. Tillich recognized that the name "national socialism," adopted by German fascism, was fraudulent: there was no subordination of the myth of origin to the principle of justice. Here a romantic return to the past made the people vulnerable to an outburst of barbarism. In *The Socialist Decision* Tillich continued to believe in the historical mission of socialism. He thought that in the future socialism may be able to overcome the exploitation and alienation of workers and the poor, if it learned to promote, within this context, the spirit of community and identity. This is why Tillich created the movement of religious socialism. Yet in the Germany of the 1920s this movement represented only a small circle.

Liberation theology in Latin America and equivalent religious movements in other parts of the world are movements with a popular base. Their originality lies in the fact that they offer a left-wing, critical, social analysis and at the same time create symbols of community and identity.

NOTES

1. Cornel West, *Prophesy Deliverance!* (Philadelphia: Westminster, 1982), p. 100.

2. See G. Baum, "Social-démocratie et engagement éthique," *Relations* (January-February 1988) 25–27.

3. Harold Wells, "The Question of Ideological Determination in Liberation Theology," *Toronto Journal of Theology*, 3/2 (Fall 1987) 209–20.

4. The article was first published in the winter issue of *Daedalus*, 1967, and republished in *The Religious Situation: 1968*, D. R. Cutler, ed. (Boston: Beacon, 1969) and R. Bellah, *Beyond Belief* (New York: Harper & Row, 1970), pp. 168–89.

5. See Bellah, *Beyond Belief*, p. 168.

6. The entire debate is presented and analyzed in *American Civil Religion*, R. E. Richley, ed. (New York: Harper & Row, 1974).

7. See *Civil Religion and Political Theology*, T. Rouner, ed. (University of Notre Dame Press, 1986).

8. Rosemary R. Ruether, *Liberation Theology* (New York: Paulist Press, 1972), p. 163.

9. Cf. Duncan Cameron.

10. For an analysis of this controversy, see Daniel Drache, "The Crisis of Canadian Political Economy: Dependency Theory Versus the New Orthodoxy," *Canadian Journal of Political and Social Theory*, 7 (Fall 1983) 25–49.

11. Christopher Lind, "Ethics, Economics and Canada's Catholic Bishops," *Canadian Journal of Political and Social Theory*, 7 (Fall 1983) 25–49.

12. Canadian Conference of Catholic Bishops, "On the Occasion of the Hundredth Year of Confederation," *Do Justice!*, E. F. Sheridan, ed. (Toronto: Jesuit Centre of Faith and Social Justice, 1987), pp. 122–34; The United Church of Canada, "Brief to the Joint Committee on the Constitution of Canada," in *Canadian Churches and Social Justice*, John Williams, ed. (Toronto: Lorimer, 1984), pp. 189–97; The Catholic Bishops of Quebec, "The People of Quebec and Its Political Future," in *Canadian Churches*, pp. 181–88.

9

Theoretical and Institutional Bases of the Opposition to Liberation Theology

FRANÇOIS HOUTART

From the very beginning of its developments, the theology of liberation has been a cause for worry, warnings, and even head-on attacks. Its approach was unusual: instead of defining the locus of its development within the religious field, it saw itself at the very heart of society, thus turning society into the starting point of the systematization of its thought about God. That was not merely a social ethic with religious references, but quite definitely a fundamental theological approach. And it dealt with all the aspects of the Christian faith, from a concern with Christ and the church to the meaning of the kingdom. It must be said that the social analysis of Latin American reality was that of a society marked by class contradictions, and that on the basis of active liberation, the social practice of a believing people took on—as had been the case of Jesus' own practice within the society of his time—a central significance. Thus Marxist analysis was seen as an adequate mediation insofar as it was used to grasp a conflictive reality and practices of liberation. We will first study the various Roman stands and then those of CELAM (*Consejo Episcopal Latinoamericano*) in the action undertaken against the new theology.[1]

THE ROMAN STANDS

In March 1983 Cardinal Ratzinger sent to the bishops of Peru "ten observations" issued by the Roman Congregation for the Doctrine of the Faith, concerning the theology of Gustavo Gutiérrez, asking the bishops to take a stand on the matter (DIAL, no. 925).[2] The document starts by stressing the "appeal" of the author whose theology is, however, characterized by "an extreme ambiguity," both features resulting from the prior-itization of attention given to the destitution of the masses and to the uncritical acceptance of Marxist interpretation. The text goes on to state that Gutiérrez uses such a perception to reinterpret the Christian message: a selective and reductionist rereading in which the exploited peoples of our time are put in the same category as the poor of the Bible and in which events, such as the exodus, for instance, become episodes of political lib-eration. Gutiérrez is also blamed for slipping into a temporal messianism that would mistake the growth of the kingdom for the progress of "justice." Also, among the "shortcuts" chosen by the theology of liberation, Cardinal Ratzinger points to a restrictive conception of sin, which would be limited to "social sin."

Moreover, Marxist influence — according to the Congregation — is mani-fest when it comes to the primacy of orthopraxis as opposed to orthodoxy. To state that the experience acquired in the struggle of liberation is an encounter with the Lord and that it is marked by the presence of the Spirit is to go against the transcendence of revelation and its normative value, as well as against the specific character of theological faith. Besides which, any rereading of the Bible, at any time of history, amounts to questioning the unity of meaning of God's word and the reality of tradition.

Lastly, as the document explains, since the theology of Gutiérrez posits that the kingdom is built through the struggles of liberation, it sees the church as a mere sign of unity and love, a fruit of such struggles. This negates the reconciliation that has already been achieved through the sac-rifice of Christ and the fact that salvation is already given in Jesus Christ; on the contrary, future salvation (liberation) is thus seen as eschatological.

Also, in the liberationist perspective, class struggle is to be found within the church too, and the opposition between the churchmen who are on the side of the powers that be and the church of the poor logically leads to a rejection of the hierarchy and of its legitimacy. This church of the poor is said to be present in the basic communities that are committed to social struggle, and therefore the danger is not a purely theoretical one. As to eucharistic celebrations that announce liberation, one must question their correspondence with the true nature of the sacrament.

In its conclusion, the document affirms that the purpose of such a the-ology is to use Christianity as an agent of mobilization for the sake of the revolution, for class struggle is seen as an objective reality. Such a theology, by resorting to Marxism, can thus pervert evangelical inspiration, the mean-ing of the poor and of their hopes.

To put it briefly, the Congregation for the Doctrine of the Faith considers that to start with class analysis would have as a consequence a triple the-ological reductionism: it is opposed to the transcendence of revelation expressed in God's Word, it is opposed to the redemption, which has already been achieved, and it is opposed to the concept of the church as mystery, the consequence being quite logically a rejection of the hierarchy.

If we read Gutiérrez carefully, such a reductionism cannot be found. In fact, the text of the Congregation of the Faith clearly makes two points. On the one hand, it notes a confrontation between an ahistorical and metaphysical conception of God's salvific action in humankind and a vision that replaces it in human history. On the other hand, it reveals a concern to safeguard the exclusivity of those who speak for the magisterium as well as of the controlling function of the hierarchy, which is obviously in keeping with the logic of the first vision. The study of the second document will provide a few additional details.

In the course of a lecture he gave in Rome in September 1983, Cardinal Ratzinger dealt with the epistemological structure of the theology of liberation (DIAL, no. 930). In the first place, he said, there is an opposition between Jesus, the historical character, and the Christ of faith.[3] For the liberation theologian, referring to history brings in a scientific dimension that makes new research possible, and this goes against tradition and implicitly brings the magisterium into disrepute, for it would appear as bound to theories that are untenable in the modern world.

The second element is that of the hermeneutics on which the new theology is based. It is accused by the cardinal of wanting to actualize Christianity according to a historical given. It is on this level, says he, that Marxism and its class struggle make their presence felt. They make Christianity into a political doctrine. Their predilection for the biblical "poor" incorporates a confusion between historical imagery and Marxist dialectic. The proletariat of the capitalistic society is seen as following in the footsteps of the biblical poor, and when faced with class struggle—a fact seen as objective—a Christian cannot remain neutral. To ignore the struggle is to conform with the will of the ruling class. Thus, said Ratzinger, the magisterium cannot intervene anymore, for if it rejects such an interpretation of Christianity, it takes a stand against the poor and therefore against Jesus himself.

Such a choice, Ratzinger said, though it seems to be a scientific one, is obviously hermeneutic. It determines a path that leads to a later interpretation of Christianity. We may ask what are the interpretive authorities. The key concepts are as follows: people, community, experience, and history. In liberation theology, the "community" interprets events thanks to its experience and is able to discover an orientation for its "praxis." The people, in its socio-religious dimension (the community of belonging) is thus opposed to the concept of "hierarchy," which is—in classical theology—the only interpretive authority. Moreover, the same people is also involved in class struggle. And here we see that the popular church is against the hierarchical church. In such an opposition, the concept of history becomes the decisive hermeneutic authority. The popular church is reasoning in terms of salvation history and therefore only in an antimetaphysical mode. It considers history as the locus of revelation.

Thus, as far as Cardinal Ratzinger is concerned, the concept of history absorbs that of God and of revelation. It also becomes a way of legitimizing Marxism's materialistic philosophy. If the magisterium insists on permanent truths, because its way of thinking is metaphysical, it will be considered not only as an authority set against progress but also as an institution that uses oppressive force.

I will not analyze here the other parts of the document, that in which the author points to the spread of liberation theology to other continents of the Third World, as well as to its ecumenical features or that in which he studies how it came into being. Let me only mention that he credits German exegetes and philosophers with an important influence. He also attacks directly the idea, which was voiced by Vatican II, of reading "the signs of the times" and using the social sciences for that purpose. Above all he accuses the Marxist interpretation of history as a critical instance of theological thought.

Most of the theologians of liberation have a difficult time recognizing themselves adequately in such a document, and some of them have already said so. Though it is a private text, it does have a great importance because it expresses an absolute rejection of liberation theology and concludes that urgent measures must be taken.

CRITICISMS AND THE STRATEGY OF CELAM

The documents that I analyze here are the result of a relatively long history in which CELAM played a very active role. It was indeed particularly concerned because that school of thought had started in Latin America. While theologians working on those themes had played an important role in the pastoral agencies of CELAM, and even in the preparation of the Medellín Conference at the end of the 1960s, the situation was progressively reversed as early as 1972. During a meeting held at Sucre in Bolivia, CELAM started to revise the functions of its various agencies and appointed as Secretary General Alfonso López Trujillo, who was at that time auxiliary bishop of Bogotá. Before studying the strategies of action, I will take a brief look at the arguments used by CELAM against the theology of liberation and against all the pastoral methods inspired by it or that it had inspired.

Criticisms of the Theology of Liberation and of New Pastoral Methods

In the course of those years, such criticism centered around four points: the use of Marxist analysis, christology, ecclesiology, and social doctrine. On the first one, López Trujillo leaves no doubts. In his opening speech to the eighteenth Assembly of CELAM in 1981 he said about the theologians of liberation: "The problem is not that they speak loudly when talking about the poor, but that they make an ideological use of a Marxist instrument of analysis . . . and this is in contradiction with the magisterium of the church."

This is a serious danger, he added, because nothing can be safe from the theological and pastoral consequences of such a use: "neither christology, ecclesiology, nor a certain conception of the basic ecclesial communities ... could CELAM remain silent about ... when one knows to what extent the church structure is endangered by the indiscriminate use – and I would even say the ascientific use – of an analysis that is 150 years old and is presented by some persons today as a novelty."

The CELAM texts refer frequently to "ideologies." Even though the latter are never specified, it is quite clear that the concept refers mostly to Marxism. Thus does the secretary general say when talking about the basic communities: they represent "the inrush of dubious ideologies and ecclesiologies" and the global pastoral plan for 1983–1986 includes a section entitled: struggle against sects and ideologies. In his speech at Puebla, John Paul II indicated the distinction that must be made between "a Christian liberation" and "a liberation nurtured by ideologies destroying the coherence it must have with an evangelical vision of humankind, things, and events." He took up the same theme forcefully in his homily at Managua on March 4, 1983. The meaning became even more obvious when Bishop Quarracino, the new president of CELAM, referred to "ideological manipulations" in a report to the conference of CELAM in Port-au-Prince, Haiti, in 1983. He gave as an example "Marxist analysis as a working tool."

In short, the accusation is clear. What is less clear is what persons mean when they talk about Marxism, Marxist analysis, "ideologies." Cardinal Aloisio Lorscheider, archbishop of Fortaleza, Brazil, did not hesitate to clarify the matter. In an interview published by the newspaper of his diocese, he stated: "When I hear people talking about a Marxist infiltration in the church, I ask them what they mean by Marxism. Most of the time, I don't get an answer.... Many when they talk about Marxism do not mean Marxist philosophy but Marxist analysis ... [the latter] endeavors to be a means of understanding the society in which we live."[4] Such a declaration should be enough to show that there is no unanimity among the bishops of Latin America.

As to theologians, they answer with the Boff brothers: "Marx is not the godfather of liberation theology. The tool of Marxist analysis is a mediation. It might be dangerous, but it is useful in order to understand social reality."[5] Thus it seems quite clear that the CELAM position amounts from the start to a lack of distinction – in the Marxist approach – between the use of social analysis and philosophical option. According to CELAM, the analysis necessarily originates in and leads to the philosophy. Then CELAM stresses the essentially atheistic character – thus contradictory to faith – of that same philosophy. In such a logic, social analysis can only bring about the destruction of religion. It is therefore necessary to oppose it forcefully. An examination of the theological writings of liberation and of the practices of the basic communities does not easily lead one to such conclusions, and so the question that remains is this: Why such an amalgam? I will come back to this point.

The second part of the argumentation against the theology of liberation concerns christology and even more generally redemption. It is accused of showing "the incarnate Word as an eminent example of charity and socio-political commitment."[6] "The Christ of the Gospels is reduced to the Christ of temporal liberation only."[7] According to López Trujillo, the Lord is not shown "as the one sent by the Father, but as a tool of class struggle; the rebel of Nazareth." Moreover, according to this theological school, the good news would only concern the poor. Such a choice is "to be understood as a class option."

Also in the argumentation about redemption, the secretariat of the bishops of Central America and Panama was even more explicit when preparing the papal visit: "Those who are hoping that the pope will come only for 'the poor' have not read *Redemptor Hominis*" (John Paul II's first encyclical). The pope is not "a class pope."[8] He clarified his own thought when speaking at the opening of the meeting of CELAM in Port-au-Prince, in 1983, pointing out, among the serious problems to be faced by the church in Latin America: "the bitterness of many who, because of an erroneous option for the poor, feel that they are abandoned and forgotten in their aspirations and their religious needs."[9]

In other words, the reproach concerns a characterization of the poor seen as being inspired by "criteria that are only political and ideological,"[10] whereas the biblical message is more global and salvation in Jesus Christ is more than a simple liberation from economic and social oppression. Such an option, "exclusive and excluding," begets inevitably "feelings of hatred and struggle between brothers."[11] But, once again, is this not a rather shallow reading of the theology of liberation, which for most of its authors, such as Gustavo Gutiérrez, the Boff brothers, or Jon Sobrino, insists on the universality of salvation and its nonreductibility to social processes? On the other hand, it remains true that it stresses the concrete character of the poor, who are not only suffering and living in destitution, but above all oppressed by the economic, social, and political practices of the classes that exploit them. And, again, we are faced with the question: Why was this forgotten in the presentation of their theological reflection?

Before answering this question, I will examine the last two issues: ecclesiology and the social doctrine of the church. In the first case, the main problem is that of "the popular church." According to Bishop Quarracino, elected president of CELAM in 1983, it is unacceptable to talk about a "church born from the people." Indeed, "we must warn our churches against this danger, which leads to a theory about two churches, and this calls for a vigorous work of clarification and unitary action."[12] As far as López Trujillo is concerned, the theology of liberation introduces on the one hand a popular church, for it opted for the poor, and on the other hand a bourgeois church, thus inserting class conflicts within the church itself.

Such a presentation of the ecclesiological thought of the theology of liberation and of the reality of the basic communities seems, at first sight, to be more adequately in keeping with what is generally said. There is, however, a fundamental difference. Never did the basic communities or theological reflection about them speak about two churches. On the contrary, they insist on their genuine membership in the one church of Jesus Christ, while also stressing the fact that there are various options within that church. They point out, in particular, that political choice, social and cultural practices, a preference for certain Catholic movements, a type of spirituality, and even theological positions on the part of some Latin American Christians as well as most of the hierarchy put them in fact, if not intentionally, in a correspondence of interests and mentality with the ruling classes. Does not such a fact call for a critique of the gospel?

Bringing differences to light is not acceptable in a concept of the church based above all on obedience and authority. This was summed up in a letter of John Paul II to the bishops of Nicaragua on June 29, 1982. It would be "absurd and dangerous to imagine next to—not to say against—the church based on the bishops . . . a popular church—that is, without reference to the legitimate shepherds" and "infiltrated by ideological connotations."[13] In his homily in Managua, the pope returned to that theme even more vigorously, talking about "parallel teachings" that weaken the church and demanding that doctrinal concepts and pastoral projects be subject to the magisterium of the church, represented by the pope and the bishops.

We, therefore, witness two parallel discourses, though they are not necessarily in contradiction. The first perceives the church in its concrete reality, though not denying in any way its eschatological character. The second favors the reality of the church as a sign or sacrament of unity, according to the words of Vatican II. But it precludes any possibility of seeing the hierarchy as so placed in social reality as to give it a precise meaning, thus crediting it with an ontological character, therefore, an indisputable one. Once again, the dialogue comes to a dead end. But in this case, the stakes seem clearer.

As to the social doctrine of the church, it is questioned by the theology of liberation. "As happens in puppy love, many were blinded by the scientific analysis of reality, class struggle, the theory of dependency, revolutionary praxis"; thus wrote Bishop Quarracino, then secretary general of CELAM, "and they did not perceive anymore the viability of the church's social doctrine."[14] Now, John Paul II said in Managua, the principle of subjection applied to doctrinal concepts and pastoral projects "must also be applied in the field of the church's social doctrine, developed by my predecessors and by myself."[15]

The perceptions of all the above are therefore very different. In the first case, class analysis brings to light the antagonistic character of economic interests, an opposition expressed in the reality of a class struggle that has repercussions in the political, social, cultural, and even religious fields. The resulting social ethic seeks to implement structural changes that go beyond mere interpersonal relationships. The goal is to establish a logic of the majorities, which means a break from the capitalistic economic system and a start on the socialist way. On the other hand, in the second case, though social differences are seen as a given, the various social categories must coexist in harmony. Thus, there is a need for cooperation between the various classes for the sake of the common good. Such an ethical norm, obviously, calls for doing away with abuses and injustices, correcting all excesses and, therefore, appealing to the sense of justice and generosity of the ruling classes but also to the patience and nonviolence of the oppressed classes. And in the end, this results in the condemnation of class struggle, considered as unacceptable behavior in interpersonal relationships and leading necessarily to violence. Such is the meaning of John Paul II's intervention in his speech to the campesinos of Panama.

This brings us back to the first point concerning Marxist analysis. To oppose its adoption in this field is justified by what is seen as a contradiction between such an analysis and an understanding of social reality inspired by Christianity, the one implicitly adopted by the church. Once more the question is raised: Why would one favor an interclass understanding of reality in the name of Christian faith?

Do we not find again and again in the reproaches addressed to the theology of liberation a logic linking all its various elements? That is what we may ask ourselves in order to formulate some interpretive hypotheses. Is there not, in fact, a double rejection? First, that of history as a dynamic part of the work of redemption, a history built by human beings. Taking it into account does indeed relativize a view of faith conceived as a deposit guarded by the magisterium and seeing the hierarchy at the top of the entire religious structuring. It also rejects class analysis because it calls for a stand. This puts the institution—in this case, the hierarchy—in an impossible situation, because it defines itself as having to rule unanimously without even mentioning the socio-political space that it would lose if it became partial. Such a double rejection would be all the more radical in that it refers to the defense of a revealed truth regarding salvation, a function considered essential by religious authorities.

What is probably not perceived is that in the concrete situation of the Third World, such a position leads to a choice that is also political and facts are a far more eloquent proof than theological writings: this choice is made against the poor insofar as they take into their own hands their own liberation and when they raise their voices without the church.

The CELAM Strategy

The year 1972, when Cardinal López Trujillo was elected secretary general of CELAM, can be seen as a watershed: it was then that the activities of CELAM started in this field. The first step was, in 1973, a meeting in Bogotá about the theme of liberation. The idea that obtained at the time was that there are two concepts of liberation, one that is spiritual and of Latin American origin, and the other stressing politics, and coming from Europe. The review *Tierra Nueva*, founded in Bogotá, specialized in refuting the theology of liberation. The first strategy was therefore at the intellectual and strictly theological levels.

It went on during the following years. A working group was set up in cooperation with German theologians, the "Church and Liberation" study circle meeting in 1973, 1974, and 1975, and leading then to a colloquy in Rome. During the latter, an important report on the "world propagation of the theology of liberation" described it as a "contagious virus" and denounced in rather violent terms the persons and institutions spreading it.

During the preparation for the Puebla Conference (1979), which brought together the bishops of Latin America for the tenth anniversary of the Medellín Conference, there was an intense activity, devoted among other things to bringing back in step the theology of liberation and the basic communities. The result was quite moderate; there was no condemnation, thanks to the intervention of influential bishops and especially of several Brazilian cardinals. Cardinal López Trujillo became president of CELAM at the beginning of 1980, and organized in 1982 two important meetings: one on ecclesiology and especially on the basic communities, and the other on christology. Father Hamer, O.P., of the Congregation for the Doctrine of the Faith (the former Holy Office), took part in the first meeting. The second one, held in Rio de Janeiro barely a month after, saw Cardinal Ratzinger, president of that same congregation, in attendance. The second meeting, described by CELAM as pluralistic, was aimed at a refutation of liberation theology, and no theologians of that school were invited.

A second aspect of the strategy consists in reorganizing the agencies of CELAM according to the objectives described above and in practicing a policy of nominating "safe" persons for the key positions. It would be too long to describe all the stages of this cleverly planned action. Persons invited to the various colloquies and meetings wind up at the key posts of CELAM, thus insuring a continuity of action. This was done in close cooperation with the Holy See where Cardinal López Trujillo has a great influence on the CAL (Committee on Latin America), the head of which is also the prefect of the Congregation of Bishops, formerly nuncio in Latin America, Cardinal Baggio. CELAM is also very active in the preparation of the pope's tour of Latin America both in the field of topics and that of orientations.

Lastly, the third part is pastoral action through pastoral projects, the third of which was implemented from 1983 to 1986, offering a logistical support to local ordinaries for the formation of religious personnel, organization of study sessions, and support for lay groups. It will be recalled that an emergency plan for Nicaragua was set up after the Sandinista revolution. All these strategies are, of course, calling for considerable funds that CELAM obtains from various sources, notably from German Catholic foundations and private American entities.

Even though this is not the topic of this article, I think it important to mention that all those actions met with some opposition. For instance, the Brazilian Episcopal Conference, the largest one of Latin America, was clearly reserved about the CELAM policy. However, new appointments of bishops might progressively erode this resistance. Moreover, the basic communities of Latin America organized themselves in 1980 during a meeting in São Paulo under the aegis of Cardinal Arns. CELAM exerted tremendous pressure to minimize the effects of the meeting. Cardinal López Trujillo also intervened with the Catholic development organizations providing aid in order to bring an end to their support of pastoral and social initiatives of groups and persons connected with the church of the poor. Lastly, in his letter to Philip Potter, Secretary General of the World Council of Churches, in early 1982, he blamed that organization for giving help — especially of a financial nature — to groups and centers "trying to hide under the ecumenical label" and "carrying ideologized forms of theological expression which are radically critical of the church, its shepherds, and even the very basic principles of the faith."

After his two terms as secretary general and one as president, having thus spent eleven years with CELAM, Cardinal López Trujillo, ordinary of Medellín, was appointed a cardinal on February 2, 1984. In a private audience, the pope expressed his appreciation of the cardinal by stating: "His contribution to the study and clarification of theology, particularly of the so-called theology of liberation, has been and remains an eminent service to the church."[16]

Controversies outside the Catholic Church

It might be useful to mention here that opposition to the theology of liberation and to new trends in the Latin American church did not only come from the church itself. In 1982 a working group met in Santa Fe, New Mexico, to prepare the outline of a U.S. policy toward Latin America in case Reagan were to be elected president. A paragraph of the confidential text, which was published anyhow, mentioned the necessity to fight the theology of liberation. At the same time, the Institute for Religion and Democracy was founded in Washington, D.C., under the direction of Peter Berger, a Protestant sociologist, and Michael Novak, a Catholic journalist and author, for the purpose of attacking the aid given by North American Christian groups to the theology of liberation and to "the popular church" in Latin America, more particularly in Central America. This institute is financed by several foundations, some of which are close to the Republican Party.

Among arguments voiced outside the church, we can mention in particular an article published by the CELAM newsletter and written by Rabbi Leon Klenicki, entitled "Theology of Liberation, the Viewpoint of a Latin American Jew."[17] After denouncing the alliance with leftist ideologies and the politization of the biblical message that he perceives in the theology of liberation, the author affirms that the latter strengthens the anti-Jewish trend in Christian theology because it does not make any reference to "the return to the Promised Land after twenty centuries of exile, through the foundation of the state of Israel . . . nor to Zionism as a process of liberation."

A First Reply

As soon as the text of Cardinal Ratzinger came out, the Boff brothers published a reply, which I already mentioned. They admit that there are dangers in the theology of liberation, which can appear as a form of reductionism. But this comes precisely from the awareness of the dramatic situation in the Third World. They add that what is new has not always had the time to be perfectly harmonized and that this is in itself a normal occurrence. Such a situation does not, however, justify an attitude tainted by the presumption of perversity. We cannot recognize ourselves in what Cardinal Ratzinger said, state the two Brazilian theologians.

The theology of liberation is, on the contrary, a creative broadening of traditional theology. To start from liberation means to read the signs of the times in the light of faith. Such an approach includes the transcendental dimension of faith, liberation from sin, and gratuitous communion with God. It is developed in a living contact with reality, and not in an academic universe. Unlike Bultmann, it stresses the historical Jesus Christ. As to Marxist analysis, it is a tool for grasping reality, perhaps a dangerous tool "but the best we have to account for concrete situations."[18]

The text ends with a reproach: that of lacking sensitivity with regard to the cause of the poor: it is not simply a factor, a mere concept, but an ethical, mystical, and theological experience. A position such as that of Cardinal Ratzinger can also become a political tool.

WHERE ARE WE GOING

The dynamics of the process now in development will lead to a confrontation if church authorities go to the very logical conclusion of their position. Should we read a sign in the fact that Clodovis Boff was deprived of his canonical mission of teaching theology at the Pontifical University of Rio de Janeiro by Cardinal de Araujo Sales, its Great Chancellor, just as the academic year was about to start in March 1984? In any case, a parallel with the crisis of modernism seems to be justified because the controversy is at least partly about similar elements.

However, the stakes are bigger this time. They are located at the very heart of the struggle of the Third World people, particularly in Latin America. There can be another parallel, that of the church in the face of the working-class problems in Europe, and this time the consequences can be foreseen. To entwine a new form of antimodernism with a struggle against popular emancipation in the Third World is an intellectual and social challenge that might become very costly in terms of human lives and religious vitality. On the other hand, to accept theological and pastoral pluralism within today's church might perhaps enable us not to be forced—within a few decades—as has already happened in many cases, to a rehabilitation of those who have been rejected.

—translated from the French by Nelly Marans

NOTES

This text of François Houtart was published in *Le Monde Diplomatique*, no. 363 (June 1984), under the title, *La peur d'une contagion marxiste* (Fear of a Marxist contagion).

1. A more detailed document about the theologies of liberation in Latin America and about the countertheologies was published as a dossier by the Tricontinental Center, 5 Avenue Sainte Gertrude, B-1348 Ottignies-Louvain-la-Neuve, Belgium.
2. *Diffusion de l'Information sur l'Amérique Latine*, 47 Quai des Grands Augustins, F-75006, Paris.
3. According to Cardinal Ratzinger, it was the influence of the German exegete Bultmann that obtained in this field, an assertion contested by several liberation theologians who are precisely stressing the central character of Jesus' practice within his society.
4. Interview given to the diocesan bulletin of the archbishopric of Fortaleza, *Páginas* 7/46 (August 1982).
5. Leonardo Boff and Clodovis Boff, "The Cry of Poverty Coming from Faith" *Folha de São Paulo*, published by *DIAL*, no. 931 (April 26, 1984).
6. Speech by Bishop Quarracino, secretary general of CELAM, at the Port-au-Prince meeting.
7. Article by His Excellency Quarracino in the CELAM Bulletin.
8. Declaration of the secretariat of the episcopacy of Central America and Panama, *CELAM Bulletin*, no. 180 (February, 1983).
9. Discourse of John Paul II at Port-au-Prince, to the general assembly of CELAM.
10. Ibid.
11. Ibid.
12. Bishop Quarracino, see n. 7.
13. *CELAM Bulletin*, no. 176 (September, 1982).
14. Bishop Quarracino, (n. 7, above).
15. Homily of March 4, 1983, in Managua.
16. *CELAM Bulletin*, no. 181 (March-April, 1983).

17. Rabbi Leon Klenicki, "La teología de la liberación: Una exploración judia latinoamericana," *CELAM Bulletin* n. 185 (Nov.-Dec. 1983).

18. The Brazilian episcopacy did not make known that between 1979 and 1983 drought had cost some ten million lives in northeastern Brazil, because the social structures in place prevented an adequate response to the climatic conditions.

10

The Religious and
the Human Ecumene

EDWARD SCHILLEBEECKX

The history of humankind in past and present is marked by religious wars and the violence of religions. The coexistence of religions does not seem in fact to be favorable for the promoting of humanity, for the movement toward living together in community worthy of humanity. This is indeed a highly paradoxical situation, especially for Christians, for Vatican II declares solemnly the Christian church to be "the sign and the instrument . . . of the unity of all the human race" (*Lumen Gentium*, 1). But try saying this in Northern Ireland, where for years Christians have been doing everything to make one another's living impossible, in the most literal sense of the word. Or, look at Iran and Iraq, Lebanon, the Golden Temple of the Sikhs, and so on. If paying homage to the highest human values becomes imperialistic, such praise deteriorates into the worst enemy of concrete human dignity!

Gustavo Gutiérrez has brought the church "as sacrament of the world" into connection with "the option for the poor."[1] I should like to elaborate on that vision here.

THE PLURALITY OF RELIGIONS AND CHRISTIANITY

The history of humanity presents us with a collection of divergent ways of life, a multicolored proposal of "ways of salvation": monotheistic Judaism, Christianity, and Islam; Hinduism and Buddhism; Taoism, Confucianism, and Shinto; animism; African and Amerindian ways to salvation and blessing. We call all of these "religions"; that is, we are convinced that there is an essential agreement among all the divergent phenomena. That is why they are designated by a single concept: religion.

Likewise, *Nostra Aetate* (1), a declaration of Vatican II, says that persons "look to the various religions for answers to those profound mysteries of the human condition which today, even as in olden times, deeply stir the human heart." In other words, by offering a message of salvation and by showing a path to salvation, religions respond to a fundamental question about life. In a similar key, modern sociologists (such as H. Lübbe) say much the same thing, albeit in very general terms but nonetheless correctly, talking about religions as "systems of orientation to the ultimate" or "systems of dealing with contingency": comprehensive systems that give meaning or systems that help us to come to terms spiritually, emotionally, and especially existentially with our vulnerable, precarious existence in an ambivalent society.

However, students of culture and philosophers of religion have some misconceptions about all of this—in the dual line of either an essentialist or a nominalist approach via "general terms" ("universals") to what is meant by "religion."

In my opinion, we can say this better with a term of Wittgenstein: that there exists among the many religions "family resemblances." Then there is really no talk of one or more "common characteristics," or of "ideal types." Phenomena that show resemblances and are on that basis designated with the same term ("religion") are (just as the members of a family, so Wittgenstein would say) each really unique in their specific combination or configuration of characteristics. But on the basis of "family resemblances" they still can be compared with one another despite their uniqueness. As a socio-cultural phenomenon and system of meaning, Christianity is also a religion alongside other religions: one out of many.

And here the difficulties begin. How can religions as religions "live together" with another, despite their conflicting pretensions? We stand here before a particularly difficult and delicate problem regarding the question of how religious persons from a variety of religions might coexist.

For themselves, Christians find their only rescue in Jesus confessed as the Christ. Therefore they have kept asking (out of their own vision and orientation in life) in the course of history how non-Christians could work out their salvation. For their confession of Jesus' uniqueness was not merely an expression of a subjective conviction. According to Christian confession, that vision has to do with something real: that is to say, *it is true* (although it is an affirmative of faith and not a scientifically provable and verifiable truth; thus it can never be used in a discussion as a weapon against non-Christians).

On the basis of that faith conviction in Jesus' universal redeeming activity, Christians had to ask the question sooner or later about the possibility of salvation for non-Christians. This happened indirectly from the very beginning of Christianity: already the Second (or New) Testament says that God desires the salvation of "all" (1 Tim. 2:4), and that God wills it in a realizable manner, adapted to the situation of given individuals (even if they do not know Christ). The actual thematization of this problem—how individuals "could become blessed" if they had never come to know Jesus Christ—began especially in modernity and really only in our own time to become a fundamental and even crucial theological problem.

For we as Christians are confronted with biblical texts that do not fit easily with this problem and for which we must account. Jesus surely preached the reign of God as a reign of justice, peace, and wholeness of creation for all persons. But according to the witness of the New Testament, Jesus himself stands in a constitutive or essential relationship to this universal reign of God for all humanity. Christians say with the Bible that "there is one God, and there is one mediator between God and men," Jesus Christ (1 Tim. 2:5); "and there is a salvation in no one else, for there is no other name under heaven given among men by which we must be saved" (Acts 4:12). The Johannine Jesus also says: "I am the way, and the truth, and the life; no one comes to the Father but by me" (John 14:16). "For so the Lord has commanded us, saying, 'I have set you to be a light for the gentiles, that you may bring salvation to the uttermost parts of the earth.' And when the gentiles heard this they were glad" (Acts 13:47). Also a Paulinism directed in a different fashion but just as Christian, says: "For as by a man came death, by a man has come also the resurrection of the dead. For as in Adam all die, so also in Christ shall all be made alive" (1 Cor. 15:21–22). What happened to Jesus is a fact "once for all" (Heb. 9:12). That which has taken place holds for all nations, peoples, and cultures; it is universally relevant in time and space; it has world-historical significance. The post-Pauline tradition even says: "He is the image of the invisible God" (Col. 1:15). A similar sound is heard in all the gospel traditions. "He who sees me sees him who sent me" (John 12:45). The essential bond between the coming of the reign of God for all people and Jesus the Christ is confessed in all levels and traditions of the New Testament, also by the first Hebrew-Jewish interpretation of Jesus of Nazareth.

Those are texts that we cannot circumvent or dilute or act as though they were not there. Moreover, that would not be honest; a selective elimination of parts of the scriptures is also hardly an honest solution. To be sure: all these statements are statements of *belief*, of course; they interpret a confessing discourse, in no way a scientific-objectivizing or propositional and thereby verifiable discourse. But this latter has in no way an exclusive claim on truth. We cannot, however, disregard these absolute statements from the New Testament, or render them harmless by reducing them to exaggerated, elegant flourishes of rhetoric, such as when lovers say to one another "you are the most beautiful and the only one in the world." That is meaningful language, but it holds only for the two lovers, even though outsiders understand clearly its meaning. It is a sensible use of language.

Confessional language of faith, to be sure, also has something to do with similar expressions of someone's complete devotion to a loved one. It indeed says something also about one's subjective stance and complete surrender to another person. But confessional language is not exhausted by that. A certain confessional language also says something about that very person, about reality, a reality that actually calls forth this complete and radical surrender, and is worthy of it, precisely because it is real. Although the immediate basis for such language may lie in a personal or collective experience, that experience also mediates something more profound. The ultimate ground of Jesus' uniqueness spoken of in the scriptural quotation is, according to the New Testament witness, "for in him all the fulness of God was pleased to dwell" (Col. 1:19); or, according to the so-called Apostles' Creed, "He is the Christ, God's only beloved Son, our Lord."

The scriptural quotations refer clearly to Christian consciousness, that Jesus of Nazareth was considered by Christians as the definitive and decisive revelation of God, who nonetheless "desires all to be saved and to come to the knowledge of the truth" (1 Tim. 2:4), also therefore even if they have not come to know Jesus Christ. Whether that revelation then is normative for other religions is the next consideration. For all kinds of ambiguities can come about here if we use the word "normative" or "criterion," because those words are used extensively on the level of "scientific objectivity," whereas the assertion that in Jesus God's definitive and decisive revelation takes place is an affirmation of faith, something that is not accessible or evident on a scientifically objective basis.

In connection with the uniqueness of the Christian church, one can ask good and bad questions. And in the past many bad questions were asked, so that the answer to them shares in the meaninglessness of the question. In the history of the Christian churches it was generally accepted until recently that Christianity was the bearer of absolute truth. "In fact," the Christian churches have so comported themselves in the course of the ages. A proper claim to universality was twisted imperialistically into an ecclesiastical claim of absoluteness, to a monopoly or exclusive claim to truth. This imperialism became the cause of religious wars and of persecution.

A BRIEF OVERVIEW OF THE CONTEMPORARY THEOLOGICAL STATE OF THE QUESTION, ESPECIALLY IN CATHOLIC THEOLOGY

Vatican II broke with this imperialism of truth. In broad lines that was clearly a new path away from the previous centuries-old tradition. However, it was not a radical break, because both the First and Second Testaments and church traditions also recognized good things in the other religions.

Already before Vatican II Karl Rahner and other theologians went further than the already broad statements of this council.[2] They not only recognized the possibility of individual salvation of the adherents of other religions, but also ascribed to those religions themselves — as such, therefore as institutions — salvific value. They, too, were "ways of salvation" to God, institutions of salvation (something that Vatican II, despite urgings from theologians, did not yet dare to say). Even the already open statements of the Second Vatican Council in *Lumen Gentium, Nostra Aetate*, and *Ad Gentes* did not go so far, at least not expressly. It seems also that implicitly for the philosopher of religion from Bonn, Hans Waldenfels, that modern position (inspired by Rahner) goes too far, when he writes that if non-Christians likewise find their salvation, "that happens not *in spite of*, but in each case *in* their religion. The formula *through* (or through the mediation of) their religion is one Christians should rather avoid," he adds explicitly.[3] For myself, I do not understand this hesitation toward religion as a social system so well; apparently he fears that this touches a seed of the truth in the old claim to absoluteness of the "imperialist" Christianity.

One does have to concede with the theologian Max Seckler that the salvific value of all religions cannot be posited merely abstractly and globally.[4] One will have to look very concretely at each religion, one by one, regarding their own values and the image of humanity and the world implicit within them. How do you want to be and how do you see your own humanity? Although it was (unavoidably) schematic, Vatican II tried to express the proper value of Judaism, Hinduism, Buddhism, and Islam, and finally this council speaks in *Lumen Gentium*, chap. 16, even of the possibility of salvation of agnostics and atheists. With this we are already close by my personal theological position, which basically affirms the following: before one can speak historically of religions, there was the reality of God's saving activity in profane history: "outside the world, there is no salvation." God brings about in world history salvation through human mediation *and* persons bring about calamity. Religions are latecomers in the history of salvation coming from God in our profane history.

In recent years some have gone even further. Thus the philosopher of religion Heinz Robert Schlette reverses the categories used earlier: for him, Christianity is not the "normal" or "ordinary way to salvation" to God; the other religions are that. Christianity is the "exceptional" or "extraordinary" way to God.[5]

With this we are still not through the bend in the road. Recently the American Catholic theologian Paul Knitter went even a step further than Schlette: he denies any form of claim to universality of Christianity.[6] In our times there indeed reigns among Christians a certain new form of modern "indifferentism," and some theologians have made themselves spokespersons for it: all religions are of the same value. Of course they are not, for even their visions about humanity are rather divergent, and a religion that, for example, sends the eldest son to death is certainly not of the same value as a religion that expressly forbids it. Criteria of humanity apply here too!

Even though one's own religion is involved in every comparison of religions with one another, one ultimately cannot avoid the truth question. But the truth question presents itself within a "hermeneutical circle." The question is not whether there are many open questions here that cannot be solved speculatively, and moreover whether one is asking the right question and not the wrong one (which can never be resolved). The question of truth with regard to one's own religion in no way need be discriminatory in itself vis-à-vis other religions. No single religion exhausts the question of truth. Therefore *in religiosis* we must put behind us both absolutism and relativism.

Our times have "liberated" themselves in many points from the peculiarly modern claim to truth and universality since the Enlightenment. Logically and practically, plurality has gained priority over unity. The ancient and neoplatonic Greek ideal of unity is in no sense still a norm for modern and postmodern persons. The claims made by a Jewish, Christian, and Muslim monotheism on all persons is perceived by many (or some) as something totalitarian. Some see in this the reason for the move of many Westerners to Asian religions. The statement "all religions are equal" is understandable to postmodern sensibilities, even though that statement is cheap and, to my mind, fundamentally wrong.

The question rather is whether monotheism with its claim to universality cannot be a critique or a challenge to those sensibilities. Current sensibilities are not normative in themselves either! The universal claim to salvation of Jesus and the human reason that remembers the suffering of humanity can also deliver a critique of that liberal pluralism of our time. For there is also a cheap form of toleration—indifference: *laissez faire, laissez passer* — I don't care! This is an attitude without the courage of the witnessing blood of martyrs.

To be sure, Christianity has often expressed its own truth, universality, and uniqueness (which are undeniable) as a claim to absoluteness, by means of which all other religions were considered inferior, whereas the good that was to be found in them was assumed to be present in Christianity itself in a preeminent fashion. One discovered "Christian values" in the other religions, but robbed them of their own identity by the fact. The consequence of this religious and cultural "imperialism" was that the modern history of colonialism and of mission has been in good measure also a time of oppression of foreign cultures and religions, both during and not less than before from the time of the abstract Enlightenment.

But Asia and practically all countries where Islam reigned shut themselves off from Christianity; these universal religions had their own claim to absoluteness. Because of that in the public forum of the West, Christianity came to be considered more and more as one religion among many and moreover, historically, as a religion under which many non-Christian cultures and other religions had suffered severely. This climatic change in Western thinking was paired with a privatization of Christianity as religion: in one's own heart one could quietly praise Christianity as the one true religion, as long as it had no consequences for others and for the bourgeois public forum. At the moment Christianity is not dropping its claim to universality, but is letting both its exclusivist and inclusivist claim to universality go. "Exclusivist," in the sense of "only Christianity is a true religion," and "inclusivist" insofar as there is truth and goodness immanent in other religions, with their adherents being "anonymous Christians." In both cases this discriminates against non-Christians and this therefore is improper.

NEW THEOLOGICAL PERSPECTIVE

Given this prehistory, we shall have to seek in any case a direction that avoids both absolutism and relativism. To ask the truth question regarding Christianity, and simultaneously with that the question whether it is possible for Christians to live together with members of other religions and with atheists and agnostics, in no way presumes, as had been thought earlier, the superiority of Christianity in the sense of how can Christians, who as members of a particular religion consider themselves superior to other religious persons, live together with non-Christians? Rather, the question is about a Christian identity that respectfully acknowledges others' religious identity and allows itself to be challenged by other religions and challenges them in return on the basis of its own message. In short, we are being confronted with other questions than were asked in the past, questions that are more productive and fruitful for all parties concerned.

We are therefore asking other questions, even if it remains binding for Christian believers that they find salvation "only in the name of Jesus of Nazareth." And in this Christian perspective questions arise about whether and how, for example, can one be a Christian as a Hindu? In other words, is there a Hindu version of being Christian? This is not a question of a speculative approach to one another's religions, but of a probably centuries-long experiment to come to a "common experience." Only a common experience can lead to a consonant hermeneutical interpretation. That common experience is by no means here yet. Therefore it seems to me that the question is whether the pluralism of religions is a *factual* phenomenon that should be overcome as quickly as possible, or a *foundational* phenomenon that asks for a continuing humane coexistence. The consequences of this are rather important for one's own vision of the ecumene of the world religions and ultimately for world peace, which, through religious intolerance and through the pretensions to exclusive or inclusive claims to absoluteness, has been put severely to the test in the course of time and today in many countries through religious wars.

My concern here directly is the identity and therefore the proper self-definition of Christianity, in which this religion sees how it is to be situated vis-à-vis other religions: on the one hand, without absolutism or relativism; on the other, without discrimination or feelings of superiority.

PHASE ONE: THE HISTORICAL CONTINGENCY OR LIMITEDNESS OF JESUS OF NAZARETH

In contrast to the earlier claim to absoluteness of Christianity, determined as it was by the regnant *Zeitgeist* of that time, lies the positive acceptance of the diversity of religions, which is, to my mind, inherent in the essence of Christianity. The problem is not so much that posed at the level of an earlier consciousness of the problematic: Is Christianity the one, true religion, or is it (in a more moderate version) a better religion than all the others? In these comparisons the concept "religion" is borrowed from the religion of the one doing the comparison (whatever religion that might be). For Christians, therefore, it is Christianity. Rather, the problem is this: *How can Christianity maintain its own identity and uniqueness and at the same time ascribe a positive value to the diversity of religions in a nondiscriminating way?* When posed in this way, it is not the common elements in the many religions, but precisely their respective differences that form their uniqueness and particularity, that is relevant for Christianity. If this is the case, one needs to indicate a basis in Christianity itself for this new Christian attitude of openness and nonintolerance toward other world religions.

This basis lies, to my mind, in Jesus' message and praxis of the reign of God, with all their consequences. For Christianity is in its particularity and uniqueness as a religion essentially bound to an insuperable "historical particularity" and thus to regionality and limitation. Thus Christianity, too, like all religions has boundaries: limited in forms of expression, and also in ways of looking at things and in concrete praxis. Christians sometimes have difficulty looking at this reality rationally. But this limitedness belongs to the essence of Christianity (even expressed especially when Christians use their "incarnation model" in their theology—which remains in this tradition the dominant paradigm).

The special, particular, and unique character of Christianity is that it finds the life and essence of God precisely in this historical and thus limited particularity of "Jesus of Nazareth"—confessed as the personal-human manifestation of God. Thereby is confessed that Jesus is surely a "unique" but nonetheless "contingent" manifestation (that is, historical and therefore limited) of the gift of salvation coming from God for all persons. Whoever ignores this fact of the concrete, particular humanity of Jesus, precisely in his geographically limited and socio-culturally recognizable and limited quality as "human," makes of the individual Jesus a "necessary" divine emanation or consequence, whereby indeed all other religions disappear into the void. This seems to be essentially in conflict with the deepest sense of all the christological councils and creeds, and finally with the very being of God as absolute freedom. Jesus' humanity is devalued in that vision to a (docetic) phantom humanity, while trivializing on the other hand all non-Christian religions. Nevertheless Christians have in the course of time absolutized without remainder precisely this historical and limited particularity of Christianity. This rang in the historical misery of empirical Christianity in opposition to the original evangelical authenticity.

However, the revelation of God in Jesus, as the Christian gospel proclaims it, does not mean that God absolutizes a historical particularity (be it even Jesus of Nazareth). From the revelation in Jesus we learn that no single historical particularity can be called absolute and that therefore, because of the relativity present in Jesus, every person can encounter God outside Jesus, especially in our worldly history and in the many religions that have arisen from it. The risen Jesus of Nazareth keeps *pointing beyond himself to God*. One could say: God points via Jesus Christ in the Spirit to God as creator and redeemer: to a God of *all* persons.

The particularity of Jesus, which defines the origin, particularity, and uniqueness of Christianity, implies therefore that the differences between the individual religions remain and are not erased. The manifestation of God in Jesus does not close out "religious history," which is evident from, among others, the rise of Islam as a post-Christian world religion. And no one, not even in Islam, can deny that new world religions can and will arise after Islam. Despite all critical questions that can be addressed, certain contemporary neoreligious movements can support this hypothesis.

It is clear that there are convergences and divergences between all religions. Differences, however, are not to be judged in themselves as deviations that should be worked out ecumenically, but as positive values. God is too rich and too supersubstantial to be exhausted *in fulness* by one distinct and thus limited religious tradition or experience. Surely, according to the Christian view of things, "the whole fulness of deity dwells in" Jesus. New Testament texts witness to that for Christians (Col. 2:9; 1:15; Heb. 1:3; 2 Cor. 4:4). But it is precisely in "bodiliness"—or "this dwelling (of God's fulness) in Jesus' *humanity*"—that the *contingent* and *limited* form of Jesus' appearance in our history is drawn. (Otherwise one should proclaim the docetism condemned by all Christian churches—that is, that the divine could only appear in a phantom humanity in Jesus).

As a result of all this we can, may, and must say that there is more (religious) truth present in *all the religions together* than in one individual religion, and this holds also for Christianity. There exist because of that "true," "good," and "beautiful"—astonishing—aspects in the manifold forms of coming to terms with God present in humanity, forms that have not found and do not find a place in the specific experience of Christianity. There are divergent authentic religious experiences that Christianity has never thematized or brought into practice precisely because of its historical particularity, probably (I say it cautiously, but assertively) because of the specifically personal accents of Jesus himself, also cannot thematize *without undoing those particular accents of their jesuanic sharpness and ultimately of their specific Christianness*.

From all this I learn that (also in Christian self-understanding) the plurality of religions is not an evil that needs to be overcome, but rather a fructifying richness to be welcomed by all. This does not deny that the historically irresolvable plurality of religions is nurtured and fed interiorly by a unity within our history that is explicitly no longer thematizable and practicable: the very unity of God (confessed by Christians as a trinitarian one), insofar as this transcendent unity is reflected in the immanent family resemblances among the religions, something that gives us permission to give the unitary name of "religion" to all these divergent religious phenomena!

The particularity, identity, and uniqueness of Christianity vis-à-vis those other religions resides in the fact that Christianity is a religion that connects the relationship to God to a historical and thus highly situated and thereby limited particularity: Jesus of Nazareth. This is the uniqueness and identity of Christianity, but at the same time its unavoidably historical boundedness. Clear with this is that the God of Jesus (based on Jesus' parables and praxis of the reign of God) is a symbol of openness, and not of being closed. This gives a positive relationship of Christianity to other religions, at the same time nonetheless maintaining the uniqueness of Christianity and ultimately honoring the Christian loyal affirmation of the positive nature of the other world religions.

The truth question is not evaded by this, but what is true here is that no one holds a lease on the truth, and that no one can claim the fulness of God's richness for themselves alone. This insight, somewhat new for Christians, flows from the fact that we are also asking new questions now that could not have been asked earlier, purified as we are by past (and still new!) meaningless religious wars and unfruitful discrimination. In doing this we do not proclaim the cheap modern liberal principle that all religions are equal, or all are equally relative, or even equally untrue (as the atheists maintain).

Christology is an interpretation of Jesus of Nazareth: it states that Jesus is redeemer of all persons and is in that sense the universal redeemer. But that which redeems, which mediates liberation and redemption, is not the interpretation, but the means of redemption itself. In *Jesus: An Experiment in Christology*, I already referred to the fact that we are not redeemed by the christological titles of Jesus, but through the means of redemption itself, Jesus of Nazareth, in whatever framework of language that means is experienced and expressed. That is to say: "Jesus" redeems us, not "Christ," a christological title coming from a certain culture and often not usable in other cultures. Moreover, redemption in Christ is only unique and universal insofar as what happened in Jesus is continued in his disciples. Without a relationship to a redemptive and liberative practice of Christians, the redemption brought about at one time by Jesus is suspended in a purely speculative, vacuous atmosphere. The credal exclamation, "Jesus is Lord" (Rom. 10:9) does not of itself bring redemption, but rather "he who does the will of my Father" (Matt. 7:21). One has to follow the path Jesus did; then Jesus' way of life takes on concretely a universal meaning (Matt. 25:37–39, 44–46). An actual, albeit fragmentary, making persons whole is also the best proof of liberation!

The claim that Jesus is the universal redeemer implies that we are beginning in our history to bring forth the fruits of the reign of God. This christology receives its authenticity from the concrete praxis of the reign of God:

the history of Jesus' path through life must be continued in his disciples; only then is there meaningful talk of the uniqueness and particularity of Christianity. There is also a coredemptive function of the "body of Christ," specifically, the historical Christian community. The path through life, following after Jesus, is marked by two essential characteristics: the way of denial of any messianism of power, coming from a seigneurial-human interior freedom (resisting oppressive powers is the basis for the human voluntary commitment to poor and oppressed persons: a solidarity of love), *and* this path includes the *via crucis,* the cross. Jesus was indeed the expected messiah, but he was that in an "unexpected way," perceived only by a few. In this is the uniqueness of Jesus; the "proof" is this: throughout the centuries Christians have witnessed to this path through life by going through him to a witnessing martyrdom. "In my flesh I complete what is lacking in Christ's afflictions" (Col. 1:24), as it was expressed in ancient times. Resistance and surrender. This brings us to the following concretization or second phase, without which that first phase of reflection remains still abstract.

PHASE TWO: THE UNIVERSAL RIGHT OF THE POOR

The *universality* of Christian faith means that the Christian faith community is an open community. Sadly enough, the institutional church has had the inclination to universalize precisely its nonuniversal, historically inherited peculiar characteristics bound to a certain culture and time, and to impose them uniformly upon the entire Catholic world: in catechesis (think of the "universal catechism"), in liturgy and church order, also in theology and until recently even in a uniform language (Latin). Universality—in Greek it is called "catholicity"—means rather that the Christian faith places itself open (critically) for each person, for each people and each culture. "Universal" means: what holds equally for all. That universal must incarnate itself then in all and in each one, without exhausting all the potentialities and virtualities of the universal in those given incarnations. Thus, in the contemporary context of aching structural world poverty, the universal openness and universal invitation of the gospel message receives a socially very concrete dimension and a new location, as it were. In that way especially Latin American, but also African and Asian forms of liberation theology inspire me.[7]

In the West we used the concept "universality" often in an abstract and nonhistorical fashion, in the sense of "valid for all persons." In itself, a correct usage! But, we said rather nonchalantly that something is valid for all persons while forgetting that humanity is divided concretely into "poor" and "nonpoor" persons, and that what was valid for the nonpoor, historically and concretely was not valid for the poor and oppressed. Structurally they are excluded. Talking about universality is therefore only meaningful and concrete if, in our fundamental theological concepts, we express at the same time the distinction between nonpoor and especially the structurally poor. It is not a matter of speaking of a pastoral predilection of the church for the poor in the sense of the duty to universal love means always a preferential love for individual, certain persons, as the church also can speak of pastoral priorities—for example, in connection with the church's option for youth. No, the option for the poor is a *datum of revelation*. The basis for that option is the Christian faith in the God of Jesus Christ, who himself gives witness to this partisan option. That option for the poor is thus a question of Christian orthodoxy; it touches all the belief statements of the Christian credo. The option for the poor, the indigent, and the oppressed is a partisan, free choice of the God of Jesus of Nazareth, as well as an option for the not always in fact "nonpoor," socio-culturally, psychologically, and religiously marginalized persons. The incarnation of God in Jesus of Nazareth is not a "becoming human," but an identification of God in Jesus with the poor, oppressed, and finally executed innocent individual, for whom Jesus stands as a model. Only within this perspective can we now speak of the concrete universality of ecclesiastical Christianity, insofar as it walks in the footsteps of Jesus.

It is therefore a matter of a "concrete universality" through which Christian believers take upon themselves the aspirations of those who are deprived of their rights in this world and are in solidarity with the cry for justice of the poor and disenfranchised. The cause of justice is the cause of all. Freedom, the rights of humanity, are there for all; and if this is not the case (in other words, if there are only rights for those who demand them), there are no human rights! If rights are valid only for a part of humanity, this part of humanity would thereby legitimate and sanction the lack of rights. In the measure that the church chooses the side of the poor and those deprived of rights and is in solidarity with human rights, it takes up that concrete universality, for the "Catholic universality" is not only a given from the very inception of Christian faith, it is a contextual charge to be achieved historically.

In the contemporary socio-political and economic time-bind of structural deprivation of rights for the majority of humanity, not only the *caritative diaconia universalizes* the Christian gospel among all people (as Mother Teresa benevolently practices it), but also the *political diaconia* that wishes to remove the causes of this structural deprivation. It thereby recognizes the universality of human rights and human dignity, and does not cover up poverty theologically and prolong it ideologically. The active presence of the Christian churches with poor and deprived persons, adding its voice to the cry for redemption of the oppressed, has therefore a universal meaning: a *meaning for all*—also for the rich and powerful as a summons to solidarity. The transformation of the world toward a higher humanity, toward justice, peace, and wholeness of creation belongs therefore essentially to the "catholicity" or universality of Christian faith, and this is a nondiscriminatory universality par excellence.

That Christianity is a universal message to all people means therefore that Christianity is only universal if Christians are concerned to reach all of humanity in its being lacerated into "poor" and "nonpoor." "To the poor is preached the good news": that is the essence of the Christian gospel! And this message is also practiced toward the poor (without Christians being able to view this as a Christian exclusive right or monopoly). The sending of Christians in solidarity to the poor in all the world belongs then also to the essential aspects of what we now call "mission." For Christians it comes down to this: by Christian praxis—in the footsteps of Jesus—to witness to the one whom they confess as their God: the God of Israel, father of Jesus Christ, who is called a defender of the poor, creator of heaven and earth, who cannot be claimed by any single religion for itself. But then we must keep clearly before our eyes with this the peculiar accent of Jesus' conception of God (if we wish to preserve the evangelical accents).

Critique of certain images of God, especially of conceptions of God that threaten our humanness, is also an essential aspect of the evangelical message of Jesus of Nazareth; it is even a focus in that message. And it was from a religious source and, for that matter, from a Christian insight of faith (otherwise therefore than in the Enlightenment) that God is personally involved with persons in their history, that Christianity is, from a theologal or mystical source, originally and simultaneously an impulse toward liberation and emancipation. On the basis of Jesus' message, parables, and his praxis of the reign of God, we see how the biblical concept of God is essentially bound up with a praxis of persons who liberate their fellow human beings, just as Jesus did before us. Precisely because in the course of church history the bond weakened and was even forgotten, and God was thereby "objectified" as the capstone and guarantor of all human knowledge, order, and behavior, and thus was declared the legitimation of the status quo—an enemy of any change, liberation, and emancipation, therefore—the crisis of the Enlightenment was historically not only possible, but even "unavoidable."

This all had, on the other hand, the consequence that in Enlightenment deism (and in its direct and indirect aftereffects) the biblical "calling upon God" disappeared and left only a secularized and diminished liberation and emancipation process—a diminished freedom movement. From a Christian point of view it is, however, a matter of an unbreakable connection between revering God (let us say: prayer and mysticism) *and* emancipatory liberation in the fullest and multifaceted sense of this word—in that a theologian such as Gustavo Gutiérrez goes ahead of us all with conviction!

This mystical and liberating message, accompanied by a consonant evangelical praxis, following after Jesus, proclaiming loudly to all who will hear, is the good right of Christianity. But Christians must remember in this a word of the prophet Amos: "Did I not bring up Israel from the land of Egypt, and the Philistines from Caphtor and the Syrians from Kir?" (Amos

9:7). Suffering humanity is evidently *the* chosen people of God. If that is so, living together with the "human ecumene," seen religiously, and the "ecumene of suffering humanity," is indeed possible.

—translated from the Dutch by Robert J. Schreiter

NOTES

1. Gustavo Gutiérrez, "Twee perspectieven op de kerk. Sacrament van de wereld—keuze voor de armen," in Hermann Häring, Ted Schoof, and Ad Willems, eds., *Meedenken met Edward Schillebeeckx* (Baarn: H. Nelissen, 1983), pp. 221–45.

2. Karl Rahner, "Christianity and Non-Christian Religions," *Theological Investigations*, vol. 5, pp. 115–34; see also "Church, Churches, and Religions," ibid., vol. 10, pp. 30–49; "Anonymous Christianity and the Missionary Task of the Church," ibid., vol. 12, pp. 161–78; "Jesus Christ in the Non-Christian Religions," ibid., vol. 17, pp. 39–50; "Über die Heilsbedeutung der nichtchristlichen Religionen," *Schriften zur Theologie*, vol. 13, pp. 341–50.

3. Hans Waldenfels, "Der Absolutheitsanspruch des Christentums und die grossen Weltreligionen," *Hochland*, 62 (1970) 202–17; "Ist der christliche Glaube der einzig Wahre? Christentum und nichtchristliche Religionen," *Stimmen der Zeit*, 112 (1987) 463–75.

4. Max Seckler, "Theologie der Religionen mit Fragezeichen," *Theologische Quartalschrift*, 166 (1986) 164–84.

5. Heinz Robert Schlette, *Toward a Theology of Religions* (New York: Herder and Herder, 1966); idem, *Skeptische Religionsphilosophie* (Freiburg: Herder, 1972).

6. Paul Knitter, *No Other Name? A Critical Survey of Christian Attitudes toward the World Religions* (Maryknoll, N.Y.: Orbis, 1985).

7. Among those to be cited are Gustavo Gutiérrez, Leonardo Boff, and others. For Africa and Asia, especially Jean-Marc Ela, *African Cry* (Maryknoll, N.Y.: Orbis, 1986); Aloysius Pieris, *An Asian Theology of Liberation* (Maryknoll, N.Y.: Orbis, 1988).

11

The Politics of Otherness:
Biblical Interpretation as a
Critical Praxis for Liberation

ELISABETH SCHÜSSLER FIORENZA

Gustavo Gutiérrez, whose life and work we celebrate in these pages, has placed in the center of theological reflection the poor, the "others," the nonpersons who are absent from history. He has insisted over and against Euro-American "progressive" theology that the point of departure for Latin American liberation theology is not the question of the modern *nonbeliever* but the struggle of the *nonperson*[1] for justice and freedom. However, Latin American liberation theology has not sufficiently attended to the fact that the majority of the poor in the world are women and children dependent on women. This realization requires not just an incorporation of "women's questions" into the framework of liberation theology[2] but calls for a different analysis and theoretical framework.

Since Simone de Beauvoir, feminist theory also has focused on the "other." Therefore feminist theory and theology predominantly has understood patriarchy as the domination of men over women.[3] Yet feminist theory has not sufficiently attended to the fact that most women in the world are not just the "others" of white Euro-American men but are the "others" of "the others." This insight asks for a transformation in the self-understanding of feminist analysis and struggle that must address not only sexism but also racism, classism, and colonialism as structures constituting women's oppression.[4] I have therefore proposed that we understand patriarchy as a differentiated political system of graduated domination and subordination that found its classic Western legitimization in the philosophy of otherness.

The Canadian writer Margaret Atwood has given us a political novel that displays the discursive practices constituting the politics of otherness. Atwood's narrative articulates the interstructuring of sexism, racism, class differences, and colonialism on the one hand and the availability of the Bible as language and legitimization for totalitarian ends on the other. *The Handmaid's Tale* decodes the history of a future totalitarian society whose structures and language are modeled after the Bible.

The speaking subject of the novel is a woman whose real name and identity is not known. She is a Handmaid called Offred who lives in the Republic of Gilead. Gilead has replaced the United States of America and is ruled by a group espousing an ideology similar to that of the Moral Majority in the pre-Gileadean period in the late twentieth century. After the president and congress of the U.S.A. have been massacred, the regime of this modern biblical republic is established. Women lose their right to property and employment, the black population, the children of Ham, are resettled in segregated national homelands; Jews are repatriated through the Jewish boat-plans. In this biblical republic, reading and writing are outlawed, the news media censured and controlled, and everyone is required to spy on everyone.

The stratifications of Gileadean society are marked by dress and color developed by the secret Think Tank of the Sons of Jacob. White women, for example, are classified according to their functions: the wives of the Commanders of the Faithful are blue-clad and their daughters white-veiled. Those who do household work are called Marthas and have to wear a dull green. The wives of poor men, the Econowives, wear red-, blue-, or green-striped dresses, because they have to fulfill all functions divided among different women in the elite households. Unwomen are those women who have been shipped to the Colonies, because they are childless, infertile, older women, nuns, lesbians, or other insurrectionary elements.

Handmaids are chosen because of their reproductive capabilities. Their dress is red topped by a white headdress. The Handmaid's role in the *Ceremony* and her whole rationale of being is patterned after that of Bilhah, the maid of Rachel in Genesis 30:1–3. Handmaids and Wives are under the control of Aunts who as female overseers are to control women in the most cost-effective way.

I have chosen Atwood's narrative to indicate the political context of U.S. scholarly discourse on the Bible as well as of the discourses of liberation theologies. For theological discourses that remain unconscious of their rhetorical functions and abstracted from their political contexts are in danger of "squandering the word." Atwood's futuristic projection of a totalitarian state re-creating classic-biblical patriarchy in modern technocratic terms underlines that liberation theologies cannot afford to engage in a purely apologetic reading of the Bible or to relegate a critical biblical interpretation to "bourgeois" scholarship addressing the question of the nonbeliever. Rather, a biblical interpretation for liberation has to engage in a critical analysis that can lay open the "politics of otherness" inscribed in Christian scriptures. By making feminist theoretical discourse central to my hermeneutical explorations, I invite not only biblical scholarship but also malestream[5] liberation theologies to attend to the conversation of the "others" on the patriarchal politics of "otherness."

ISSUES IN FEMINIST BIBLICAL INTERPRETATION

Because the Bible is the foundational document for the Republic of Gilead, it is reserved for the elite and only to be read by men in power:

> The Bible is kept locked up, the way people once kept tea locked up, so the servants wouldn't steal it. It is an incendiary device: who knows what we'd make of it, if we ever got our hands on it? We can be read to from it, by him, but we cannot read. Our heads turn towards him, we are expectant, here comes our bedtime story. . . . He has something we don't have, he has the word. How we squandered it, once.[6]

Atwood's narrator not only discloses the dehumanizing horrors of the totalitarian patriarchal state but also alludes to the potentially "incendiary" character of the Bible if it were given into the hands of "the subordinate others," the nonpersons of Gilead. In the awareness that reading can be subversive, elite men have kept the key to biblical interpretation in their own hands. It is mostly elite men who still read their Revised Standard Versions to us in liturgical celebrations and academic lectures. In the past thirty years women have entered theological schools in significant numbers and have begun to produce biblical scholarship. Yet replacing men with women and other nonpersons in pulpits, universities, the Supreme Court, or Buckingham Palace does not guarantee that the word read to us will no longer be a bedtime story legitimating situations of oppression.

Although still a marginalized minority in academy, church and synagogue, contemporary feminist theological scholarship and studies in religion have begun to claim the theological word and religious symbol-systems of biblical religions in the interest of women. However, the more feminist articulations are in circulation, the more it becomes pressing to ask how we can prevent our readings functioning like the Aunts of Atwood's Gileadean Republic who manipulate and adjust women's intellectual and spiritual needs in order to survive by serving the patriarchal system. For women's readings of androcentric texts and patriarchal traditions are always in danger of recuperating the "Commander's readings to us," of using the "biblical bedtime-story" for quieting women's and other nonpersons' anger and rebellion. Finally to own "the word" could mean in the end to own a word that legitimates the totalitarian regime of Gilead.

How, then, can a feminist biblical hermeneutics situate its readings of the Bible in such a way that they do not support the totalizing discourses of Gilead but empower women and other nonpersons in struggle for justice and freedom? In order to minimize the possibility of such a co-optation in the interests of Western patriarchy, I suggest that feminist biblical interpretation must reconceptualize its act of critical reading as a moment in the global praxis for liberation. In order to do so, it needs to decenter the authority of the androcentric biblical text, to take control of its own readings, and to deconstruct the politics of otherness inscribed in the text before it can positively retrieve biblical language and visions of liberation.[7]

Insofar as feminist biblical interpretation has been motivated by an apologetic retrieval of biblical authority, it has focused on biblical texts about women, on male injunctions for woman, on the biblical teaching on womanhood, on the great women of the Bible, or on feminine biblical language and symbols. By using "woman" or "the feminine" as a hermeneutical key, such gynecentric biblical interpretations, however, are in danger of recuperating the totalizing discourse of Western gender dualism.

Moreover, in its academic forms feminist scholarship has not only adopted diverse historical, social, anthropological, psychological, or literary critical methods of interpretation, but also the academic posture of "detached" inquiry. For the sake of scientific objectivity, such biblical scholarship often masks its own political location and forecloses theological or ethical evaluation. Although it focuses on "women" or the "feminine," it cannot but reproduce the whitemale[8] androcentric discourse.

Finally, feminist biblical interpretation seems to remain caught up in the same "logic of identity." Feminist critics have elucidated the indebtedness of modern political theories to the classic patriarchal discourses of Plato and Aristotle, and especially criticized the theories of Rousseau and Hegel, which understand the civic public expressing the "impartial and universal point of view of normative reason," on the one hand, in opposition to the private realm, which encompasses the family as the domain of women, on the other. *Ratio* as the "logic of identity" "consists in an unrelenting urge to think things together, in a unity," to formulate "an essence that brings concrete particulars into unity."[9]

To achieve theological unity, feminist hermeneutics has attempted to reduce the historical particularity and pluriformity of biblical writings to a feminist "canon within the canon" or a liberating "organizing principle" as the normative center of scripture. Feminist biblical and liberation theological scholarship has inherited this search for an interpretative key or authoritative "canon within the canon" from historico-theological exegesis that has recognized the contradictory pluriformity of scripture.

Although liberationist biblical discourses have rejected the value-neutral, objective, apolitical rhetorics of academic biblical scholarship, they have not avoided its "drive to unity and essence." Just as male liberation theologians stress God's liberating act in history, single out the Exodus as "canon within the canon," and focus on a "new reading of the bible," or stress the liberating "biblical recollection and regathering of God's salvific deeds," so also feminist liberation theologians have sought to identify a liberating theme, tradition, text, or principle as the hermeneutical key to the Bible as an androcentric-patriarchal book in order to reclaim the authority of scripture. In this search for a "canon within the canon" or the "unity" of scripture, biblical theological interpretation engages in the universalist "logic of identity," which eliminates the irreducible particularity of historical texts and the theological differences among biblical writers and contemporary interpreters.

A debated question in feminist liberation hermeneutics remains: Must such a feminist critical hermeneutical key be derived from or at least be correlated with the Bible so that scripture remains the normative foundation of feminist biblical faith and community? Or—as I have argued—must it be continually articulated and called into question in the contemporary liberation struggle?[10] The Bible is to be understood as formative root-model rather than to be obeyed as a normative archetype of Christian faith and community. Whereas a feminist apologetics locates authority formally if not always materially in the Bible, a critical feminist reading derives its theological authority from women's experience of God's liberating presence in today's struggle to end patriarchal relationships of domination. Such divine presence, for instance, is at work today in the emerging Christian recognition that the systemic oppressive patriarchal contextualizations of our readings—sexism, racism, economic exploitation, and military colonialism—are structural sin.

My own work, therefore, has sought to shift the focus of feminist liberation discourse on the Bible away not only from the discourse on "women in the Bible" to the feminist reconstruction of Christian origins,[11] but also from the drive to construct a unifying biblical canon and universalist principle to a discussion of the process of biblical interpretation and evaluation that could display and assess the oppressive as well as liberating functions of particular biblical texts in women's lives and struggles. Concern with biblical positivity, normativity, and authority is in danger of too quickly foreclosing such a critical analysis and feminist evaluation of particular biblical texts and traditions. It neglects the Bible and its interpretation as the site of competing discursive practices.

A critical feminist theological hermeneutics of liberation positions itself at the intersection of three theological discursive practices—historical and literary biblical criticism, liberation theologies, and feminist critical theory—practices that question the Western totalizing "logic of identity." However, this positioning can only be appreciated when the interrelation of all three critical discourses is not seen as correlative but as mutually corrective interacting in the matrix of a feminist commitment and struggle for overcoming the patriarchal politics of otherness.

THE PATRIARCHAL POLITICS OF OTHERNESS

The Euro-American "classic" form of the politics of otherness is rooted in the practices of the andro-social Greek *polis*, its politico-philosophical subtext is democracy, and its social formation is patriarchy, the governing dominance of elite propertied male heads of households. Freeborn propertied women, poor women and men, slave-women and -men, as well as barbarians, women and men, were excluded from the democratic government of the city-state. This exclusion required ideological justifications as to why only freeborn propertied Greek male heads of households could be full citizens if, as the Sophists maintained, all are equal by nature.

The articulation of human-animal/male-female dualism, of androcentrism fostering the marginalization of Greek women and the exclusion of barbarians, as well as the articulation of the "natural" inferiority of freeborn women and of slave-women and -men, of nonpersons, are ideological constructs of difference formulated by Plato and Aristotle. They continue to define relations of dominance and submission in Western culture and philosophical discourse today.[12] They were reproduced not only in early Christian writings and malestream theology but also in the modern democratic discourses of political philosophy, in the Enlightenment construction of the *Man of Reason*,[13] as well as in colonialist articulations of racism.[14] This political and philosophical rhetoric of otherness masks the oppressive relations of domination and exclusion in systemic patriarchy. However, it must be recognized that it does not simply elaborate the *generic person* but the Sovereign-Father or, in black idiom, the Boss-Man, as the universal subject. Its totalizing discourse of male-female dualism masks the complex structuring of patriarchal domination in Western societies and religions.

Insofar as feminist theory has focused on woman as the "other" of man, it has tended to identify patriarchy with sexism or gender-dualism. It has not focused on the complex interstructuring of patriarchal domination in women's lives. Although one of the earliest manifestos of the women's liberation movement in the U.S.A. categorically states: no woman is free until and unless every woman is free, feminist analyses and strategies generally have not taken their political measure, standpoint, and strategy for change with the women on the totem pole of patriarchal oppression, with the "others of the others." Instead Euro-American feminist discourse has tended to take its measure from an idealized version of the Man of Reason, the sovereign subject of history, culture, and religion. Its oppositional discourse has been in danger of reproducing the cultural-symbolic construction of masculine-feminine polarity and heterosexual antagonism that is constitutive of the patriarchal "politics of otherness."

Women's studies in all academic disciplines have greatly enriched our knowledge *about women* but have not been able to undo the marginalizing dynamics of the androcentric text and its institutions. In order to dislodge the androcentrism of Western metaphysical discourse, feminist theories or theologies of femininity, whether they have as god-fathers Jung, Tillich, Lacan, or Derrida, have valorized woman—body, sexuality, maternity, nature—as feminine archetype, essence, or divinity. Yet in this attempt to construct an oppositional discourse on woman or on gender differences, feminist theory has kept in circulation the discourse of classic Western philosophy and theology on gender-dualism or gender-polarity that understands man as the subject of history, culture, and religion, and woman as the other.

This universalist Euro-American feminist discourse on "woman as the other of man" is more and more interrupted by the diverse resistant discourses of an emerging global feminist movement coming-into-consciousness. In an anthology of the international women's movement entitled *Sisterhood Is Global*, Robin Morgan has compiled statistics and collected reports on the worldwide struggle of women for liberation.[15] The global character of this movement is displayed in its very particular and concrete political struggles that are not to be universalized, for the configurations of patriarchy are different in different historico-cultural formations. The voices of this movement insist that feminism requires a political commitment not only to the struggle against sexism but also to the struggles against racism, classism, colonialism and militarism as structures of women's exploitation and oppression. Feminism's self-understanding and analysis must therefore shift from a preoccupation with gender-dualism in order to attend to the interstructuring of sex, race, class, culture, and religion in systems of domination.[16] This insistence of black, Hispanic, Jewish, Asian, African, or Palestinian women asks for a new analysis of the patriarchal "politics of otherness." For, only when patriarchy is understood not as a universal transcultural binary structure but as a historical political system of interlocking dominations, can it be changed.

The rhetoric of the feminist movement that is emerging around the globe, therefore, is directed not only against male supremacy but also against the totalizing discourse of Western universalist feminism. Insofar as this rhetoric elaborates racial, political, cultural, national, ideological, sexual, religious, age, class, and other systemic differences, and discriminations among women, it challenges the essentialist definition of woman and female culture as "the other" of man and male culture. However, because of its commitment to the political liberation struggle, its insistence on the perspectival character and historical particularity of knowledge does not degenerate into an endless play of deconstruction and negative reaction nor lead to a determinism and nihilism that denies women's subjectivity and historical agency.

Unraveling the unitary otherness of woman from man in Western philosophico-political discourse, the emerging discourses of global feminism insist on the specific historical cultural context and subjectivity as well as the plurality of women. By deconstructing the ideological construct "woman," such global feminist discourses also elucidate how the identity of women of subordinated races, classes, cultures, or religions is constructed as "other" of the "other," as negative foil for the feminine identity of the white Lady. For instance, with her analysis of lynching, Ida B. Wells has elucidated the patriarchal manipulation of race and gender in the interest of political terrorism, economic oppression, and conventual sexual exploitation.[17] The variety of feminist discourses emerging around the globe thus enjoins middle-class feminists in the First World not to reduplicate the whitemale universalistic discourse of gender dualism and at the same time cautions Third World middle-class feminists not to reproduce the colonial discourse on woman and femininity.

The differences and often irreconcilable contradictions among women and within women are always concretely embedded in power relationships. To collapse them into a unitary identity, homogeneous image or totalizing discourse of universalist feminism—be it Euro-American or Afro-American, lesbian or straight, activist or academic, or any other feminism—would mean to reproduce the androcentric discourses of universalist abstract humanism on woman or to reinscribe differences and contradictions among women as patriarchal divisions and oppositions.[18]

However, if just as race, nationality, or social status, so also gender is a social-cultural-historical construct and not a feminine substance or universal female essence, then the question arises: How can women transcend our being socially constructed as *women* and at the same time become historical subjects as *women* struggling against patriarchal domination? If subjectivity is seen as totally determined by gender, one ends up with feminine essentialism; if it is understood as genderless, then one reverts to the generic human subject of liberalism for whom gender, class, or race are irrelevant.

This theoretical either-or posed by cultural and poststructuralist feminism[19] can be negotiated—I would suggest—if we attend to the patriarchal politics of otherness in Western culture. The totalizing ideologies of sexism, racism, classism, or colonialism that make the patriarchal oppression and exploitation of "the others" of elite white men appear to be "natural" and "common sense," produce at the same time contradictions and fissures in the social psychological identity construction of the nonperson. Far from being irrelevant to human subjectivity, the experience and articulation of gender, race, class, cultural, or religious alienation and exploitation motivate the nonperson to struggle for human rights, dignity, freedom, and equality:

What is emerging in feminist writings is, instead [of the posthumanist Lacanian white male subject], the concept of a multiple, shifting, and often self-contradictory identity, a subject that is not divided in, but rather at odds with, language; an identity made up of heterogeneous and heteronomous representations of gender, race, and class, and often indeed across languages and cultures. An identity that one decides to reclaim from a history of multiple assimilations, and that one insists on as a strategy: "I think," writes Elly Bulkin, "of all the women [of mixed heritage] who were told to choose between or among identities, insist on selecting all."[20]

In short, in order to sustain a global feminist movement for ending patriarchal oppression, all feminist discourses must engage at one and at the same time in a continuing critical deconstruction of the politics of otherness, in reclaiming and reconstructing our particular experiences, histories, and identities, as well as in sustaining a permanent reflection on our common differences. The subordinated others must reject the rhetoric of self-lessness and articulate the "option for the oppressed" as an *option for ourselves*. Self-identity *as women* cannot be assumed but must be chosen in the commitment to the struggle for ending patriarchal structures of oppression. Moreover, the "politics of otherness" can be displaced only when identity is no longer articulated as unitary universal identity and established either by exclusion and domination of the others or by the others' self-negation and subordination.

The hermeneutical insights and theological challenges of the heterogeneous voices emerging from the global movements of liberation must, therefore, become central to a differentiated theological discourse on biblical interpretation and evaluation. A historical and global contextualization of biblical interpretation has to deconstruct the totalizing biblical rhetoric of Gilead and to generate new possibilities for the communicative construction of self and world. Christian identity grounded by the reading of the Bible must in ever-new readings be deconstructed and reconstructed in terms of a global praxis for liberation. Insofar as the Bible still is used in Western public discourse for reinforcing an Euro-American identity formation based on the exclusion and subordination or vilification of "the others," it becomes important to deconstruct the "politics of otherness" inscribed in its pages.

THE POLITICS OF OTHERNESS INSCRIBED IN THE FOURTH GOSPEL

If feminist biblical interpretation should not continue to reproduce the patriarchal politics of otherness, it has to reconceive its task as critical consciousness-raising or conscientization that can explore the functions and patriarchal contextualizations of biblical discourses, and replace them with a diversified public biblical rhetoric[21] and feminist frameworks of reference.

In the following cursory discussion of the fourth Gospel[22] I will indicate the complex process of such a critical feminist reading understood as a strategy and process of conscientization. Such a focus on the contemporary reading process does not replace historical text-oriented readings but presupposes an evaluative analysis of their textual interpretations and of their reconstructions of particular historical contexts. My focus on certain Johannine problems and my theological emphases indicate my subject position as a white German Christian feminist biblical scholar and theologian living in the U.S.A. Such a particular reading invites other readings that begin from a different subject position in the liberation struggle.

Whereas historical critical exegesis attends to the text in its historical contexts, but not to its ideological formation and textual "politics of otherness," rhetorical analyses and reader response criticism seek to make conscious how the text "works" in the complex process of reading as a cultural or theological praxis. By elucidating how gender determines the reading process feminist reader-response criticism underlines the importance of the reader's particular socio-cultural location.

Every reader brings cultural (grammatical principles, social customs, cultural attitudes, historical experiences) and personal contexts (personal experience, social location, education, beliefs, and commitments) to the act of reading. "Contextualization" is often assumed but not articulated; it is often masked in order to produce an "unbiased" objective reading. Such contextual knowledge operates as "a kind of grid that obscures certain meanings and brings others to the foreground."[23] However, whereas feminist biblical scholarship has become skilled in detecting the androcentric contextualizations in malestream biblical interpretation, it has not paid sufficient attention to its own inoculation with gender stereotypes, racism, sexism, or theological confessionalism.

In recent years New Testament scholarship has elaborated the social world and symbolic universe of the fourth Gospel. It has highlighted the leadership role of women in the Johannine community, its sectarianism and anti-Jewish polemics, as well as its dualistic worldview and religious exclusivism. In all three instances of inscribed Otherness, a certain tension or contradiction in the text has been elaborated.

First, the fourth Gospel presents the Christian community as a circle of friends, an egalitarian community of the children of God, that does not exclude the leadership of women, but appeals to the apostolic women disciples of Jesus for its legitimization of this practice. Nevertheless, its symbolic language and universe is not only androcentric but patriarchal because it stresses that the Father is revealed only through the Son and at the same time co-opts the language of sophia-theology and masculinizes it.

Secondly, although the language of the fourth Gospel is very "Jewish," the term "the Jews" is predominantly a negative term. It does not include Jesus and his followers as Jews but distances them from the Jews. The expression can also be used in a neutral sense, in order to mark that not all Jews have rejected Jesus but many have believed, or even as a positive theological affirmation in the dialogue with the Samaritan woman: "Salvation comes from the Jews" (4:22). However, anti-Jewish language is predominant in the Gospel. It bespeaks not just fear of expulsion but aggressive sectarian affirmation.

Thirdly, this anti-Jewish polemics is generated by a cosmological dualism of light and darkness, spirit and flesh, life and death, above and below, "the world" and the believer, God and satan. One could say that the whole narrative of the Gospel is woven within a framework of dualism. However, the cosmological dualism of the fourth Gospel is not absolute: God has sent the Son not for the condemnation but for the salvation of the "world."

This dualistic framework engenders not only anti-Judaism but also christological absolutism that breeds religious exclusivism, although the Gospel's intent is universal—namely, to present Jesus in an idiom that reflects the profound interests of the Greco-Roman world in religious syncretism and with religious symbols that have the widest appeal. In light of the Gospel's dualistic framework and its religious exclusivism, it is remarkable that its dualism does not include the pair male and female. Nevertheless, the Gospel exhibits a patriarchal identity formation characterized by the politics of otherness.

In the last twenty years historical critical scholarship has moved away from a gnostic or antignostic interpretation of the fourth Gospel's *Sitz im Leben* toward an understanding of its anti-Jewish polemic as an expression of the socio-religious alienation of the Johannine community because of synagogue expulsion.[24] Although Jewish scholars have disputed that such an official synagogue ban had existed at the time of the Gospel's redaction, Christian scholars maintain that explicit references to the expulsion from the synagogue of those who believe in Christ testify to the strained relationship between the Jewish leadership and the emergent Jewish-Christian movement. However, scholars do not reflect critically that such a reconstruction of the historical subtext of the Gospel reinforces the anti-Jewish Christian identity formation today.

Just as historical-critical exegesis so also liberation theological interpretations have explained away the Johannine "politics of Otherness" if they have it addressed as a theological problem at all. José Miranda, for instance, seeks to "undo" the traditional spiritualistic interpretation of the Gospel by stressing that belief in Jesus Christ (John 20:31) means that the kingdom has arrived in Jesus of Nazareth, the messianic kingdom that "consists in justice being done to all the poor of the earth."[25] Luise Schottroff in turn rejects the term "anti-Judaism" for the interpretation of the fourth Gospel by pointing to the oppression under which Jews and the emerging Christian community lived. "To accuse the Jewish leadership as it is portrayed in John's Gospel of opportunism vis-à-vis the Romans, or to accuse the Christians ... of anti-Judaism, is to apply labels which are inappropriate to the historical situation."[26]

Stress on the prophetic principle or the prophetic activity of Jesus also makes it possible to explain the anti-Jewish statements of the Gospel historically as a remembrance of Jesus' "prophetic renunciation of a corrupt religious establishment" or as prophetic call to conversion and renewal. A feminist apologist reading in turn has proposed to dissolve the tensions in the text by claiming that the Gospel contains its own critical principle, when it says that salvation comes from the Jews, that believers are children [not sons] of God, and that "God loves the world." Such liberation theological attempts of characterizing the Johannine text positively as a liberating text is not able to unravel and critically reject the patriarchal Christian identity formation inscribed in it.

Literary critical studies on the other hand have shown that the gospel narrative integrates these apparent tensions and contradictions of the Gospel into a realistic unitary story. Since the masculine figure of the Son as the revealer from above is the narrative axis of the Gospel, the stories about women, for example, function to harness the affection of the historical women readers for the masculine revealer of the Father. Further, the "Jewish" language of the Gospel in its positive or neutral use serves to reinforce the conflict of the revealer Son with "the Jews" whose Father is the devil, a conflict which climaxes in the passion narrative. Finally, the Gospel's relative cosmological dualism aims at a radical theologico-ethical dualism. Those who do not believe—the world, the Jews, and their leaders—will continue in darkness (15:18–16:4).

According to Culpepper, the Gospel's characterization, plot, comments, misunderstanding, irony, and symbolism "all work together in leading the reader to accept the evangelist's understanding of Jesus as the divine revealer."[27] As a reader-response critic, Culpepper does not shirk the question as to the function and impact of the Gospel's rhetoric today when he points out that the reading experience of the original reader was quite different from that of the contemporary reader, for the world of the text is quite different from our own. Insofar as modern readers distinguish between empirical and fictional narratives, between history and literature, they assume that they must read the gospels as "literally true."

Culpepper thus shares the concern of modern "progressive" theology when he insists that the real question and issue for contemporary readers is whether John's story can be true if it is not history. In response he suggests, if contemporary readers no longer would read the text as a window to the life of Jesus but with openness to the ways it calls "readers to interact with it, with life, and with their own world," they will again be able to read the Gospel as the original audience read it. The rhetorical effect of the Gospel is then profound:

> The incentive the narrative offers for accepting its world as the true understanding of the "real" world is enormous. It places the reader's world under the providence of God, gives the reader an identity with a past and secure future, and promises the presence of God's Spirit with the believer, forgiveness for sin, and an experience of salvation which includes assurance of life beyond the grave. The gospel offers contemporary readers a refuge from all the unreliable narrators of modern life and literature.[28]

Culpepper's summary appropriately underlines that the fourth Gospel narrative engenders Christian identity formation today, but he does not attend to the fact that such Christian identity is articulated in terms of androcentric dualism, religious exclusivism, and anti-Judaism. Moreover, he does not problematize the political effects of the Gospel's narrative that according to him offers "a refuge from all unreliable narrators" of contemporary society and life. Assuming that this characterization of "what the narrative offers" is adequate, the whole narrative of the fourth Gospel and not only elements in it must be problematized and assessed if we want to unravel its anti-Jewish Christian identity formation, which is shot through with racism. Although in classical and New Testament times "darkness" was not associated with race, and therefore the original readers would not have interpreted the dualistic matrix of the Gospel in racist terms, a long history of racist interpretation provides the contextualization for racist readings today.

Whereas historical and literary criticism focus attention on the text and its historical context but does not explore and critically assess the textual inscription of the patriarchal "politics of otherness," a critical feminist hermeneutic for liberation seeks to make conscious the complex process of reading as a cultural and theological praxis. Feminist reader-response criticism has shown that reading and thinking in an androcentric symbol system produces reader *immasculation*. It requires identification with men and therefore intensifies women's feminine socialization and internalization of cultural values that are self-alienating and often misogynist.

The androcentric text of the fourth Gospel derives its seductive "power" from its generic aspirations that play on women's authentic desires and liberative aspirations in order to harness them for the process of *immasculation*. The Gospel's christological focus and attention to "the love of the Father for the Son" reinforces theologically the linguistic and cultural process of *immasculation* and establishes Christian identity as male identity in a cultural masculine-feminine contextualization. Focusing on the figure of Jesus, the Son of the Father, when reading the Gospel, "doubles" women's oppression. Not only is our experience not articulated, but we also suffer "the powerlessness which results from the endless division of self against self, the consequence of the invocation to identify as male while being reminded that to be male—to be universal— . . . is to be *not female*."[29] Conversely, the androcentric scriptural text communicates that to be female is to be *not* divine.

However, such a conceptualization of the first moment of reading in feminist-reader response criticism is in danger of recuperating the totalizing discourse of gender dualism when it insists that one read "as a man" or "as a woman." Reading as a woman does not necessarily mean to activate solely the ideological context of gender and femininity. Women readers can read from a feminist, black, Asian, or any number of "contexts." The identity of the reader is not a fixed gender position maintained by the exclusion of other contexts. The reading subject is not unitary but as the agent of her reading can activate different subject locations and positions. In the process of reading, identity is always assumed and then discarded, it is decentered and reassumed.

This means that we have to learn in a series of readings from different contextualizations to unravel the full dynamics of the Christian identity formation produced by the Johannine text and elaborated in its subsequent interpretations. A feminist biblical interpretation for liberation that understands its task as ongoing conscientization engages in an ongoing process of reading that deconstructs the politics of otherness inscribed in the biblical text without getting lost in the endless play of textual deconstruction and undecidability. Different starting points in the reading process will result in competing readings of the Gospel. Nevertheless, all such feminist readings must be assessed in terms of the liberation of the women on the bottom of the patriarchal pyramid of domination.

A feminist analysis of the politics of otherness and commitment to the liberation struggle of all nonpersons also will avoid the liberal pitfall that declares race, gender, class, or cultural differences insignificant for the reading process, because in essence we are all human and the same. Empirical studies have documented that so-called generic masculine language ("man"; pronoun "he") is read differently by men and by women. This is possible because of the ambiguity of generic masculine language. In the absence of any clear contextual markers, a statement such as "all men are created equal" can be understood as generic-inclusive or as masculine-exclusive.

Insofar as a feminist analysis elucidates the function of androcentric language in different contexts, it challenges the presumption that such language functions as "generic" language in patriarchal contexts. Inasmuch as women's reading tends to deactivate masculine/feminine gender contextualization in favor of an abstract degenderized reading, such an analysis makes a conscious discrimination between patriarchal and generic-inclusive language contexts possible. Moreover, reading experiments have provided evidence that men report a higher incidence of male imagery when completing neutral sentences with generic pronouns. Women in turn associate virtually no images with generic masculine pronouns in such cases probably because we are required to suppress the literal meaning in order to be able to understand ourselves as included in the values of freedom, self-determination, and human rights.[30] Therefore, Christian women have read and still read biblical texts without attending to the fact of Jesus' maleness or the masculine images of Father-Son. As Virginia Fabella insists: "In the Asian Women's Consultation in Manila, the fact that Jesus was male was not an issue, for he was never seen as having used his maleness to oppress or dominate women."[31]

Catherine Belsey elaborates this contradictory ideological position of women reading unmarked generic male texts: "We (women readers) participate both in the liberal-humanist discourse of freedom, self-determination, and rationality, and at the same time in the specifically feminine discourse offered by society of submission, relative inadequacy, and irrational intuition."[32] However, I submit, only if this ideological position becomes conscious in a process of feminist conscientization are women readers able to become readers resisting the *immasculation* of the androcentric, racist, classist, or colonialist text. If this contradiction is not brought into consciousness, it cannot be exploited for change but leads to further self-alienation.

For change to take place, women and other nonpersons must concretely and explicitly reject an abstract reading. For instance in reading the fourth Gospel we should not too quickly resort to abstract God language such as God is love or God is light, without deconstructing the structural dynamics of the Gospel's Father-Son language and replacing it with images of God gleaned from the concrete contextualizations of women's life. Or, if as liberation theologians we insist that God is on the side of the poor, we need to spell out theologically what it actually means that God is on the side of poor women and children dependent on women.

However, we can appropriate as our very own only those "human" values and "Christian" utopias that can be reasoned out in a feminist process of conscientization as liberating not only for Euro-American white elite women but also for those women who suffer from multiple oppressions. Only after having deconstructed the politics of otherness, which constitutes the dualistic frame and theological identity formation of the fourth Gospel, will we be able to reclaim its vision of life and love in the context of the global movements for liberation. Christian identity that is grounded by the reading of the fourth Gospel's inscribed patriarchal politics of otherness must in ever-new readings be deconstructed and reconstructed in terms of a global praxis for the liberation not only of women but of all other nonpersons.

NOTES

1. For this expression, see for instance G. Gutiérrez, *The Power of the Poor in History* (Maryknoll, N.Y.: Orbis, 1983), p. 93. See also C. Cadorette, *From the Heart of the People. The Theology of Gustavo Gutiérrez* (Oak Park, Ill.: Meyer-Stone, 1988).

2. See the interviews of leading male Latin American liberation theologians by E. Tamez, *Against Machismo* (Oak Park, Ill.: Meyer-Stone, 1987); see also Schüssler Fiorenza/Carr, eds., *Women, Work, and Poverty* (*Concilium*, 194; Edinburgh: Clark, 1987).

3. See the overview and discussion by Sylvia Walby, *Patriarchy At Work. Patriarchal and Capitalist Relations in Employment* (Minneapolis: University of Minnesota Press, 1986), and the definition of the term by G. Lerner, *The Creation of Patriarchy* (New York: Oxford University Press, 1986).

4. See especially B. Hooks, *Feminist Theory. From Margin to Center* (Boston: South End Press, 1984).

5. I owe this expression to the feminist sociologist Dorothy Smith.

6. Margaret Atwood, *The Handmaid's Tale* (New York: Ballantine, 1987), pp. 112–13.

7. For the fuller development of a model for a critical feminist interpretation for liberation, see my book *Bread Not Stone. The Challenge of Feminist Biblical Interpretation* (Boston: Beacon, 1984).

8. For this expression, see K. G. Cannon, *Black Womanist Ethics* (AAR Academy Series, 60; Atlanta: Scholars Press, 1988).

9. I. Young, "Impartiality and the Civic Public: Some Implications of Feminist Critiques of Moral and Political Theory," in Benhabib and Cornell, eds., *Feminism as Critique* (Minneapolis: University of Minnesota Press, 1987), p. 61.

10. For this discussion, see the essays in L. Russell, ed., *Feminist Interpretation of the Bible* (Philadelphia: Westminster, 1985).

11. See especially the methodological chapters in *In Memory of Her. A Feminist Theological Reconstruction of Early Christian Origins* (New York: Crossroad, 1983).

12. See also Page duBois, *Centaurs and Amazons. Women and the Pre-History of the Great Chain of Being* (Ann Arbor: University of Michigan Press, 1979).

13. See G. Lloyd, *The Man of Reason. "Male" and "Female" in Western Philosophy* (Minneapolis: University of Minnesota Press, 1984).

14. See, e.g., the essays in Jan Mohamed and Lloyd eds., *The Nature and Context of Minority Discourse*, which have appeared as special issues of *Cultural Critique*, 6 (1987) and 7 (1987).

15. R. Morgan, *Sisterhood Is Global. The International Women's Movement Anthology* (Garden City, N.Y.: Anchor Books, 1984). See also V. Fabella and M. Amba Oduyoye, eds., *With Passion and Compassion: Third World Women Doing Theology* (Maryknoll, N.Y.: Orbis, 1988).

16. See, e.g., the dialogue between G.I. Joseph and J. Lewis, *Common Differences. Conflicts in Black and White Feminist Perspectives* (Boston: South End Press, 1981).

17. This is pointed out by H. V. Carby, " 'On the Threshold of Woman's Era': Lynching, Empire and Sexuality," in H. L. Gates, Jr., ed., *"Race," Writing and Difference* (Chicago: University of Chicago Press, 1986), pp. 301–28.

18. See E. W. Said, "An Ideology of Difference," in Gates, *"Race," Writing and Difference*, pp. 38–58.

19. See also N. Hartsock, "Rethinking Modernism: Minority vs. Majority Theories," *Cultural Critique*, 7 (1987) 187–206; L. Alcoff, "Cultural Feminism Versus Post-Structuralism: The Identity Crisis in Feminist Theory," *Signs*, 13 (1988) 405–36.

20. T. de Lauretis, ed., *Feminist Studies/Critical Studies* (Bloomington: University of Indiana Press, 1986), p. 9.

21. See my "The Ethics of Biblical Interpretation: Decentering Biblical Scholarship," *JBL*, 107 (1988) 3–17.

22. For an overview see R. Kysar, "The Gospel of John in Recent Research," *RSR*, 9 (1983) 314-323; see also D. Moody Smith, *John* (Philadelphia: Fortress, 1986, 2nd ed.) and the commentary by R. Schnackenburg, *The Gospel According to John*, 3 vols. (New York: Crossroad, 1968–82).

23. S. S. Lanser, "(Feminist) Criticism in the Garden: Inferring Genesis 2–3," *Semeia*, 41 (1988) 77.

24. See the very influential work of L. J. Martyn, *History and Theology in the Fourth Gospel* (Nashville: Abingdon, 1979, 2nd ed.).

25. José Miranda, *Being and the Messiah. The Message of St. John* (Maryknoll, N.Y.: Orbis, 1977), p. 88.

26. L. Schottroff, "Antijudaism in the New Testament," in Schüssler Fiorenza/ Tracy, eds., *The Holocaust as Interruption* (*Concilium*, 175; Edinburgh: Clark, 1984), p. 59.

27. R. A. Culpepper, *Anatomy of the Fourth Gospel: A Study in Literary Design* (Philadelphia: Fortress, 1983), p. 226.

28. Ibid., p. 235.

29. P. P. Schweikart, "Reading Ourselves: Toward a Feminist Theory of Reading," in Flynn and Schweikart, eds., *Gender and Reading. Essays on Readers, Texts, and Contexts* (Baltimore: Johns Hopkins University Press, 1986), p. 42.

30. M. Crawford and R. Chaffin, "The Reader's Construction of Meaning: Cognitive Research on Gender and Comprehension," in *Gender and Reading*, pp. 14–16.

31. Virginia Fabella, "A Common Methodology for Diverse Christologies," in *With Passion and Compassion*, p. 116.

32. C. Belsey, "Constructing the Subject: Deconstructing the Text," in Newton and Rosenfelt, eds., *Feminist Criticism and Social Change. Sex, Class, and Race in Literature and Culture* (New York: Methuen, 1985), p. 50.

12

Human Rights Language and Liberation Theology

ALOYSIUS PIERIS, SJ

The cloud of incomprehension that surrounded recent discussions on liberation theology in the official churches in the West cannot be dispelled fully without acknowledging that the two parties in dispute were using two theological languages, albeit within the same orthodox Christian tradition. Many First World theologians committed to social justice follow their pastoral magisterium in using *human rights language* as a theological discourse whose primary addressees could only be the wielders of power and the accumulators of wealth, including the governments of rich nations. Third World theologians on the contrary take *human liberation as God's specific language* primarily addressed to and easily understood by the poor and the oppressed.

Unfortunately, this language difference is not respected. Thus certain First World theologians tend to universalize and absolutize their paradigm, unmindful of its contextual particularity and ideological limitations. On the other hand, many activists and some theologians in Asia fail to make a "paradigm shift" when perusing the plethora of literature issued by human rights advocates from the West and liberationists from Latin America.

This essay is occasioned by this confusion, over which therefore, I wish to reflect aloud in the hearing of my colleagues both in the First and Third Worlds. With their critical response, I hope to arrive at some clarity, some day.

THE HUMAN RIGHTS TRADITION: A BRIEF HISTORY

In origin and development, "the human rights tradition represents an almost Anglo-American phenomenon."[1] This movement reached its climax with the incorporation of the so called Bill of Rights in the American

Constitution. It was, undoubtedly, the most revolutionary event in constitutional history. The very idea that certain *individual* human rights should be invested with constitutional inviolability is said to be unprecedented in the history of political thought.

However, "without prior English development, *individual* rights could scarcely have developed to the level they did in the American law," says the American constitutional historian, Bernard Schwartz.[2] Historians find the Magna Carta of medieval England (1215) a convenient starting point. The next convenient milestone would be the Petition of Rights (1628) followed by the English Bill of Rights (1689), which gave its name (not its contents, which were too meager) to the American Bill of Rights. For brevity's sake I omit here other intermediary events.

The Magna Carta was a monarchical document saturated with the language, the concerns, and the spirit of feudalism. It merely *conceded* certain rights to the barons in return for obedience. It was a royal bargain with feudal chiefs rather than the outcome of a common people's struggle for liberation. The English playwright Arden's play, which commemorated the 750th anniversary of this great charter in 1965, was aptly titled *Lefthanded Liberty*! Yet in some of its provisions, the phrase "any baron" seems to alternate with the more generic term *liber homo* (any free human). Such elements give these provisions an elasticity that the monarch may have never intended but that later human rights advocates found helpful. Thus the charter happened to contain "the germ of the root principal that there are *individual* rights that the state—sovereign though it is—may not infringe."[3]

The Petition of Rights of 1628, in contrast to the Magna Carta, was not a feudal claim of privileges. The battle for parliament's independence from the crown was the context that gave rise to it. It started with the "Protestation of 1621," and this struggle climaxed with the fundamental rights of English persons becoming a positive law by way of a parliamentary enactment. Herein, "the almost superstitious reverence Englishmen feel for their law" and their "legal conservatism" were made use of by a group of "common lawyers who rewrote the history on parliamentary lines in the House of Commons and who built up the body of rights and precedents alleged to be the immemorial heritage of the English People."[4]

History showed that superstitious reverence for the law was not effective even among the English. A law-enforcing machinery was never built into the parliamentary acts, which therefore remained merely declaratory. Charles, the king of England, did not bow down to this act of parliament. It is the crown that ruled. Thus the achievements of 1628 were null and void from a constitutional point of view—a lesson the Americans learned to avoid in *their* declaration of rights.

It is true that the so-called levelers—religiously motivated radicals in the parliament—tried to bring out a more fundamental concept to the fore: (what we might anachronistically call) the people power as the primordial source of authority to which even the parliament should bow and which alone can countercheck any form of arbitrary government. Their document—the "Agreement of the People"—after a series of debilitating amendments, succumbed finally to the fate of all previous written declarations. It had no binding power. The whole exercise was no more than a mere dream. And there was Cromwell who would not let it become history.

Only against this background could one recognize the revolutionary character of the English Bill of Rights of 1689. King James II had dissolved the parliament in July 1688 and five months later fled from the kingdom after throwing the Great Seal (the symbol of constitutional continuity) into the Thames. In the absence of a crown to legitimize a new parliament, a body of responsible persons assembled in an unprecedented manner to form a self-legitimized parliament and offered the throne to William and Mary, subject to the conditions laid down in the "Declaration of Rights"—better known as the "Bill of Rights"—which passed as a regular act of legislature. According to the bill, the parliament was to be freely elected by the people, and was to enjoy complete freedom of speech uninhibited by court or crown. The revolutionary nature of this document has earned it the title: the Second Great Charter.

Yet, the English Bill of Rights, Schwartz warns us, was rudimentary compared to the American one; for the former contained much fewer rights than the latter, and was ever subject to interference by the legislature.[5] The American Bill of Rights, with its more complete list of *individual rights*, succeeded in immunizing itself constitutionally against any such interventions from successive governments or courts whereas the English Bill of Rights did not have enforcement machinery built into it. Thus, the American Constitution has immortalized the inviolability of the human person in terms of a series of basic, "God-given" rights.

THE "SECULAR HUMANIST" AND "RELIGIOUS-CHRISTIAN" CONTRIBUTIONS TO THE HUMAN RIGHTS THEORY

The major influential factor in the development of the American Bill of Rights is what Garrett calls the *Human Rights Tradition*, which, he complains, is too easily confused with something quite different, the *Natural Rights Tradition*, as he names it. In presenting Garrett's valuable insights,[6] I am compelled to make use of his terminology. In the subtitle above, I have called these respectively, the *secular-humanist* and the *religious-Christian* streams of the one human rights tradition. I shall switch back to this terminology after allowing Garrett to make his point.

The movement that climaxed in the American Bill of Rights could be viewed as a confluence of these two streams of thought. But a sociological analysis has convinced Garrett that the natural rights tradition is overrated as an influential factor, whereas the human rights tradition was also largely responsible for the development of the American ideal.

Garret's analysis of the natural rights tradition begins with medieval Europe. The immediate context was the phenomenon of papal absolutism, which tried to absorb secular monarchy into its own hierocratic structure. The defensive posture adopted against this papal hierocracy was twofold. The first reaction produced the "dualist school." It revived the ancient "divine right theory of monarchy." It saw both pope and king as two independent recipients of divinely conferred authority in their respective spheres of competence, spiritual and temporal. The other defensive posture was adopted by the "Natural law school" with leanings toward the Aristotelian theory of nature and society, a theory gaining currency among intellectuals. It looked for a secular basis for political authority, to free it from all ecclesiastical interference. Their appeal to "reason" and "natural law" was equally aimed at the dualist school in order to safeguard humans from the dangerous consequences of the state claiming God-given, inalienable rights over persons.

There was, in the course of time, a *populist view* emerging from these conflicts. In the divine rights school, this meant that God bestows political power to the king through the people. This same theory, applied to the papacy, resulted in the "conciliar movement." In the natural law school, however, it took the guise of a social contract theory, which received a more sophisticated articulation later in Locke and Rousseau.

The "human rights tradition" differs from this European ancestor on many counts, Garrett maintains. First of all, it was an exclusively *Anglo-American* phenomenon. In England, it was associated with the lower-status levelers (as opposed to the Independent Party, which was made up of the gentry); in America, the main actors were Roger Williams and Issac Backus, with the Baptists and Separatist Congregationists serving as the social carriers of the tradition.

Secondly, it was essentially a *religious* movement in neat contrast with the natural rights tradition, which had a clearly marked secular thrust. It was particularly nurtured by a piety expressed through a variant form of Calvinistic theology. To me the implication seems to be that, here, the inviolability of human rights is based on a "divine origin," so to say, and this makes the individual the only "sacred" component of any given society.

The third difference, in Garrett's list, is that the human rights tradition was a *populist* movement, both in England and in America; its social carriers were the "lower status folk" and its ideologues, for the most part, were not even university trained. This explains the widespread support that the American Bill of Rights received from the common folk in the colonial states. The natural law theory, by contrast, was a movement of intellectual theoreticians, from the lawyers and philosophers of medieval Europe to the founding fathers of the American dream.

Finally, the motivational points of departure are diametrically different in the two traditions. The natural law theory aimed at protecting the sovereignty of the secular state from ecclesiastical encroachments, whereas the human rights tradition, especially in America, began as an effort at safe-guarding the "freedom of conscience"—that is, *individual religious liberty* against a secular state trying to impose an official religion (in this case, the Church of England) on the consciences of all. In fact, almost all the rights (speech, assembly, property, and the like) were derived from this basic concern for religious liberty.

Obviously, the two movements, despite radical differences, converged in the demand for total separation of church and state. The "experts" who framed the Bill of Rights and the "people" who greeted it with an over-whelming approval arrived at the same conclusion from divergent points of departure. The two streams have joined together to form one river: a great human rights tradition. It has flowed beyond the confines of the North American continent thanks to the UN Charter of Rights.

THE HUMAN RIGHTS LANGUAGE AS A PARADIGM OF HUMAN FREEDOM IN WESTERN CHRISTIANITY

The human rights movement—I am now shifting back to my original nomenclature, leaving that of Garrett—has been shown to be a convergence of a secular-humanistic and a religious-Christian tradition. In appropriating this tradition as a theological discourse on social ethics, both the radical reformed movements in Protestantism and the progressive thinkers, includ-ing popes, within Roman Catholicism, were merely yielding to an ancient Christian propensity to combine humanistic reason with biblical revela-tion—that is, a universally valid and transcendent *theoria* with the concrete tenets of Christian faith.[7]

In fact, according to one scholar, " 'human rights' is not a biblical con-struct"; it is one of the "nonscriptural categories" that, in confrontation with the scriptures, gave rise to the Christian discourse on human freedom. "The biblical communities functioned with a conception of rights, though they would not recognize the terminology of natural rights or human rights," for the manner of stating universal human claims in terms of a comprehensive and compartmentalized list of rights reflects a typically Western mode of perception.[8]

The human rights movement is, in other words, the West's specific con-tribution to the understanding of human liberation. It is the spiritual nucleus of Western culture, the quintessence of the Western ethos. It is the ideological substance of which the Western democratic order of social relationships is constructed. Understandably, therefore, all political organs of the West—both governments and the NGOs—could hardly perceive, proclaim, or promote the values of freedom and fellowship except in terms of individual rights.

The Western church absorbed this language in the very process of con-tributing to its development and to its eventual refinement. This Church gave the human rights tradition a solid biblical basis, by rooting it in the revealed doctrines of creation (every human is created to the *image of God*) and redemption (every human is an object of God's redemptive intervention through Jesus' *atonement*). Accordingly, it is God who has *gratuitously* endowed each individual with a transcendental and inviolable dignity so that the "autonomy," which the secular-humanist tradition (of the natural rights school) claimed for the human person in terms of inalienable rights, takes the guise of a "theonomy" in the social teachings of the church.[9]

With this type of theological reasoning, the Western patriarchate tried to refine the rights tradition in three interconnected areas. The first revolves around the phenomenon of "individualism," which has now come to be the hallmark of Western spirituality and is the most pernicious outcome of enthroning individuals where formerly kings ruled with divine authority. A team of North American sociologists, led by Robert N. Bellah, have monitored "the classical polarities," or more bluntly, the contradictions of American individualism, one of which is described as "the commitment to the equal right to dignity of every individual combined with an effort to justify inequality of reward, which, when extreme, may deprive people of dignity."[10] The church resolved this contradiction—theoretically, of course—by presenting the human person not as a self-enclosed unit dissociated from the human community, but as a dynamic member of society intrinsically related to other members of that society even in the exercise of rights.

The other inadequacy springs from the close ideological nexus that this individualism maintains with the liberal democratic tradition of the West. The church consciously steered clear of both individualism and collectivism by distancing itself from this liberal democratic ideology—as well as from Marxism, which rightly insisted on the inseparability of personal freedom and social solidarity.[11] Although it repudiated Marxism, the church was certainly influenced by the Marxist critique of liberal democracy and of individualism, and also by the Marxist thesis that economic freedom is basic to political freedom.[12]

Thus we come to an important distinction that Christianity's "public theology" introduced: the distinction between *economic* rights (to food, shelter, work, health care, social security), which Marxists lay stress on, and *civil* and *political* rights, which are the foundation of Western democracies (freedom of speech, belief, assembly, association, habeas corpus, due process, etc.).[13] By affirming them both as inseparable and as equally essential, the Catholic social teachings in particular have not only critically accepted the Marxist distinction, but also partially appropriated its critique of the Western tradition of rights—namely, that this tradition concentrated on political rights, without basing them on the foundation of economic rights. This is the third area in which the Christian rights theory corrected the human rights tradition of the West. The most powerful statement of recent times in this direction is the North American Catholic Bishops' Pastoral, "Economic Justice for All."[14]

As Hollenbach has argued, social doctrine still continues to be developed in the Christian community and he has himself suggested "three strategic moral priorities" that all liberation theologians would endorse, though from quite another perspective: (1) the needs of the poor take priority over the wants of the rich; (2) the freedom of the dominated takes priority over the liberty of the powerful; and (3) the participation of marginalized groups takes priority over the preservation of an order that excludes them.[15] This is indeed a revolutionary stance; if carried out, it would overturn the ideological framework of Western democracy. For such a shift in policy implies a radical structural change that goes beyond the "social democratic conception with the welfare role of the state" as advocated by other Western theologians who wish to combine the "freedom rights" of liberal democracy with "benefit rights" of socialist systems.[16] Liberation theologians too are asking for a structural change in opposition to the Western democratic model. Can the Catholic human rights tradition, even in the radical form envisaged by Hollenbach, meet the demands of liberation in Latin America and other Third World countries? This is the issue I take up next.

THE LIBERATIONIST THESIS VERSUS THE HUMAN RIGHTS DISCOURSE OF THE WESTERN CHURCH

I was intrigued to note that there is no entry on "individualism" in the extensive index of the Hollenbach classic — *Claims in Conflict* — which is the most comprehensive and critical exposition of the Western church's social teachings. I was equally intrigued to note Hollenbach's own surprise at the absence of any entry on "human dignity" or on "human rights" in the extensive index of the Gutiérrez classic, *A Theology of Liberation*. As Hollenbach suspects, the liberation theologians abandon the rights language because that language, in their minds, is associated with "the static and individualistic notions of the human person."[17] These omissions in Gutiérrez and Hollenbach are a clear index of the language difference between the First World theologians concerned with rights and the Third World theologians steeped in the liberation struggle.

The two paradigms differ primarily in the way they combine the secular-humanist and the biblical-religious components of their respective theologies. In the West, the human rights theologians not only ground their natural rights language in the doctrine of the human person extracted from the Bible, but they also employ that language as a *critique on the Bible*, detecting the absence of scriptural references to many rights, such as freedom of religion or freedom for women, even though such rights could eventually be deduced from the biblical principle of "the dignity of the human person."[18]

In the liberationist paradigm, the secular humanist contribution comes from socialism, which includes the reality, if not also the ideology, of class struggle,[19] whereas the biblical foundation it seeks for its praxis is not a transcendental principle extracted from the Bible—as is the case with human rights theology and Catholic social teaching—but the *foundational experience* that forms the axis of biblical revelation: the election of the oppressed as God's covenant partners in a liberation praxis initiated by God. This foundational experience is the "canon within the canon," which is the critical principle that judges the biblical contents internally. Unlike the human rights theologian who "critiques" the Bible from a human rights perspective, the liberation theologians subject the whole corpus of Catholic social teachings and human rights theology to this critical principle of biblical revelation (and would perhaps question the right of anyone other than the oppressed to speak of human rights!).

Thus, according to Gutiérrez, even *Populorum Progressio* seems to be entrenched in the Western developmental model of human growth. The first comprehensive use of the language of liberation, according to Gutiérrez, is found in the message delivered by eighteen Third World bishops in response to that same papal encyclical; this language resonated in Medellín and became its central and all-pervasive concern.[20] And, if Puebla was a step back from Medellín, was it not because the Catholic social doctrine permeated by the human rights language was trying to regain lost ground in Latin America?

I find it quite significant that Gutiérrez not only makes absolutely no use of the human rights language, as Hollenbach has already noted (see above), but has also ignored the whole human rights movement, as if to say that it has no relevance in a Third World context. This movement, as I described it in the earlier part of this paper, began from an elitist concern, not from the underside of history, as is made evident by the nature of the major events that contributed to that movement from the Magna Carta to the American Bill of Rights.

The implication of this observation is not that the human rights movement has no global message but that it constitutes the mood and method of a theology that continues to speak from elitist and conceptual heights, and presupposes Western democratic structures, whereas liberation theology is born out of a struggle that in some way is directed against those same democratic systems and their domination in the Third World. Hence, one cannot gloss over the contextual, ideological, and methodological discrepancies that separate the two theologies.

This may be why the American Bill of Rights has not merited even an adverse comment in the pages of *A Theology of Liberation*. The United States of America is mentioned there only about three times; and in each instance, this gigantic paragon of Western democracy is made to appear as the major hindrance to Latin America's sovereignty! In Gutiérrez's references to liberative initiatives recorded in history, the great American independence struggle is conspicuously absent, whereas the French Revolution (which was, in fact, inspired by it) receives an honorable mention, as does also Russia's October Revolution. He counts these two among "the great revolutions," which, at least tentatively "wrested the political decisions from the hands of the elite" — that is, from the "elite" who claimed they alone were "destined" to rule.[21]

Does this mean that for Gutiérrez the American Revolution was not really an example of a "people's struggle" as it had not "wrested the political decisions from the hands of the elite"? I would hardly contest the fact that the social carriers of the human rights movement (the religious, populist stream of it) in the British colonies of North America were the lower-status folk, as Garrett (quoted above) has cogently argued. But in the wider context of colonization and in the perspective of liberation theology, it was a battle of the elite and not a *colonized* people's struggle against the domination of *colonists*; indeed it was a case of colonists wrenching for themselves the "privileges, liberties, and immunities" of English citizens — that is to say, the colonists' acquisition of "Englishmen's rights."[22] The colonists were (European) "emigrants" who — according to John Adams's boast — were the real "author, inventor, and discoverer" of American independence.[23] Neither the *black slaves* imported by the colonists, nor the *colonized natives* marginalized by the same colonists were the immediate beneficiaries of this revolution. Thus, to the liberationist it is not a meaningful model even though it remains the crown and glory of the human rights movement in the Western democratic tradition.

And yet, no liberationist would deny the fact that the human rights language is the West's own indigenous way of communicating the gospel of justice to the rich and the powerful. Nor would Third World theology stand in the way of Western theologians forging a third way between capitalism and communism, even if that might sound abstract.[24] For that abstract idea has crystalized into a "public theology," which has, at least *theoretically*, corrected three major defects of the human rights tradition — individualism, liberalism, and neglect of economic rights, as indicated above.

Although one would be skeptical about a mere idea generating a change in social structures, one would still respect the great philosophical tradition of Western theology that succeeds in clarifying issues conceptually. Hence when the church appropriates radical ideas as basic to Christian message, it is bound to express them with prophetic clarity. When this happens, a sigh of relief is heard in Third World churches. That certainly was the case when the news of the U.S. Bishops' Pastoral Letter on Economic Justice reached our ears in Asia! Though reformist and tame,[25] it is the only language the Western church knows to speak.

As long as this theology speaks to the rich and the powerful in the West and in the westernized enclaves of the Third World, it is within its own right and the only enemy it will encounter will be political liberalists and Christian fundamentalists. But it draws the wrath of liberation theologians only when it becomes a tool at the service of the Western church's ecclesiastical colonialism in the poor countries. This is the concluding argument of my analysis.

HUMAN RIGHTS THEOLOGY: A TOOL OF ECCLESIASTICAL IMPERIALISM IN THE THIRD WORLD?

Ecclesiastical imperialism is the tendency of one church to regard all others as its extensions, and to make its "particular" theology "universally" obligatory. This is but an ecclesiastical version of the ethnocentric dogma: "my culture is the modern universal culture." The human rights theology as it appears in the social teachings of the Western churches tends to be used in this manner.

Eminent and much respected theologians join the official church in this campaign, though not with bad faith. They criticize black, feminist Latin American and Afro-Asian theologies for being mere particularized perspectives claiming to be theologically comprehensive, but quite firmly believe that the human rights theology is based on transcendent universal principles valid for all situations.[26]

Although this universal principle ("dignity of the human person") is invoked against all other theologies, the ultimate criterion, I suspect, is a matter of *ideological* preference.[27] The human rights theology is ideologically tied to the Western democratic model of social organization; but liberation theology accepts critically the socialist paradigm, which includes also the *reality* of class struggle. Therefore, at the root of the argument against liberation theology there is more ideology than theology at work.

The history of the Roman Church's social doctrine can be cited in support of this. For instance, two popes who laid the foundation for the church's social doctrine, Leo XIII and Pius XI, may have had many biblical, theological, and philosophical arguments against the Marxist theory of class struggle. But, as Hollenbach observes with scholarly candor, their rejection of the class struggle idea, in reality, came from "the close links between the church and the classes which were the targets of Marxist attacks." Moreover, "these links prevented the papal tradition from understanding important aspects of the Marxist social analysis."[28] It is such ideological links that prevent both the pastoral and the academic magisterium of the Western patriarchate from respecting the particularity and therefore the validity of another local church's theology.

The Vatican's reaction to liberation theology cannot be explained otherwise, as a careful analysis of this excerpt from Ratzinger illustrates. Explaining his own Congregation's second instruction on liberation theology, he says:

> Catholic social teaching accordingly knows no utopia but it does develop models of the best possible organization of human affairs in a given historical situation. It, therefore, rejects the myth of revolution and seeks the way of reform, which itself does not entirely exclude violent resistance in extreme situations, but protests against the rec-

ognition of revolution as a *Deus ex machina* from which the new man and new society are one day inexplicably to proceed.[29]

Here one local theology posing itself as "Catholic social teaching" refuses to recognize that the shift ("conversion") from sin to grace in the order of social relationships is a qualitative jump; the "myth of revolution" is rejected in favor of "reform." But the scripture scholar and Ratzinger's collaborator in *Communio*, Norbert Lohfink, has inquired into the biblical roots of liberation theology and come to quite another conclusion: the revealed notion of liberation is distinguished from the nonbiblical approaches to social questions (1) by treating the poor as *the* poor—that is, a people oppressed as a class—and therefore also (2) by advocating a radical opting out of that oppressive system rather than resorting to reformist solutions, and (3) by believing that God takes full responsibility for this radical change[30] (notwithstanding Ratzinger's suspicion of deus ex machina). In that case, "Catholic social teaching," which, according to Ratzinger, is called to "develop models of best possible organizations of human affairs in a given historical situation," cannot a priori preclude a Third World church's option for a social system that conforms to the biblical principle enunciated above, or impose on a Third World church the West's reformist model of human rights theology as if it were "catholic" (universal). That would be an ideological imposition of the Western church on other churches.

It is this "ecclesiastical imperialism" that liberation theologians wish to combat, and not necessarily the human rights theory or the public theology that appropriates it, or the ideologically ambivalent principle about social models that Ratzinger enunciates.

The most critical area of conflict, therefore, revolves around the ideologically interpreted biblical foundations of the two theologies. Liberation theology does not speak of a "transcendental principle" extracted from the Bible and then "applied" to concrete situations. Such a manner of theologizing is indigenous to a Christian culture that employs philosophy as *ancilla theologiae*. Liberation theology does not explain reality philosophically; it analyzes reality sociologically. Hence, it is not concerned about a "transcendent principle" (biblical or otherwise) that "integrates" various conceptual diads such as "individual and society," "economic freedoms and political freedoms," "liberal democracy's anticollectivism and Marxist socialism's anti-individualism." Liberation theology is engaged, not with reconciling conceptual opposites, but with resolving social contradictions between the classes.

Let me, therefore, reiterate that the biblical basis of liberation theology is not a transcendent principle derived from reason and confirmed by the Bible but the *very foundational experience that gave birth to the Bible*, a canon within the canon, by which the Bible itself is criticized internally. This foundational experience is the *election of the oppressed class* as God's equal partners in the common *mission* of creating a new order of love, a mission that can be shared by anyone who becomes one with God by being one with the oppressed class. Each concrete situation that reveals a new class of oppressed—women, minorities, and the like—is a continuation of this biblical revelation.

In this scheme, the transcendental and universal principle of "the dignity of the human person" fades away into a larger picture: God's *election* of the oppressed as God's co-creators of the kingdom and God's co-redeemers of the world; it is not an ontological status conferred by grace through creation and atonement, as in human rights theology, but an *elevation* of the oppressed, insofar as they are a class, to the status of God's covenantal partners engaged in God's project of liberation. Thus in partnering God, they have learned to use the language that the rich and the powerful refuse to speak or understand, the language of liberation, the language that God speaks through Jesus.

The human rights language is a language that may persuade the rich and the powerful to share their riches and power with the poor and thus gain access to this covenantal partnership. In that sense, the human rights language has a pedagogical value for liberation theology. In fact, Sobrino seems to use it as a means of communicating this message to the churches of the rich nations.[31]

When the secular humanist tradition, which discovered the role of the proletariat in the construction of the new order, coincides with the aforementioned biblical foundation of liberation theology, then "socialism" appears to be "the best possible organization of human affairs in the given historical situation"—to use Ratzinger's words. The past failures in the socialist experiments could serve as guideposts rather than as barriers, if only the powerful ideological blocs of either side do not interfere—as Russia does in Vietnam and the U.S.A. in Nicaragua—and if the church does not side with one or the other of these superpowers, but allows the "foundational experience" of the Bible to become a social reality.

This theology is diametrically different from the human rights theology of the Western patriarchate, but considers itself as a local theology, which, however, confronts the human rights theology on ideological grounds. This healthy confrontation is neutralized when the human rights theology parades itself as the universal theology valid for all churches. The tendency in the West to extoll Christian institutions that follow the human rights tradition,[32] and to condemn missionaries who opt for the liberation schema,[33] contributes to this species of ecclesiastical imperialism. Most episcopal peace and justice commissions in Asia stay at the human rights level; if they change their stance in favor of the liberation scheme, they could be disbanded by the hierarchy, as the Australian experience warns! This way, human rights theology is *used* as the tool of ecclesiastical imperialism.

My concluding remark is directly addressed to the human rights theologians in the very language they have created: respect the God-given inalienable *right* of every local church, especially in the Third World, to evolve its own theological discourse. Any tendency to universalize the social teaching of the Western patriarchate and impose it on others is a violation of the autonomy of the local church. Even in the struggle for justice, let justice be done to the creativity of the Third World theologians who have initiated a "neat break" from the cultural domination of the Western church even in social ethics; it is the *caesura* (radical rupture from the West) that Karl Rahner, voicing our concerns, advocated fearlessly as the conditio sine qua non for the birth of a truly universal church.[34]

NOTES

1. William R. Garrett, "Religion, Law, and the Human Condition," *Sociological Analysis*, 47 (1987) 21.

2. Bernard Schwartz, *The Great Rights of Mankind: A History of the American Bill of Rights* (New York: Oxford University Press, 1977), p. 25; italics added. This is the source I follow in writing this section of the paper.

3. Ibid., p. 3.

4. Ibid., p. 9, referring to Pocock, *The Ancient Contribution and the Feudal Law* (1957), p. 48.

5. *The Great Rights*, p. 1.

6. Garrett, "Religion, Law, and the Human Condition."

7. Max L. Stackhouse, "Public Theology, Human Rights and Mission," *Human Rights and the Global Mission of the Church* (Cambridge: Boston Theological Institute, 1985), pp. 13–21.

8. Stephen Charles Mott, "The Contribution of the Bible to Human Rights," in *Human Rights and the Global Mission of the Church*, pp. 5–6.

9. Ibid., pp. 7–8.

10. Robert N. Bellah, et al., *Habits of the Heart: Individualism and Commitment in American Life* (Berkeley: University of California Press, 1985), p. 150. See also pp. 28–35.

11. David Hollenbach, *Claims in Conflict* (New York: Paulist Press, 1979), p. 21.

12. Ibid., p. 83.

13. David Hollenbach, "Both Bread and Freedom: The Interconnection of Economics and Political Rights in Recent Catholic Teaching," in *Human Rights and Global Mission*, pp. 31–34.

14. "Economic Justice for All: Catholic Social Teaching and the U.S. Economy," *Origins, NC Documentary Service*, 16/24 (1986) 410–55.

15. Hollenbach, *Claims*, p. 204.

16. Mott, "The Contribution," p. 11.

17. Hollenbach, *Claims*, p. 179, n. 2.

18. Mott, ibid.

19. Gustavo Gutiérrez, *A Theology of Liberation* (Maryknoll, N.Y.: Orbis Books, 1973), pp. 26, 27, 30, 90, 91, 111–13, 274.

20. Ibid., pp. 33–35.

21. Ibid., p. 46; see also p. 28.

22. Schwartz, *The Great Rights*, p. 27.

23. Ibid., p. 29.

24. But Hollenbach ("Both Bread and Freedom," p. 32) argues against the accusation that human rights theology is abstract.

25. See Leonardo and Clodovis Boff, "Good News of US Bishops' Economic Pastoral and Bad News Left Unmentioned," *National Catholic Reporter*, 23/38 (Aug. 28, 1987).

26. E.g. Stackhouse, "Public Theology," p. 17.

27. Here I understand ideology as I have defined it in chap. 3 of my *An Asian Theology of Liberation* (Maryknoll, N.Y.: Orbis Books, 1988).

28. Hollenbach, *Claims*, p. 52.

29. Joseph Ratzinger, "Freedom and Liberation: Anthropological Vision of the Instruction 'Libertatis Conscientia,'" *Communio*, 14 (Spring 1987) 70.

30. Norbert Lohfink, *Das Judische am Christentum. Die verlorene Dimension* (Freiburg: Herder, 1987), pp. 132–134.

31. Jon Sobrino, "The Divine Character of Human Rights," *COELI Quarterly* (Brussels) 43 (Fall 1987) 19–27.

32. Max L. Stackhouse, "Militarization and the Human Rights Tradition in Asia: Implications for Mission Today," in *Human Rights and Global Mission of the Church*, p. 86.

33. Ibid., p. 87.

34. Karl Rahner, "Toward a Fundamental Theological Interpretation of Vatican II," *Theological Studies*, 40 (Dec. 1979) 716–27.

PART III

LOOKING
TOWARD
THE FUTURE

13

Women in the Future
of the Theology of Liberation

MARÍA CLARA BINGEMER

*I believe that ... to explore the spiritual journey of women is also to
explore the spiritual journey of human beings. ... I think that if women
are valued and make tenderness attractive, they will liberate many men
who refuse to recognize that they have this experience in their lives too,
and must have it.*

— *Gustavo Gutiérrez*

It is audit time in Latin America. The theology of liberation is coming
up to its twentieth birthday. It is time to look back to the past in order to
be able to distinguish the present, and having distinguished it, to be able
to desire and construct the future. It is time to ask some questions. After
these twenty years of laborious construction and slow consolidation, what
does the theology of liberation look like? What is its future?

To answer these questions we have to look at the faces of those who
have the leading roles in this theology, those without whom the theologians
themselves and even Latin American theology would not exist—the poor
and oppressed. It was their shouting that caused a disturbance and ended
up echoing round the church until there was no escaping it—their passion
and their imprisonment, their indestructible hope, the fire of their desire
for liberation, conceived and brought into the world a new language for
talking about the ancient and eternal truths of the Christian faith.

Today, however, the faces of these poor and oppressed look different.
Out of the mass of faces of the great poor majority of Latin America three
types in particular are emerging and attracting attention, presenting new
challenges to church and society. They are the blacks, Amerindians, and
women. These groups, oppressed for centuries by their color, race, and sex,
are now essential for an evaluation of the theology of liberation and for

any attempt to glimpse its future, because they bring into theology new issues, a new method, and a new language.

Women in particular interest us most closely here. Their state of double oppression—by their socio-economic situation and by their sex—calls for the attention of society and the church.[1] Their presence in the development of Latin American theology has recently been felt with increasing weight and frequency. Their ideas and their language have already been recognized as among the most serious and solid products of Latin American theology. This presence enjoyed by women in the theology of liberation enables us to hope for a bright and joyful future. From the mouths and hearts of these once silent and invisible workers for the kingdom there is now coming a message of jubilation that says, "Rejoice!" The half of humankind that thought of itself as absent from theology's discourse — and in particular from the theology of liberation—has now made itself present and is speaking. And this widens the horizon and helps us to see with more clarity the Absolute Future that goes out to meet those who wait in hope.

Women are active producers of theology, just as they are an object of theological reflection. They bring their own method and a particular perspective with which to conceive and express the traditional topics of the faith within the process of Latin American liberation. In all this they are emerging and finding their place. Because of this all those men and women who are committed to the same service and enlightened by the same hope, and give their lives daily so that imprisonment may end and the kingdom come, are exclaiming jubilantly, "Rejoice!" The new event is taking place and the Spirit is blowing. The female presence in the theology of liberation is growing and becoming visible, tempering struggle with festivity, force with tenderness, and rigor with desire. God's kingdom is in its advent— more than that, it is in our midst.

WOMEN AS PRACTITIONERS AND SUBJECTS OF THEOLOGY

Women's past in the world of theology was largely silence and invisibility. Though present in the church—and even with a numerically stronger presence than men—their faces were not seen or their voices heard in any "shouting from the housetops," when any audible and recognized statement had to be produced and uttered.

In the case of theology, and more specifically, theological production, the silence and the absence were particularly marked. Women as subjects did not appear with any prominence in theology treatises, courses, or books. Subsumed in the treatise on "theological anthropology," where human beings were considered in their status as the image and likeness of God, women, diluted and forgotten even in language, were at the most allowed to be included in the ambiguously androcentric term "man."[2] The category "man" sought to designate the human being as a whole, man and woman, but insensibly the form influenced the content and the object of consideration came to be in fact male humankind, rather than the totality of human-kind, man and woman. The specificity, the differentness, of women, their characteristics, their ways of feeling, their particular way of being the image of God, were obliterated in the dark night of time in a diffuse anthropol-ogico-theological category that did not do justice to the richness of their being.

Similarly, in theological production, the past for women was marked by centuries of absence as practitioners, and by a deep silence. Until recently there were in the history of theology no books or articles written by women, no chairs occupied by women, no courses run by women. No one even bothered to specify the sex of the authors of theological texts or of profes-sors of theology. It was "obvious" that such work was a male prerogative.[3] For all this time women's ways of thinking and talking did not enrich the-ology with their own characteristics, did not shape it with their way of feeling and thinking, did not color it with their own different accents. As a result, theology, the church, and humankind were the poorer. And women suffered like the woman in the parable of Luke 15:8–10, who searched tirelessly and persistently for the lost coin whose existence she knew of with unshakeable certainty, and which she was unwilling to give up her claim to any longer.

Today, therefore, we are witnessing the awakening of women in the church and in theology. And although it is an awakening inevitably marked by the signs of the breaking of an age-old silence, the dazzle of a sight suddenly seen from the depths of an endless tunnel, it still shows signs of promise that hint at what it has still to disclose, in addition to what it has so far revealed. It is like the tip of an iceberg that makes us suspect a whole vast transparency still submerged, and desire its full and rapid emergence.

What women are saying is making itself strongly heard in the world of theology.[4] It is making itself heard as a message distinct in kind. Women's ideas and language are no longer the insecure stammering of a person whose tongue has recently been loosed, nor is the torrent of talk that has made verbal diarrhea a female characteristic in popular opinion. It is a new and different theological message, a deliberate decision to speak. The mes-sage is systematic and ordered, and contains a distinct style all its own, visible in everything from the selection of topics for systematic investigation, the emphasis given to biblical texts, and the way they are approached and explained, to the premises and structure of arguments, the framework of theological discourse.

Women's theological message in the present, which gestated in the long night of absence and silence, shines a new light on all theology, the same light that shone from the face of the woman in the parable of Luke 15:8–10 when she found the coin that had always been hers, after she had lost it and searched for it.[5] This coin was the currency of mystery, of God's truth and word, the currency of the secret of life in abundance, revealed to her from the beginning and now rediscovered as something to be revered, pondered on, and proclaimed.

From their long experience of silence, women have acquired the wisdom, ancient and always new, that speaks the word and silence, in a harmonious combination of gestures, prophecies, lamentations, and counsels, able to express—though never exhaust—the mystery of the presence of the divine in the human. Understanding life and the slowness of its processes, women apply this knowledge in their theologizing. For a woman, bringing into being theology is like bringing into being a life, a new creature. It means carrying it in her womb, giving birth to it after many months, feeding it, and protecting it with her body, defending it, and watching it grow. It means thinking about, pondering on, and talking about the revealed word with power and courage, but also with patience—doing, building, and talking, but also being silent, waiting, hoping, and celebrating. And besides all this, more important than all this, with the transparent and pure happiness of someone who has found what she was looking for and now cannot celebrate alone, she *has to* call her "friends and neighbors" and say, "Rejoice with me, for I have found the coin I had lost!" For a woman, doing theology means finding a way into a new solidarity, into a theology that cannot be done in isolation, but only in solidarity, in community, in the church.

It is at this point that a new future in the theology of liberation opens up for women. One of the fundamental features of the Latin American theological venture known as the theology of liberation is that it is a collective theological enterprise. The theologian of liberation no longer regards herself as someone who thinks, ponders, writes, and speaks in isolation, out of her individual experience, about the reading she has done on her own, or her own brilliant reasoning. She sees herself as the spokeswoman for the great mass of oppressed persons who have recently woken from centuries of the most bitter oppression of all kinds, are standing up, and rediscovering themselves as responsible and active initiators. They are eager to rewrite history from their own point of view, to reinterpret the liberating message of God's covenant with the people and Jesus Christ's liberating act in terms of their own situation of captivity, in order to turn them into a source of strength, insight, and strategy to live and suffer in their struggle. Theology comes into this process as an ally and a spokesperson. Through sharing in the aspirations, the organization, and the faith-lives of these oppressed persons, the theologian finds her raw material, which she then returns to them in the form of a worked out, systematic argument; for they have helped to bring it to birth and, along with her, are creators and theologians.

This is what is happening as women enter the domain of theology. Their awakening and their speaking are not the sum of isolated experiences, but are the sign of a new, fascinating, and indestructible solidarity with their comrades from poor communities who, beneath the surface of history, are weaving the threads and sewing the stitches of the liberation of the poor on the Latin American framework. With the word of God and the gospel of Jesus as their only wealth, the women of the Latin American poor are taking over the leadership and the administration of the great majority of the increasing number of biblical groups and basic ecclesial communities, giving the church a new look and a new vigor. In the farthest corners of Latin America, they are there, catechists taking responsibility for education in the faith and the deeper assimilation of the gospel, ministers and servants of communities organizing to struggle and celebrate. In rural areas, in *favelas*, in the poor communities on the edges of the big cities, they are organizing in groups around their common work, inspired by their faith in the Lord and their love for the people of which they are a part. Mothers' clubs, community gardens and kitchens, and a variety of other women's organizations are springing up everywhere, organizing the struggle, strengthening faith, defending life, consolidating courage and unity, celebrating the feast.[6]

It is these women whom the woman theologian today accompanies and speaks for. Her theological message is called to reflect, organize, and make audible the unsystematic message that comes, in the raw state, from the rough and experienced lips of poor women. Prompted by the experience of faith, these women from poor communities are taking responsibility for practical struggles on behalf of their people. The woman who does theology, one more among them, a sister and companion, receives from their calloused and affectionate hands, still warm from hard labor for the building of the kingdom, her mission and the stuff of her reflection. Within this greater collective struggle, she is called on to develop her argument and reflection in order to return it as a humble and willing contribution to the continuing process of liberation.

Women's future in the theology of liberation is thus the future of the liberation of all human beings, men and women, who, from the depths of their oppression, desire and call out for the God of life, who brings liberation—socio-economic, political, cultural, racial, ethnic, sexual—from every type of death.

Theological Method

Theology's past is heavily imprinted with the primacy of the rational. Ever since it divorced itself from spirituality, which gave it flexibility, beauty, and movement, theology ran the serious risk of becoming stiff—of treating reason as the one universal mediator of its thought and language. In this way it often became circumspect and cold, not allowing for all the other fundamental elements of human life and also, therefore, of the divine life that is theology's source and model: sensitivity, gratuitousness, experience, desire. Theology's past, therefore, is imprinted with this almost absolute primacy of rationality, and this had much to do with the fact that theology was done almost exclusively by men.[7]

The theology done in the past was, in addition, marked by an abstract language and style in its presentation of the life and truths of the faith. Theological language has often fallen into the temptation of divorcing itself from reality, the hard ground of experience, and of spinning complicated and esoteric theories unrelated to real life, unrelated to the detail of everyday concerns, unrelated to the questions brewing in the minds of the faithful, unrelated to the burning desire in their hearts. The result of this was a theology distant even from the detail of church life, foreign to the deepest aspirations of the people of God, remote from the sufferings and anguish of all sorts of poor and oppressed who longed, from the depths of their imprisonment, for light and a word of guidance. Theological concepts and theories ran the risk of becoming empty words if they could not name the distant spring they flowed from, what deep existential reality, what vital aspiration and desire they expressed; if they could not turn themselves into intelligible communication with the people of God they were meant to serve.

Women's entry into the domain of theology brings with it a new way, a new method, of conceiving and expressing this 2,000-year-old theology. Entering into the domain of theological reflection with their specific and different bodiliness, open to ever-new and innovative messages, available for invasion and creative fecundation, destined to be host and protector of life, women are revolutionizing the very rigor and system of theological method.[8] Their present irruption into the circumspect and rational male theological world of the past is as disconcerting and new as that of the woman in John's Gospel (12:1–8) who invaded the meal taking place within the very strict social and ritual norms of Judaism with her presence and her perfume.[9] Breaching expectations and regulations and following the impulse of the desire that overflowed from her heart, the woman filled the space with a new scent, which none could avoid smelling and breathing in.

The presence of women in theology brings with it this same air of the new and unexpected. Today we are witnessing women's theological message being uttered and heard amid the formerly monolithic and impregnable structure of male theology. And, even though the first impression that emerges is one of a foreign body and the nonintegration of a foreign body, not properly assimilated into the system, the female way of doing theology is finding its place and gaining ground. The courage to pour out the perfume at someone else's party is followed by the moment at which the perfume poured out struggles and collides with the ancient scents that have traditionally formed the environment. The present is made up of this plurality of scents, sometimes apparently incompatible, and often in conflict.

The future of the female way of doing theology is therefore inseparably linked with desire.[10] The primacy of rationality must be replaced by the primacy of desire, the cold circumspection of purely scientific inquiry must give way to a new sort of systematics springing from the impulse of desire that dwells at the deepest level of human existence and combines sensitivity and rationality, gratuitousness and effectiveness, experience and reflection, desire and rigor. "God is love" (1 John 4:8). If this is so, God can only be, in the beginning, the object of desire; not of necessity, not of rationality. Theology—which seeks to be reflection and talk about God and God's word—therefore cannot but be moved and permeated throughout its whole extent by the flame of desire. At a particular point in its theological articulation, reason, science, and systematic rigor have their role and their place, but they can never suffocate the greater desire, never tame the divine pathos, which, from all eternity, has broken silence and become a loving and calling word, kindling in its turn in the hearts of humankind an irresistible and insatiable desire. Theology is called—humbly—to bear witness to and give an account of this burning desire. Born of desire, theology exists as theology only if it is upheld and supported by desire, in the direction of the desire that is its goal and its horizon.[11]

The presence of women in the world of theology brings back to the front line, to the front of the stage of the church's life, that primacy of desire for which purely rational concepts do not allow.[12] A woman finds it unthinkable to divide her own being into watertight compartments and treat theological work as a purely rational activity. Moved by desire, a totalizing force, she does theology with her body, her heart and hands, as much as with her head, and the ripe fruit that she begins to make available is the result of slow and patient pondering of experiences lived deeply and intensely, confronted with the tradition of the past and with the normative landmarks of the journey of the people of Israel and the church.

In this way the Spirit, the motor and origin of desire, poured out on history and humanity, finds good and fertile ground for creative imagination. As well as referring back constantly and faithfully to the Jesus of the past as the ultimate and definite norm, it opens the future to infinite possibilities of inventiveness and newness in expressing the Christian mystery. At the center of theological reflection and discourse, which remain open to a future still not fully explored, the Spirit reinstates the rights of the poetic and symbolic as literary genres, the only ones able to reach the heart of the matter and touch the hem of the Spirit and of Beauty.[13]

Everything I have just said about theology done by women with their whole selves is particularly true, and indeed characteristic, of the theology of liberation. Talking of desire is not to talk of an aseptic impulse that obeys sterile and preserved esthetic rules. When we talk about desire we are talking about human beings at their deepest level, in their deepest and ultimate truth, in their vital force,[14] and therefore in their most authentic and legitimate aspirations. We are talking about what makes our bodies quiver and tremble with pleasure, about our noble and threatened vulnerability, our greatness, which depends on our fragility. When a human being's most basic and vital needs are denied, when he or she is deprived of the essential elements that make up and sustain life at its most fundamental, it is human desire itself, the person's deepest core, the truest and most basic impulse, that is attacked and violated.[15]

From this point of view Latin America has been systematically attacked in its vital desire. The poor, who make up the vast majority of the population, daily experience the weight of domination. Bending and wasting their bodiliness, imprisoning them in remorseless deprivation and oppression, also bends and wastes their ability to desire and know themselves desired, and so their ability to live and express themselves fully as human beings. The process of liberation begins to take place when the poor become conscious of the desire repressed within themselves and let it emerge, release it as a cry, and feel it at the same time to be the energy for the struggle. It is in this liberation of desire that theology is called to give its message, and specifically in our case, theology done by women.[16]

Women's future in the theology of liberation, then, means for them to place their integrated and integrating approach at the heart of this struggle and this process. To be a woman means to be able to combine experience and action, to be able to grapple with oppression and liberation, to be able, in the midst of disaster, to glimpse the superabundance of grace. It is an ability, in a situation filled with vast and profound contradictions, to integrate and see the unity in contrasts and differences, to be able to discern and contemplate in the disfigurement of the cross the breath of hope and the weight of the glory already starting to shine. It is the ability not to lose the thread of the desire that, from the depths of a disfigured world, groans with unspeakable groans to proclaim the birth of the new creation, already visible. Women have received this ability as a gift, and women in poor communities in Latin America exercise it every day.

A challenging and promising future lies in store for a woman doing theology in the context of the theology of liberation. The challenge is to *restore the primacy of desire within theological discourse.* The promise is that she will be enlightened and led by that desire toward the kingdom where liberation will be a full reality. In the midst of the hopeful and stubborn struggle, which consists of the pain and joy of her sisters from poor communities, she is called to place her reflection and her arguments, not only at the service of the struggle, but also as decorations at the celebration. With her theological message uttered in favor of life and light, denouncing the forces of darkness and death, she is called to inaugurate new ways of listening to revelation, of expressing the experience of faith, of reading and interpreting the word of God, of thinking about and unfolding the great themes and chapters of theology. And all the while she allows herself to be possessed by the desire that inflames and summons, that keeps alight, not consumed, the flame of love in the face of everything that threatens to extinguish it.

The Great Themes of Theology from a Woman's Viewpoint

The theology of liberation is not a different theology from that which grew out of the experience of the people of Israel, of Jesus of Nazareth and the apostles. It is the same faith-experience, the same desire, the same love made flesh, now reflected on in conjunction with the sufferings and hopes for liberation of the oppressed.[17] Consequently it does not deal with different topics, but the same topics as in the great line of the church's theology, which are studied from a new point of view in the theology of liberation.[18] What Christian faith is able to say about itself in this new and different perspective will reveal the relationship it has with the real questions raised by the human beings of today in their various struggles as they develop out of their historical activity.[19] The content of a theology from a woman's perspective is determined by the same principle. It will tackle the same themes, reflect on the key tenets of Christian theology, taking into account women's views and methods.

One of the constants of theology in general—and the theology of liberation is no exception to this generalization—is that it has always been done by men. This does not deprive it of value or of the status of true theology—that is, inspired and systematic reflection, a metalanguage related to revelation and faith—but it necessarily limits its scope and vision. It is not possible for only one of the sexes of humankind to encompass and do justice to the whole mystery of being human, and therefore still less to that of the revelation of the divine in the human. Theological reflection has lacked the desire, the heart, the body, and the head of a woman to enable it to be more fully itself, to enable new treasures to be discovered and brought to birth out of the womb of God's word, so that the image of God—man and woman—could be more perfectly revealed and made known.

This is beginning to happen, at a steadily increasing rate. However, whereas in the First World there is already a considerable volume of theology produced by women, with a large number of books and articles published,[20] in the Third World the process of theological production by women is taking place in a different way. It is more collective, less "visible," in terms of large, impressive publications, more of an antlike infiltration, coming gradually up from the base of church life and gradually penetrating theological production as a whole.

Specifically, women's theological production in Latin America regards itself as part of the larger body of the theology of liberation, as a humble and modest contribution to the process of the total redemption of all classes of oppressed. In bringing out their theological message, Latin American women are not trying to engage in a power struggle with men, still less to replace the male model of theological reflection by the female one. They are looking and working for "a new synthesis in which the dialectic present in human existence can really take effect, without destroying any of the vital components."[21]

If the past was silence and absence of a female perspective on the content of theology, the present is marked by increasing visibility, gently exerting its influence. In the Latin American theological community, the female touch is gradually becoming apparent, a woman's approach to problems, a woman's feeling in raising certain issues. The first publications are beginning to appear, the slowly ripened fruit of contact with the base, along with the women from poor communities who make the church exist in history at the day-to-day level. Meetings are being organized at local, regional, and national levels. The Ecumenical Association of Third World Theologians (EATWOT) is encouraging dialogue between women theologians from Africa, Asia, and Latin America, and from minority groups in North America. These meetings, dialogues, and interchanges produce conclusions that take forward women's contributions within the general framework of theological reflection committed to the process of liberation.[22] There are also topics that appear and become dominant when studied in this new light. They are gradually opening up a path for the future of women's theological thinking.

The woman who does theology in today's Latin America, in solidarity with the poor and from the depth of their oppression, has every day the experience of *seeing the Lord,* as Mary Magdalen, on the first day of the week, beside the tomb, *saw* the light of the new life and heard her name spoken by the mouth of the risen Lord: "Mary!" (John 20:16). And she did not keep the experience to herself, but went to talk about the things the Lord had told her (John 20:18). This is what is happening to women who do theology. Having seen the Lord and heard new things from his lips, they go and reflect on them, assimilate them, and communicate them in their words and in their way.

So now we are able to witness a new way of approaching the Bible and the sacred texts, a way devised by women, a new reflection on Jesus Christ, on Mary, on the church; a new experience and a new understanding of the living God who is the center from which all theology emanates and on which it all converges. There is a new way of understanding and celebrating the eucharist and the other sacraments. These topics and others not yet broached are gradually forming and filling out the new and original fabric of Latin American theology.[23]

Women and the Bible

Women and the poor in Latin America rediscovered the Bible at the same time. When those who had been kept out of the way, outside the word of God, once again discovered the entrance to the book that was theirs, which spoke of their struggles, their hopes, their desires, and their covenant of love with a compassionate and loving God, women were present. The great movement of study and reading of the Bible that sprang up throughout Latin America—with biblical circles, basic ecclesial communities, and short courses of biblical formation for pastoral workers from poor communities—shook consciences and challenged other parts of the church. The poor were rediscovering holy scripture, the word of God; were once more taking possession of and establishing residence on ground that was their own.

Despite all this, women with a certain level of feminist consciousness began to ask a number of questions about the Bible. They felt deeply involved and identified with the great accounts of liberation contained in scripture, and Jesus' treatment of them as described by the Gospels proclaimed to them the good news of the kingdom as a discipleship of equals.[24] On the other hand, in their reading of the Bible they came up against the problem of the clear and explicit marginalization of women in various passages of scripture, in both Old and New Testaments. This fact drew the attention of women who were becoming aware of their situation, and in particular of women theologians specializing in holy scripture.

The work of these new biblical scholars revealed something new: there is a difference between reading the Bible from the point of view of the poor and reading it from a woman's point of view. Whereas a poor man may find himself affirmed and defended by the mouth of the living God throughout the holy scriptures, the poor woman, in contrast, as a woman, while feeling the company and the presence of the holy Spirit in her life and history, does not know how to deal with the texts that seem to marginalize her and treat her as an inferior human being.[25] This problem is all the greater in that the poor communities where this explosion of biblical renewal is taking place are particularly marked by patriarchal and male-supremacist ideologies. In this context reading biblical texts that seem to reaffirm female segregation may help to confirm women still further in the oppression that crushes them, and this time with the very authority of the word of God.

Because of this, Latin American women biblical scholars are working particularly with women from poor communities for a deeper understanding of the nature of biblical texts. They present the text as the testimony of a people and a faith-community with particular cultures, within which divine revelation is transmitted—God's word *in* human words—as a saving word always supporting the lowest and the oppressed, who include women. The spirit of the revealed text, which is profoundly liberative, relativizes the antifeminism of a patriarchal culture that may give a negative tone to some parts of the Bible.

In addition they are attempting to recover the origins of Christianity from a woman's perspective. In so doing they bring to light and emphasize the figures of the women who appear to be builders of the history of salvation, whom a traditional interpretation often forgets or relegates to a secondary plane. Examples are the Egyptian midwives of Exodus 1, the subversives Tamara and Agar, who felt completely free to question the Jewish law, and finally the whole legion of women who can be found in the Gospels and the Acts of the Apostles playing an active part in the early stages of the church.

Latin American interpretation of the Bible from a woman's viewpoint is thus taking place in a process of distancing and approach.[26] The distancing means putting aside the more current interpretations, which are already implicit in our reading. It means recovering the capacity for awe and terror, to see new things never seen before in texts read and heard so many times. The other side is an attempt to get closer to the Bible, linked to daily life, with its experiences of pain, joy, happiness, hope, hunger, repression, celebration, and, lastly, struggle. In this way women's reading of the Bible, through this dialectic of distancing and coming closer, will advance, not as a theoretical or abstract intellectual exercise, but as a desire to find meaning for their present, to discern the desire and will of God in the detail of their own history. In the process women in Latin America are creating a new look for exegesis, and a new way of understanding the principle of biblical authority.[27]

MARY OF NAZARETH, TRAVELING COMPANION

Speaking about women from a Christian point of view inevitably means speaking about Mary of Nazareth, the mother of Jesus. Presented and venerated from the beginning by Christianity as the perfect woman, she who carried in her womb God made flesh, Mary was, and has continued to be, presented to women as the model to be followed, imitated, and inwardly assimilated. However, traditional Mariology has often presented an image of Mary that instead of promoting and liberating women, has confirmed and confined them in their ancient oppression. Submissive and passive, entirely absorbed in domestic activities, idealized and exalted for her individualistic virtues, Mary of Nazareth was, in the eyes of women who were beginning to become aware of their situation and wanting to take responsibility for their lives, a source of perplexity rather than inspiration and motivation for the struggle.

The theology of liberation set out to recover the figure of Mary in its liberating and prophetic potential. Stressing above all the text of the Magnificat (Luke 1:46–55), this theology gave to the poor women of Latin America, to the women who lead the basic ecclesial communities, a Mary whose face was no longer only that of Our Lady, glorious queen of heaven, but also and primarily an elder sister and traveling companion.[28] In Latin America this prophetic and liberating Mary takes on many loving faces: the Morenita of Guadelupe who appeared to the Amerindian Juan Diego in Mexico, the black Aparecida who allowed herself to be found in the waters of the river Paraiba in Brazil, Nicaragua's Purisima, Cuba's Virgin of Charity, and so on. In all these, Mary, the valiant and prophetic daughter of Sion, committed to justice, faithful to her God and to her people, inspires and strengthens women's unity and struggle, redeeming and ennobling them in their own eyes.

But there was still a need for women themselves to get down to the task of developing a reflection on the mother of the redeemer. Alongside many other female figures in the Bible and the history of the church, Mary emerges as the prototype, the one who says most clearly to every woman who she is and who she is called to be. There was a need for her figure and symbol not only to speak to women, but —much more important—to speak to the whole people of God *through the mouths of women.* This is now happening in Latin America. The first essays in Mariology by women are beginning to appear, introducing a female way of seeing the figure of Mary.[29]

What is new about this work is that it reveals a Mary no longer considered individualistically, in terms of a model of ascetic virtues to be imitated, but as a collective symbol, a type of the faithful people within which the holy Spirit of God finds fertile ground to raise up the new people, the seed of the kingdom, which will inaugurate the new creation. This new approach leads in turn to a reconsideration and reinterpretation of the traditional Mariological themes, the Marian dogmas and the church itself, which Mary symbolizes. A church like that in Latin America, which seeks to be a church of the poor and of the people, will find in this Mariology produced by the wombs and heads of women a new and rich source of inspiration for working out its identity.

THE THREEFOLD GOD IN A FEMALE PERSPECTIVE

For some time now theology has begun to see the need to conceive and speak of God in the feminine, to believe in, invoke, and proclaim God in the feminine. It is no longer adequate to reflect on the divine mystery that creates, saves, and sanctifies us as identifying primarily with one of the two sexes, rather than integrating and harmonizing the two sexes, without suppressing their enriching differences—at the same time as it transcends them. To achieve this, theology has to go beyond the traditional theological conception, which sees a woman as God's image only in her rational soul and not in her sexed female body, and therefore sees God as andromorphic, conceived and understood in male terms, which, in considering God's covenant with humankind, identifies the divine party (God) as male and the human party (Israel, the church) as female.

Christology developed from a woman's viewpoint has sought to be a way into this new conception of God. The form this has taken in Latin America has been to search for the key that the liberative approach has used throughout its study of the Gospels: an analysis of Jesus' egalitarian behavior as revealed by his encounters and relations with women.[30] Among the ways in which Jesus broke with tradition, one of the clearest has to do with women. His behavior toward the women marginalized by Jewish society was not only new, but even shocking, surprising even his own disciples (John 4:27). Women were singled out as beneficiaries of his miracles (Luke 8:2; Mark 1:29–31; 5:25–34; 7:24–30) and were active participants in the assembly of the kingdom (Luke 10:38–42), leading figures in and recipients of the good news he brought.

As well as breaking the taboo that marginalized them, Jesus redeemed their bodiliness, which had been humiliated and proscribed by Jewish Law. In curing the woman with the hemorrhage, who was impure to the Jews, he exposed himself to the risk of making himself impure by touching her (Matt. 9:20–22). In allowing his feet to be touched, kissed, and anointed by a known public sinner, he led his Pharisee host to cast doubt on his prophetic status (Luke 7:36–50). And not only that: Jesus also allowed women to question and influence him. His encounters with them changed not just them, but him too. The Gospels show us Jesus learning from women and giving way to their requests. He did so with his mother Mary, who advanced his "hour" in Cana (John 2:1ff.). He did so with the Canaanite woman, who "dragged out of him" the miracle she wanted with much pleading, so setting in train the process of the proclamation of the good news to the gentiles (Matt. 15:21–28; Mark 7:24–30).

Jesus' incarnation and messianic consciousness is an exchange, in which the God-man both gives and receives, proclaims and listens, loves and is loved. In this reciprocity women have an important place. And this man of flesh and blood, who treated women like this and was loved and known by them, who proclaimed their full dignity as daughters of God and citizens of the kingdom and was proclaimed by them God's Messiah, is the same man who had his way confirmed by the Father in the resurrection and is now Kyrios, the glorious Lord seated at the right hand of God.[31] Christology is thus – today as ever, and more than ever – the good news of salvation for all the oppressed, and among them for women who are looking for their place in world and church.

Nevertheless, it is not so much in christology as in the doctrine of the Trinity, in the mystery of the communion of the three divine persons, the unquestionable center of the Christian faith, that the main road to a concept of God in women's terms is being sought. To say that God is Father, Son, and Holy Spirit is not, and cannot be, in any way equivalent to saying that the divine community is composed of three persons identified as male. The thinking being done by women theologians in Latin America today seeks to recover the biblical root of the experience of God, which uses the word *rahamin*, "womb," female entrails, to refer to God's love.[32] Countless Old Testament texts, especially in the prophets, refer to God by this part of the female body. The effect of this is that in theology – feminist or not – God the Father is being called also Mother or, better, Maternal Father or Paternal Mother.[33] These divine female entrails, pregnant with gestation and birth, which have been identified in the Father, also appear in the incarnate Son, who in the Gospels is driven to cry out in frustrated maternal desire to gather under his wings the scattered and rebellious "chickens of Jerusalem" (Luke 13:34). They appear in the Spirit, the divine *ruach*, who in the labor of creation "hatches" the cosmos, which is to burst forth from the primitive chaos, who is sent like a loving mother to console the children left orphaned by Jesus' departure (John 14:18,26) and to teach them patiently to pronounce the Father's name, Abba (Rom. 8:15).

A rich future is in store for the theology of liberation in the female dimension of God. The poor who are discovering themselves as active makers of history and are organizing for liberation are experiencing God as the God of life, as embodying the very fulness of life, as the only source from which it is possible to derive hope and promise in the situation of death they live every day. God's female entrails—maternal *rahamin,* fertile, in labor and compassionate—enable this liberation to come about with force and firmness, but also with creativity and gentleness, without violence. Once God is experienced, not only as Father, Lord, strong warrior, but also as Mother, protection, greater love, struggle is tempered with festivity and celebration of life, permanent and gentle firmness ensures the ability "to be tough without losing tenderness," and uncompromising resistance can be carried on with joy, without excessive tension and sterile strain. God's compassion, flowing from female and maternal entrails, takes on itself the hurts and wounds of all the oppressed, and a woman who does theology is called to bear witness to this God with her body, her actions, her life.[34]

THE EUCHARIST CELEBRATED AND SYMBOLIZED
BY THE FEMALE BODY

The theology of the sacraments is something that as yet has received little attention from women theologians. Nonetheless there exists a whole body of women's experience of sacramental life—in its significance and in its liturgical celebration—that promises to be a rich seam for the future of women in theology, and specifically in Latin American theology.

Everywhere at the base of the Latin American church, and in a very special way in the basic ecclesial communities, the liturgy has a predominant place. It is the place for festivity, for the celebration of life in its purest truth and transparency, where the experience of faith is expressed not only with the mouth and in words, but with all the body's resources, singing, gestures, and dance, and in which tangible material symbols signify deeper and definitively transcendent realities.

In this celebration of faith and life, women have an important role. With their integrated and unified selves and attitudes, they are able to express cheerfully and happily in the community celebrations even the hardest and most painful struggles, which are part of the community's life. As they live the gospel joy, which is not necessarily happiness, and which therefore may exist alongside pain and even make it the raw material of its hope, the women of the poor communities find in the liturgy a privileged space to show the work and the struggle they carry on—in the unions, in the mothers' clubs, in the neighborhood associations, community gardens, and canteens, and in various other forms of popular community organization. The euchar-

ist celebrated where women are active participants and organizers, as well
as being the subversive memory of the Lord's death and resurrection, is
the joyful distribution and sharing of bread among all, with joyful and
generous hearts, just as the Acts of the Apostles describes the agape of the
New Testament church (Luke 2:46).

But there is also another dimension in which women find themselves
and identify themselves with the sacrament of the eucharist. This is the
strict significance of the sacrament as the transubstantiation and real presence of the body and blood of the Lord, which, under the species of bread
and wine, are given to the faithful as food. Feeding others with one's own
body is the supreme way God chose to be definitively and sensibly present
in the midst of the people. The bread that we break and eat, and that we
profess to be the body of Jesus Christ, refers us back to the greater mystery
of his incarnation, death, and resurrection. It is his person given as food;
it is his very life made bodily a source of life for Christians. But it is women
who possess in their bodiliness the physical possibility of performing the
divine eucharistic action. In the whole process of gestation, childbirth, protection, and nourishing of a new life, we have the sacrament of the eucharist, the divine act, happening anew.

Throughout Latin America, in the rural areas and the poor districts on
the edges of cities, there are millions of women conceiving, bearing, and
suckling new children of the common people. Sometimes they do it with
difficulty, pain, and suffering, sometimes with the last trickle of life left in
them.[35] This female body, which is extensive and multiplies in other lives,
which gives itself as food and nourishes with its flesh and blood the lives it
has conceived, is the same body that wastes away and dies tilling the earth,
working in factories and homes, stirring pans and sweeping floors, spinning
thread and washing clothes, organizing meetings, leading struggles, chairing
meetings, and starting singing. It is the woman's body, eucharistically given
to the struggle for liberation, really and physically distributed, eaten and
drunk by those who will—as men and women of tomorrow—continue the
same struggle of patience and resistance, pain and courage, joy and pleasure. Breaking the bread and distributing it, having communion in the body
and blood of the Lord until he comes again, means for women today reproducing and symbolizing in the midst of the community the divine act of
surrender and love, so that the people may grow and the victory come,
which is celebrated in the feast of true and final liberation.

Women who do theology in Latin America and who share with their
sisters from the poorest environments the same sacramental vocation, the
same eucharistic destiny, are called to open, with their reflection and discourse, a new path, a possible future, so that this sacramental act may
become more and more present, recognized, and believed in in Latin America's journey toward liberation.

"THERE IS NEITHER MALE NOR FEMALE...
YOU ARE ALL ONE IN CHRIST JESUS" (GAL. 3:28)

There is a future on the horizon of the theology of liberation. After twenty years of movement, life, and suffering, along a road composed not just of light but also of darkness and uncertainties, we can look back with gratitude and note the ground covered and the achievements won. However, we can and should equally look forward with hope and attempt to discern what remains to be done and where the road leads.

There is a future on the horizon of the theology of liberation. The poor who have arisen and awoken to take on the task of building their own history, and whose shouts provoked the theology, are joining together in community bases and growing stronger in their organization. In turn, the process of liberation they are leading is becoming more complex and developing new facets. New groups begin their own struggles, denouncing more clearly the different forms of oppression from which the peoples of Latin America suffer. We do not hear now only of socio-economic and political oppression. Oppression is also cultural, sexual, racial, and ethnic. The one captivity has various names, and alongside the disfigured faces of the categories of poor listed by the Puebla documents (peasants, workers, old persons, etc.),[36] the faces of the victims of other forms of oppression are emerging, as they take their place in the fight for liberation: women, blacks, Amerindians.

Among these women, after challenging society and church life, some have entered the domain of theology. The history of salvation is beginning to be reinterpreted from their perspective, theological reflection is beginning to accept them as practitioners, as an issue and subject matter, welcoming into its discourse the enriching difference of their language, their experience, and their methods. Desire, brought by their hands, once more has full civil rights in theology's domain, spiritual experience and liturgical celebration mix with scientific rigor in joyous and rich combination. Theological study and argument are beginning to be carried out, not just with the intellect, but with all that material life provides: pain and happiness, anguish and hope, body, hands, heart. Poetry is once more a literary form suitable for expressing the mystery of God.

This present is an opening and a guarantee for a future that is opening up and coming to meet all Latin Americans. Worked eschatologically from within, pregnant with the presence of the one who, already risen and victorious, still remains crucified in the passion and death of the poor and oppressed of Latin America, this future can be seen to be full of women's presence. This is cause for happiness and rejoicing for women, and for all those who through them will receive the good news of the proclamation of the gospel of liberation. "Rejoice!" says the voice of the woman who has found the coin lost for so long, and which had been given to her by God from the beginning. And today, at this point in the history of Latin America, this voice repeats, in tones of joy, "Rejoice!" The Latin America of today is pregnant with the kingdom of tomorrow. In that kingdom differences will be integrated in a differentiated communion in which there will in future be "neither Jew nor Greek, neither slave nor free, neither male nor female," but all will be "one in Christ Jesus" (Gal. 3:28).

—translated from the Portuguese by Francis McDonagh

NOTES

1. It is a fact that someone who is poor in socio-economic terms, and also a woman, suffers twice over. See Gustavo Gutiérrez's remarks on this in his interview with Elsa Tamez: "That's what we said from a theology of liberation perspective, a phrase which is now very well known: 'doubly marginalized and doubly oppressed,' which we got into the Puebla document. (Unfortunately in the published version they moved it into a note, whereas in the version approved at Puebla it was in the body of the text, but it's there [para. 1134n.].) And I think that it's true that women are doubly marginalized and oppressed, as poor persons and as women" (*Teólogos de la liberación hablan sobre la mujer* [San José, Costa Rica: DEI, 1986] p. 52; Eng. trans. *Against Machismo* [Oak Park, Ill.: Meyer-Stone Books, 1987, p. 40]).

2. Sexism still persists in theological language, as in language in general, despite the deliberate efforts being made today to overcome it. Efforts are still not sufficient, if they do not reflect an underlying change of attitude, which might eventually make such care with language unnecessary.

3. Cf. I. Gebara, "A mulher faz teologia. Um ensaio para reflexão," in I. Gebara and M. C. L. Bingemer, *A mulher faz teologia* (Petrópolis: Vozes, 1986); Eng. trans. in Virginia Fabella and Mercy Oduyoye, eds., *With Passion and Compassion* (Maryknoll, N.Y.: Orbis, 1988), p. 9.

4. I realize that theology is not the only area in which women's voices are being heard. This is happening in all areas of society. But a complete study of the phenomenon would go beyond the limits of this chapter.

5. I realize that Luke's Gospel uses the image of the coin in a different context, that of God's mercy for sinners, but I have taken the liberty of using it in a different way.

6. I should like to mention in particular here the new outlook of the pastoral program for marginalized women. Instead of taking women out of prostitution and then working with them, this new program establishes itself within the women's own environment and forms groups, communities, and Bible classes there, in an attempt to bring the word of God and the good news of the gospel into this whole situation, which is the object of discrimination and marginalization on the part of the dominant sectors of society. See H. de'Ans, "Pastoral da mulher marginalizada—13 anos de caminhada libertadora," *Revista Eclesiástica Brasileira*, 47/187 (1987) 651–54.

7. I do not mean to claim that sensitivity, the sense of gratuitousness, and desire are exclusive attributes of women. The way in which our civilization has separated male and female into watertight compartments, isolating both in opposing

and even irreconcilable characteristics, has left men for a long time trapped in "the rational," repressing their emotions and not allowing them to make "concessions" to their sensitive and affective side. The remark, "Men don't cry," which mothers and fathers make to boys, is significant here. See Gustavo Gutiérrez's remarks in *Teólogos de la liberación hablan sobre la mujer*, pp. 56–57.

8. On woman as this open structure, permeated by and host to life, see I. Gebara and M.C. Bingemer, *Maria Mãe de Deus e mãe dos pobres* (Petrópolis: Vozes, 1987), pp. 117–26; Eng. trans. *Mary: Mother of God, Mother of the Poor* (Theology and Liberation Series) Maryknoll, N.Y.: Orbis, 1989.

9. Parallels in Matt. 26:6–13; Mark 14:3–9; Luke 7:36–50.

10. See Alves, *What Is Religion?* (Maryknoll, N.Y.: Orbis, 1984), p. 63. "We are our desire." The author goes on to define religion as a message of desire, an expression of nostalgia, and a hope of pleasure.

11. Here we give the name desire even to God. If God is love, we have to say also that God is desire. Love desires and moves, comes toward the object of its desire, arousing in it desire in turn. Where there is desire, there is a chance of having more passionate and dedicated work, giving to the other, love. If desire is extinguished, all that remains is need, which, once satiated, disappears. Rationalism does not allow for this dynamism of desire, inherent in human beings. Desire only survives in a climate of gratuitousness, not in one of immediate needs. Theology — like any other experience and action to do with the sphere of religion — is an activity involving desire and an object of desire. The excessive rationalism that has dominated Western theological thinking has overshadowed this dimension.

12. See Gebara, "A mulher faz teologia," p. 22.

13. See ibid.: "this procedure is the giving back to theology of the poetic dimension of human existence, for the most profound aspects of human nature can be expressed only by analogy, mystery can be expressed only in poetry, and gratuitousness can be expressed only through symbols." The psalms and wisdom literature are sources where this primacy of desire can be verified.

14. For a phenomenology of desire, see D. Vasse, *Le temps du désir* (Paris: Seuil, 1968).

15. See E. Dussel, *La producción teórica de Marx. Un comentario a los Grundrisse* (Mexico City: Siglo XXI, 1985), p. 340.

16. See R. Alves, *What Is Religion?*, p. 79: "But martyrs have appeared — Gandhi, Martin Luther King, Oscar Romero, and many others. Religious leaders are intimidated, persecuted, threatened, expelled, arrested.... This would not happen if they were in alliance with power. They are witnesses to the political significance of prophetic religion, an expression of the hurts and hopes of the powerless. Opium of the people? Maybe, but not here. In the midst of the martyrs and prophets, God is protest and the power of the oppressed."

17. See Gebara, "A mulher faz teologia," p. 24.

18. See L. Boff and C. Boff, *Introducing Liberation Theology* (Maryknoll, N.Y.: Orbis, and London: Burns & Oates, 1987) p. 43.

19. See G. Gutiérrez, *A Theology of Liberation* (Maryknoll, N.Y. : Orbis, 1973, and London: SCM, 1974), pp. 133ff., referring to the new perspectives of theology arising from the facts of underdevelopment and dependency, and historical action in support of the oppressed.

20. Notably E. Schüssler Fiorenza, L. Russel, R. R. Ruether, and others in the U.S.A., K. E. Borressen, C. Halkes, D. Sölle, and others, in Europe.

21. Gebara, "A mulher faz teologia," p. 27.

22. For example, in 1988 Brazil held its third national meeting of women theologians on the theme "Women, Theology, and Land." The Ecumenical Association of Third World Theologians (EATWOT) has a specific project on women and theology. Meetings have already been held on the three continents and a dialogue between women theologians of the First and Third Worlds is now in preparation, as is a larger and broader dialogue between men and women theologians.

23. I have selected only a few of the themes. It would be impossible to deal with all of them here.

24. On this see A. M. Tepedino, *"Mulheres discípulas nos Evangelhos — discipulado de iguais,"* doctoral thesis presented in the Pontifical University of Rio de Janeiro in April 1987.

25. See E. Tamez, *Mujer y Bíblia,* mimeographed text presented at the Intercontinental Consultation on Third World Theology from a Woman's Perspective, Oaxtepec, Mexico, December 7–14, 1986.

26. See Tamez, *Mujer y Bíblia,* pp. 9–10.

27. Ibid.

28. See the article by L. Boff, "Maria, mulher profética e libertadora — a piedade mariana na teologia da libertação," *Revista Eclesiástica Brasileira,* 38/149 (March 1978) 39–56. See also my article, "Maria, a que soube dizer não," *Grande Sinal,* 40/4 (May 1986) 245–56.

29. See, e.g., *Concilium,* 168 (1983) *Mary in the Churches,* and the May 1985 issue of *Grande Sinal,* both written by women. See also the recent book, Gebara and Bingemer, *Mary: Mother of God, Mother of the Poor* (Theology and Liberation Series) (Maryknoll, N.Y.: Orbis, 1989).

30. On this see N. Ritchie, "Mulher e Cristologia," contribution to the meeting of Latin American women theologians, Buenos Aires, October 1985, published in *Revista Eclesiástica Brasileira,* 46/181 (1986) 60–72.

31. See also M. C. L. Bingemer, "Jesucristo y la salvación de la mujer," paper presented to the Intercontinental Consultation on Third World Theology from a Women's Perspective, pp. 15–16.

32. On this see M. C. L. Bingemer, "A Trindade a partir da perspectiva da mulher," in Gebara and Bingemer, *A mulher faz teologia,* pp. 31–79; Eng. trans. in Elsa Tamez, ed., *Through Her Eyes* (Maryknoll, N.Y.: Orbis, 1989).

33. See L. Boff, *O rostro materno de Deus* (Petrópolis: Vozes, 1979); idem, *Trinity and Society* (Maryknoll, N.Y.: Orbis, 1988).

34. See the remarks on this aspect of the female character by L. C. Susin, "O Negrinho do Pastoreio — leitura teológica de uma lenda," *Revista Eclesiástica Brasileira,* 48/189 (1988) 49: "The drama of expiation, first and foremost, welcomes maternally the suffering provoked by others. Like the mother with child who carries and puts up with her child, she is stomach, lap, shoulders, body support, platform of a world. She is a store and laboratory of mercy, in which the human is welcomed in its impurity and perversion, put right and sanctified in order to be returned to its proper form, without the tortuousness of violence. To accept violence and respond with its opposite demands a resistance that is already divine because it is a supportive resistance that unconditionally bears evils and violence and breaks the vicious circle of their ever-more sophisticated violations, absorbing and 'digesting' in itself, without releasing them, but, by a metabolism and synthesis of mercy, gives

back expiation. This is the supreme service — sacrifice, 'making sacred' — to another, restoring the other's humanity and the new creation."

35. See the true story told by Clodovis Boff in L. Boff and C. Boff, *Introducing Liberation Theology*, pp. 1–2: "One day, in the arid region of northeastern Brazil, one of the most famine-stricken parts of the world, I met a bishop going into his house; he was shaking. 'Bishop, what's the matter?' I asked. He replied that he had just seen a terrible sight: in front of the cathedral was a woman with three small children and a baby clinging to her neck. He saw that they were fainting from hunger. The baby seemed to be dead. He said, 'Give the baby some milk, woman!' 'I can't, my lord,' she answered. The bishop went on insisting that she should, and she that she could not. Finally, because of his insistence, she opened her blouse. Her breast was bleeding; the baby sucked violently at it. And sucked blood. The mother who had given it life was feeding it, like the pelican, with her own blood, her own life."

36. See paragraphs 28–73.

14

Reflections of a North American:
The Future of Liberation Theology

ROBERT McAFEE BROWN

Among the things Billy Pilgrim could not change were the past, the present, and the future.

— *Kurt Vonnegut,* Slaughterhouse Five

Persons writing about the future had better invoke Kurt Vonnegut's help. We do not control the future absolutely, with the significant exception of our ability to destroy it absolutely. But we do control it to some extent. The reason we do so is that we all have pasts that condition our lives in the present, and thus either enlarge or diminish our ability to lend some measure of direction to the future. To talk about the future, therefore, is also to talk, however briefly, about the past and present. Herewith:

THE PAST: BEING INVITED TO LEARN

My own initial exposure to liberation theology was cerebral. I had been asked by Philip Scharper to do a blurb for the dust jacket of a new book by a theologian of whom I had then never heard, Gustavo Gutiérrez, on a topic of which I was equally innocent, *A Theology of Liberation.* I will never forget the experience of turning over page after page of galley sheets in the summer of 1972 and thinking, "If this is right, I have to start my theological life all over again." The impact was sufficient for me to risk commenting in the blurb that Gutiérrez's book "may well be the most important book . . . of the decade." This uncharacteristic prescience has, I think, been vindicated and then some: fifteen years down the line *A Theology of Liberation* remains the basic interpretation of liberation theology.

The cerebral exposure began to take on more flesh and blood a year later when our daughter, fresh out of high school, spent a year in Chile,

194

beginning just three months after the coup that established the Pinochet regime in power, and she shared with us what she was experiencing of both the brutality of dictatorship and the extraordinary courage of "ordinary" Christians who were living (and dying) for liberation. Shortly after that, I was fortunate enough to attend the first "Theology in the Americas" conference at Detroit in 1975, when theologians from Latin America and North America met face to face. My own conscienticizing took a quantum leap after a comment of Gonzalo Arroyo, a Chilean Jesuit, who at one point addressed the North Americans with the query, "Tell me, why is it that when you speak of *our* theology you call it 'Latin American theology,' but when you speak of *your* theology you call it 'theology'?" I realized, quite suddenly, that with the best will in the world, we North Americans were still identifying *our* point of view as normative, and *their* point of view as culturally-conditioned and thus in need of periodic reexamination and correction by reference to the norm. Another decade of theological existence down the drain.[1]

But liberation theology cannot truly be communicated through books or secondhand experiences or conferences. It can be communicated only through human lives, and a subsequent trip to South America after the above events, two later trips to Cuba, and three still later trips to Nicaragua, have provided me with whatever inklings I now have of the power of liberation theology. I see it as truly a "theology of the people" rather than of professional theologians, rising out of the cries of the distressed, refined in the experience of those who may not even be able to read or write, clarified in the thousands of *comunidades de base*, and embodied in lives that risk everything in order to be faithful to the good news of a God who hears their cry, who consequently sides with them in their distress, and who works with them for liberation—a liberation in which they play a central role even while recognizing that the ultimate attainment of liberation will be God's gift.

So there is a new reality in the life of the people of God today, a reality embodied in the lives of those who struggle and suffer and often die, and in so doing reacquaint the rest of us with an understanding of the gospel so demanding that most of the time we would prefer to avoid it, until those struggles and sufferings and deaths become witnesses too powerful for us to shut out.

THE PRESENT: BEING INVITED TO RESPOND

What are we to do with all of this in North America? I suggest three ways in which we need to respond.

1. Our first obligation is simply *to hear and to hear correctly*. We must make sure that we do not distort, caricature, or willfully misrepresent the claims to which those lives and deaths bear both militant and silent witness.

Unfortunately, our North American track record is not enviable in this regard. Because liberation theology represents a threat to much of the ease and comfort we have, many who ought to know better distort its message in order to discredit it. Let one example suffice. Ernest Lefever, whose nomination by President Reagan to become assistant secretary of state for human rights was rejected by Congress, feels that liberation theology has been accorded more attention than it deserves, chiefly by those whom he gratuitously characterizes as eager "to embrace novelty and the radical chic shibboleths of the past two decades."[2] Against "a disquieting tendency to take it too seriously," Lefever feels that "a posture of benign neglect" would be more appropriate. He defines liberation theology "as a utopian heresy because it sanctified class violence," and utopianism as "an escape from responsibility." So much for hundreds of martyrs in the liberation struggle.

He complains that attention to a "preferential option for the poor" negates "concern for every man, woman, and child," for we are "all in need of liberation and redemption." Even the most cursory examination of the literature will make clear, as Gutiérrez notes time and again, that a "preferential" option does not mean an "exclusive" option but a starting point: if the needs of the poor begin to be attended to, then some of the injustices of society will begin to be overcome.[3] The Roman Catholic bishops at Puebla in 1979 furthermore coupled their message about a preferential option for the poor with "a preferential option for youth," indicating another priority for the church, and making clear that the two go hand in hand.[4]

Lefever compounds the above misunderstanding by claiming further that a preferential option for the poor "pits class against class and encourages enmity." This is only a fresh version of the perennial canard that liberation theologians exalt violence. Actually, the notion of "class struggle" is a *description* of what is taking place in many Third World countries. There *is* a powerful minority, and there *is* a powerless majority, and there *is* a "struggle" between them, because the few with most of the goods refuse to share them, and the many with few of the goods demand a larger share. Liberation theology is not trying to foment class struggle, *pace* Lefever, but to overcome it by a gospel that not only talks about justice but points out existing injustices. Lefever argues that "it stresses novelty at the expense of the tried and true." No one but a North American "intellectual" could make such a callous statement, for "the tried and true" has been responsible for centuries of Third World oppression.

Lefever also accuses liberation theology of fostering "economic determinism." Further, "it sponsors a new materialism." Liberation theologians are accused of promising to remove social ills "by a more equal distribution of material goods," and of suggesting (along with Karl Marx) that freedom, culture, music, love, and so forth, are all "economically determined."

Such charges are so far off the mark that they do not deserve serious comment, and I have devoted more space to Mr. Lefever's irresponsible accusations than they deserve simply to make the point that if persons like him, who ought to know better, can present such insensitive critiques, there are many more who will fall prey to such simplistic and erroneous reductionism. The task of ensuring that liberation theology gains a fair hearing will be ongoing.

2. A second obligation is to try to see the role of the United States in the Third World through the eyes of those committed to liberation. Here the shoe really begins to pinch, for we are told by those who perceive themselves as oppressed that they perceive persons like us, and the social systems we uphold, as their oppressors.

My experience has been that when North Americans are confronted by such a claim, the first reaction is one of incredulity ("How can they talk that way when we send them so much aid?"), usually followed by anger ("If that's the way they feel about us, so much the worse for them"). There may also be pain and wistfulness ("We certainly don't intend to hurt them; we are really trying to help, and maybe we can send more food and clothing to make up for past mistakes").

As soon as the analysis gets more refined, the Achilles' heel in the posture of injured feelings begins to surface ("It sounds as though they are attacking capitalism"). The truth of the matter, of course, is that they are, and the further truth of the matter is that this often offends North Americans more than anything else, because the very core of their belief-system is being challenged.

Some of the Latin American analysis is quite sophisticated, engaged in by Third World thinkers who can hold their own in a serious debate with economic counterparts from the First World. Some of it is also descriptive and indeed poignantly so, and it must be heard by us. We are invited to look at lives destroyed, villages bombed, children starving, human hopes receding, and sooner or later the question must be faced: Who is responsible for this? And while it is too simplistic to charge that it is only U.S. corporations, or U.S. banks, or U.S. right-wing politicians, it is nevertheless clear that high among the real contributors to the ongoing misery are all of the above.

Where do the North American chuches and theological community fit into this? We are part of it to the extent that both our message and our mission are complicit in support of the injustices of our society, and the moment of truth comes for us (as we will presently examine) when we realize that a choice between the gospel and the "powers that be" is forced upon us, and that if we say yes to the first we must say no to the second. So we are called upon to assess, preferably at first hand, some of the consequences of what happens when a watered-down faith turns out to be in lockstep with U.S. foreign policy and U.S. corporations exploiting those overseas.

We cannot have the luxury of assuming that what is happening in Latin America or Africa or Asia is really not our concern, either as citizens of the United States of America, or as members of the kingdom of God. We bear a major responsibility for the upheaval and distress of the world, and that assessment must surface in our consciousness if we are to begin to act as responsible global beings.

3. If we are willing (1) to hear the liberation message clearly on its own terms, and (2) hear its assessment of our responsibility for much of the world's oppression, this must (3) challenge us *to rethink and re-create our own message*. The task is not to decide that Latin American liberation theology is the way of the future, and seek to import it. The task is rather to discover where our own areas of need for liberation are located, and begin to create a liberation theology for North America. This will call for the most exacting kind of honesty, confession, struggle, and rebuilding.

Fortunately, this process has already begun, not with the creation of a single North American theology of liberation, but with the creation of a number of indigenous North American theologies of liberation. Let us take brief account of this important fact.

The initial liberation theology to be spawned on North American soil is surely black theology, which has grown directly out of the U.S. black experience of oppression, victimization, marginalization, and powerlessness.[5] In one of those curious acts of prescience of which he was frequently capable, Dietrich Bonhoeffer prophesied back in 1931 that it might be the black churches that would save America.[6] And it is indeed the case that to the degree that there has been a new sense of concern for justice in the United States and in the American churches, that concern has sprung in significant measure from black theology and the black churches.

A second indigenous North American liberation theology is feminist theology. Feminist movements have, to be sure, spread worldwide, but the articulation of a way of doing theology from a feminist perspective had important origins in the United States. Once again this has grown out of the experience of a group of human beings who, like blacks, have undergone oppression, victimization, marginalization, and powerlessness. It is encouraging to see how quickly links with women from other parts of the globe have been established by North American feminist theology, as local realizations of outrage have been replicated globally.[7]

Nor are these the only liberation theologies that have sprung from North American soil. Particularly distinctive has been the concern among Amerindians to create a theology springing from their situation of oppression. This theology, which has distinctively American geographical and cultural roots, clearly shares affinities with the black South African situation, where government treatment discloses disturbing parallels to the treatment Amerindians have received (and continue to receive) in the United States.[8]

A fourth distinctive North American liberation theology has grown out of gay and lesbian oppression. While this issue is by no means a uniquely North American one, the most significant articulations of the shape of such a theology have again come from the United States.[9] And the list can continue: Puerto Rican theology, Hispanic theology, theology for Philippine-Americans, and so on.

These positions, all of which have distinctive emphases that must not be artificially conflated, nevertheless do share the common characteristic that they are the products of groups who have experienced oppression, victimization, marginalization, and powerlessness. They have needed time and space to work out their own distinctive emphases and develop both self-awareness and a sense of self-worth ("Black is beautiful," "The Lord's my shepherd and he knows I'm gay," "Christ in a poncho," and so forth). It is now clear, however, at least to this observer, that these varied theologies will increasingly draw closer to one another, not only by significant overlapping of their concerns, but also by the realization that together they can wield a power they can never hope to wield separately.

THE FUTURE: BEING INVITED TO ACT

I referred to myself in the above paragraph as an "observer" rather than a participant. What kind of cop-out is this?

The truth of the matter is that in relation to the groups just described, I *am* an observer; I am not black, female, Amerindian, gay, Puerto Rican, Hispanic, or Filipino. I am (in terms that are descriptive to some and pejorative to others) a white male North American. This is at best a dubious category in which to be cast, for it is a historical fact that with whatever separates all the liberation viewpoints cited above from each other, they agree that the main architects of their oppression have been and continue to be members of the white male North American establishment.

In the light of this fact, how can we white, male North Americans relate to the liberation struggle? Is there a liberation message for us as well? Can there be a liberation message from us as well? It is these themes that I propose to examine for the balance of this essay.

I shall not attempt anything so grandiose as a full-blown "liberation theology for white male North Americans," particularly in ten pages.[10] My more modest agenda will be to try to identify some of the issues we must confront realistically, if we are to come within hailing distance of a meeting place between ourselves and the liberation struggles of others. Out of a massive potential agenda, I arbitrarily choose five themes:

1. *On being an "oppressor."* As indicated above, there is a widespread consensus among oppressed peoples that we are the ones most responsible for their misery. When confronting us with this estimate, they sometimes add, in an act of generosity, "Of course, I don't mean you personally...," which mitigates the sting a bit, but only a bit. Who wants to be tagged an "oppressor," even if it is only guilt by association?

We have to deal with the fact, however, that the charge has substance, and that much of the structural violence in the world today can be laid at the door of white males, even if not all of them are North Americans. I do

not consider it creative to respond by saturating ourselves with guilt, however, for guilt is not only an unsatisfactory motivation for change, but also
tends so to immobilize its advocates that they are effectively exempt from
doing anything beyond wallowing in self-depreciation.

Since those who most truly work for liberation are those who *need* liberation, is there any meaningful way in which we can claim that we, denom-
inated as "oppressors," are also among the "oppressed," and must work
for our own liberation as well as the liberation of others?

This is a tricky proposal because it immediately sounds self-saving, but
I have long been impressed by the remark of Basil Moore, writing out of
the South African struggle:

> I am prepared to trust and stand alongside a man who is fighting *for
> himself and his own freedom* if I know that his freedom is bound up
> with mine. I cannot wholeheartedly trust a man who is fighting *for
> me*, for I fear that sooner or later he will tire of the struggle.[11]

So a recognition that all of us occupy some territory on both sides of the
hyphen in the "oppressor-oppressed" contrast may be a creative act. I know
of no one who has made this point of view clearer, from within the feminist
struggle, than Karen Lebacqz. In *Justice in an Unjust World* (Minneapolis:
Augsburg, 1987), she acknowledges that "by virtue of skin color, solvency,
education, religious background, and nationality," she has advantages
denied to most women. She is part of a group that rules . . . and oppresses.
She has not, and cannot, experience the oppression that Jews have felt, or
the desperately poor and disenfranchised, the wheelchair occupant, the
black woman. And yet, she is a woman, "and even in white, solvent, well-
educated Christian America, women are oppressed" (p. 14). This fact is
then catalogued in some detail. So she can "speak both as an oppressor
and as oppressed," and this posture, rather than being the basis for a cop-
out, helps Professor Lebacqz "to temper my oppressor mentality by remembering my own experiences of oppression and by attending to the voices of
the oppressed" (p. 15).

In addition to this kind of recognition, to the degree that we could
identify the source of our own oppression, we might be able to work col-
laboratively with others in the liberation theology.

What, then, is the source of our own oppression? Unless we can "name"
it, we will remain caught in its thrall, for we will not even be aware of its
hold over us. I suggest that our oppressor is not a group within our social-
economic system so much as it is the very socio-economic system itself. We
are the inheritors of, and have been conditioned to accept uncritically, a
whole series of "virtues" that are meant to be self-evident and self-vali-
dating. They include such things as the necessity of upward mobility, both
personally and professionally; the willingness to compete, by fair means or
foul, against those who threaten our success or our job or our nation; a

commitment to "looking out for Number One," for no one else will; a conviction that the payoff for hard work is material comfort of an increasingly lavish sort; a willingness to put our jobs ahead of our families; a belief that it is both appropriate and necessary to check our moral values at the entrance to the work place, for the bottom line is always profit, and nothing must interfere with that.

If the above sounds like a caricature, I submit that that is simply an indirect indication of its accuracy, for few of us are ready to believe that we have gotten locked into a social structure in which greed and exploitation are two sides of the same coin. At all events, I propose that one of our first jobs is to examine these and other criteria of success in the marketplace, and ponder the degree to which we have been oppressed by such structures without knowing it. I am not sanguine that a revolution of the ruling class is about to sweep through our society. But I am convinced that if there are to be significant changes in our society to "liberate the oppressed" (as Jesus said so well), they will come only to the extent that we properly "name" the oppressor and begin to find ways to challenge its sovereignty.

2. *On being a "traitor to one's class."* The cost for doing so can be great. If it is our initial plight to be categorized by the left as sell-outs, it will be our increasing plight, should we press these issues, to be categorized by the right as traitors. "You have inherited a wonderful situation," we will be told, "the benefits of which are due to market capitalism, and you are not only ungracious to seek to bite the hand that feeds you so well, but disloyal to suggest that we should seek 'a more excellent way.' " Concern for the social good will be presented as betrayal of the values of "individual initiative," and concern for the poor will be linked (as in the baleful example of Mr. Lefever) with fomenting violence or espousing economic determinism, and thus betray the ultimate apostacy that we are really communists at heart.

Let us be honest. Such charges may not threaten us in the abstract, but when they are pronounced by friends, colleagues, and (maybe the bottom line if we are *really* honest) those who hold control over our jobs and livelihoods, the pressures to keep quiet and conform are great.

For some of us, the tensions will be exacerbated by the fact that cries of treason (though clothed in more genteel theological garb) will come from members of our churches, who will see even an implicit attack on middle-class values as an attack on themselves, and indeed on the church, to the degree (a high degree) that the church is a reflection of, and support for, middle-class values.

For all of us, the bottom line is going to be more than simply fending off personal attacks, however; it is going to have something to do with lifestyles—that is, not just how we think, but how we live. With a few notable exceptions like Richard Shaull (see his *Heralds of a New Reformation* [Maryknoll, N.Y.: Orbis, 1984], esp. chap. 6, "Changing Values and

Changing Sides"), most of us who live within the "establishment" have found it convenient not to face this issue. When push comes to shove, we are inclined to settle for reform tactics rather than revolutionary commitment, choosing gradual change rather than significant confrontation. I have no personal heroics to report on this front, but I am increasingly convinced that those of us who are mainstream must face more directly the liberation challenge as it affects us personally and as it colors what we do within our churches.

3. *On working within church structures*. But the church is not solely a repository of middle-class values. It has a history, usually submerged but occasionally breaking out above the surface, of siding with victims, calling rulers to account, and discovering, often to its surprise, that without human contrivance fresh resources in the heritage reassert themselves in times of crisis.

There are two reasons why it is important to try to carry on the liberation theology struggle within the churches. First of all, the churches themselves need to hear a liberation message that can deliver them from excessive co-optation by the principalities and powers of this world. If we really believed in *ecclesia semper reformanda* (the church always to be reformed), then the breath of the Holy Spirit that is blowing today in some parts of the church (notably in the Third World) could fan new flames of ardor and commitment in our own lives. The second reason for relating the liberation struggle to the churches is that there is no other vehicle in society that has more potential for keeping the struggle alive and well, and overcoming the burnout factor that hamstrings so many other social groups. The recuperative power of the gospel can keep churches from being subservient to any ideology—in a world where all sorts of ideologies, particularly those of the right wing, trap or subsume liberation concerns within their own very different agendas.

To be sure, organized churches move with maddening slowness when issues of justice and liberation are involved, and those who work within them will need involvement with other groups in society as well, in order to avoid the erosion of personal engagement by institutional timidity. But there can be a healthy dialectic here, with institutional and personal cross-fertilization helping to enhance the life of both groups.

There is another point to be made. Within the churches today there is an increasingly widespread discussion that has important implications for liberation concerns: are the churches moving into a new "confessional situation" (what has historically been called a *status confessionis*) in which, on certain issues we have to say something like the following: "Until now, it has been possible to be a Christian and hold either side of the argument; but we have now reached a place where our understanding of the Christian message is *so clear* that taking exception to it is no longer possible. Those who now dissent removed themselves from the company of believers." The situation came to a head in the Confessing Church in Germany after the rise of Hitler, and the conclusion was reached: to say yes to Jesus Christ means to say no to Hitler. A similar conclusion has been reached by many of the churches of South Africa: to say yes to Jesus Christ means to say no to apartheid.[12] And increasing numbers of Christians today, particularly in the United States, are reaching the conclusion that to say yes to Jesus Christ may have to mean saying no to nuclear weapons.[13] There is also beginning to be some discussion within the churches about the impossibility of a simultaneous yes to Jesus Christ and to market capitalism.[14]

These are important movements, and it may be that part of our engagement in the liberation struggle will be to forward such discussion within the churches and find ways to act upon it.

4. *On "speaking truth to power."* If the declaration of a *status confessionis* is the extreme situation, representing an all-out frontal attack on an otherwise accepted position, there are many points short of that in which we have an obligation to "speak truth to power."

It can be questioned whether "middle-class" persons have any significant power in a world dominated by a power elite and corporate structures whose effective control is in the possession of a tiny handful; our illusion of power (the ballot, "shareholder resolutions," dissent in public life, and so on) may be greater than its actuality. And yet as long as there are structures within a society that provide any access to the molding of public opinion, we have an obligation to use them.

One of the ways of "speaking truth to power" will be to concentrate on the very issue of power itself, and this has the added virtue in the present essay of providing an example of how North American and South American liberation concerns, though focusing on the issue of power, may need to say and do different things in their different contexts. In most Third World countries, although the internal power of a dictator may be inordinate, the power of these countries in terms of international leverage is virtually nil. They have no real control over their own destinies; they cannot decide what crops to grow if shareholders in a multinational corporation rule otherwise; they cannot control access to world markets for their exports save as First World nations allow; and they are saddled with debts so massive that there is no way they can ever expect to be free of stultifying indebtedness. In such situations, obviously, the Christian message must be related to liberation *from* such dependency, and liberation *for* a significant measure of control over their lives. They must pray for, act for, struggle for, power.

In North America, however, the situation is different and the liberating message must consequently be different. If Third World peoples are those who scarcely know the taste of power, First World nations like ours are drunk with it. If Third World nations have too little power, First World nations have too much, and with awesome consistency use it destructively. The task of liberation theology in our situation, therefore, is "to speak truth to power" in an effort to show (1) that rather than clutching more and more power to ourselves, we must share it; and (2) that the legacy of our remaining power must begin to be used creatively rather than destructively. Stated so baldly, these sound like either platitudes or irrelevant nonsense, but the truth of the matter is (1) that if we do not begin to share power, it will finally be taken from us, and (2) that to the degree that we continue to use it destructively, we will be sowing the seeds of a whirlwind that will finally engulf and destroy us. Instances of our nation's abuse of power can be documented in relation to almost any country with which we have had economic relations. We have had an almost unerring instinct to back forces of injustice, shore up dictators, and finance rebellions against countries that want to give "people's" democracy a chance to work. The names of Chile and the Philippines spring unaided to the mind. As I write, the notorious instance is Nicaragua, where for over a century we have imposed our will on a tiny and desperately poor country, usually by military intervention — a policy the Reagan administration has been obsessively desirous of pursuing yet again, determined to topple a regime whose chief sin is its refusal to "say uncle" to Uncle Sam. I am persuaded that one of the reasons the Reagan administration did not long ago invade Nicaragua is because, throughout the land, groups of Christians, working with other citizens, have attempted to "speak truth to power" by denouncing the administration's policy of intimidation and destruction.

5. *On broadening the base.* I noted earlier that in the case of burgeoning indigenous liberation theologies — black, feminist, Amerindian, gay/lesbian, Puerto Rican, Hispanic, and Filipino — an initial need for separateness, in order to refine their individual agendas, is beginning to be replaced by a desire to work together, not only for mutual self-enrichment, but because only together can they be effective instruments for social change. There is nothing the principalities and powers would like more than to have political protest groups continue fighting among themselves.

I doubt that such groups are enchanted, at least yet, by the notion of joining forces with white male North Americans, and it is also likely that many white male North Americans still feel ill at ease in the company of those with whom past associations have often been conflictual. But as many doors as possible must be set ajar now so that later they can more easily be opened wide. If the liberation struggle is going to move beyond a series of discrete, private, and unconnected dreams, the base must be broadened to be as inclusive as possible of all these theological commitments. And the base must be broadened as well beyond the strictly theological community. The experience noted in the previous section — that church groups and other citizens joined forces to create a stronger voice in combatting U.S. policy in Nicaragua — must become a model for other issues as well. The resultant theologies must include large doses of social analysis, "doing theology" must become more communal and less dependent on theological superstars, and new vocabularies must be developed that avoid the sexism, racism, and classism of so much traditional theology.[15] What must happen, in other words, is that persons be liberated to join the human race, rather than continuing to live in enclaves.

CONCLUSION

In an essay in a book honoring Gustavo Gutiérrez, it may seem strange not to have given more explicit attention to his writings, but I am gambling on the hunch that this is one of the best ways to "honor" him. Our theological task is not to become clones of Gustavo, but, having learned from him, to make use of the various resources with which he reacquaints us (scripture, tradition, social analysis, and personal engagement, for example) as we struggle to be faithful to the gospel in our situations, just as he has tried to be faithful to it in his.

There is, of course, another resource still—Gustavo's own writings. We need them as anchors to keep us moored to reality. Part of our own hope for the theological future is the promise that he will keep writing, and the assurance that from each new book we will learn new things. (How long, let us ask proddingly, until the promised volume on Las Casas appears?) Most of all, however, to those fortunate enough to know him, the total congruence between what he writes and what he lives remains his supreme contribution to the rest of us.

Better perhaps to leave it there. We should not, after all, further embarrass one who is already a little embarrassed at being the subject of a festschrift.

NOTES

1. For an account of the conference, see S. Torres and J. Eagleson, eds., *Theology in the Americas* (Maryknoll, N.Y.: Orbis, 1976).

2. See "Liberation Theology as a Utopian Heresy," in *Face to Face, an Interreligious Bulletin* (Winter 1987) 18–20.

3. See G. Gutiérrez, *The Power of the Poor in History* (Maryknoll, N.Y.: Orbis, 1983), pp. 126ff., 136–142, 149; *We Drink from Our Own Wells* (Maryknoll, N.Y.: Orbis, 1984), p. 101; "El Evangelio del Trabajo," in Gutiérrez et al., *Sobre el Trabajo Humano* (Lima: CEP, 1982), pp. 43–57, and many others.

4. See J. Eagleson and P. Scharper, eds., *Puebla and Beyond* (Maryknoll, N.Y.: Orbis, 1979), pp. 267–72. I have commented on the Puebla treatment of this matter in ibid., pp. 341–43, and more fully in W. Tabb, ed., *Churches in Struggle* "The Preferential Option for the Poor and the Renewal of Faith" (New York: Monthly Review Press, 1986), pp. 7–17.

5. The literature is extensive. See esp. J. Cone, *For My People: Black Theology and the Black Church* (Maryknoll, N.Y.: Orbis, 1984); G. Wilmore, *Black Religion and Black Radicalism*, 2nd ed. (Maryknoll, N.Y.: Orbis, 1983); C. West, *Prophesy Deliverance* (Philadelphia: Westminster, 1982).

6. D. Bonhoeffer, *No Rusty Swords* (New York: Harper and Row, 1985), "Protestantism Without Reformation," pp. 92–118.

7. Here, too, the literature is extensive. See inter alia R. Ruether, *Sexism and God-Talk* (Boston: Beacon, 1983); C. Heyward, *The Redemption of God* (Washington: University of America Press, 1982); M. Katoppo, *Compassionate and Free: An Asian Woman's Theology* (Maryknoll, N.Y.: Orbis, 1980); L. Russell, ed., *Feminist Interpretation of the Bible* (Philadelphia: Westminster, 1985).

8. See V. Deloria, *God is Red* (New York: Delta, 1973), and the interpretive material in Reist, *Theology in Red, White, and Black* (Philadelphia: Westminster, 1975).

9. Cf. G. Edwards, *Gay/Liberation: A Biblical Perspective* (New York: Pilgrim Press, 1984); R. Scroggs, *The New Testament and Homosexuality* (Philadelphia: Fortress Press, 1983); Glaser, *Uncommon Calling* (New York: Harper and Row, 1988).

10. Because the term "white male North American" fails to yield a satisfactory acronym, no matter how the letters are arranged, I shall henceforth identify this breed simply by the pronoun "we."

11. Moore, *The Challenge of Black Theology in South Africa* (Atlanta: John Knox, 1974), p. 5, italics added.

12. See J. De Gruchy and C. Villa-Vicencio, *Apartheid is a Heresy* (Grand Rapids: Eerdmans, 1983).

13. I have dealt with these issues in *Saying Yes and Saying No: On Rendering to God and Caesar* (Philadelphia: Westminster, 1986), esp. chap. 1 and 2. See also the important article by G. Hunsinger, "Barth, Barmen, and the Confessing Church Today," *Katallagete* (Summer 1985) 14–27, and the extended responses in ibid. (Fall 1987) 1–108. This material deserves the widest possible circulation.

14. U. Durchrow, *Global Economy: A Confessional Issue for the Churches?* (Geneva: World Council of Churches, 1987). I have a brief commentary, "Global Realities, Local Theologies," in *Christianity and Crisis*, Feb. 15, 1988, pp. 15–16.

15. Writings that begin these tasks are R. Shaull, *Heralds of a New Reformation* (Maryknoll, N.Y.: Orbis, 1984); M. Lamb, *Solidarity with Victims: Toward a Social Transformation* (New York: Crossroad, 1982); W. Tabb, ed., *Churches in Struggle: Liberation Theologies and Social Change in North America* (New York: Monthly Review Press, 1986); J. Nelson-Pallmeyer, *The Politics of Compassion: Hunger, the Arms Race, and U.S. Policy in Central America* (Maryknoll, N.Y.: Orbis, 1987).

15

Liberation Theology:
A Difficult but Possible Future

PABLO RICHARD

It is interesting that for this celebration of twenty years of liberation theology and the sixtieth birthday of our dear master and friend Gustavo Gutiérrez, we all start thinking not about the past but also the future. We are all convinced not only that liberation theology has a *future* but that it is theology's *only future*. We are also well aware that this future will be difficult. If liberation theology wants to remain faithful to its past and keep its identity, it will have to face an increasingly difficult future. However, the lives of poor Latin American Christians have been and go on being even more difficult, and so has the renewal of the church through the ecclesial base communities. But difficult does not mean impossible, providing that we find the right way and the necessary strength to keep to it.

I find it extraordinarily appropriate to reflect thus on the future of liberation theology in solidarity with Gustavo Gutiérrez. I do not want to go into personal details here, but it is obvious to me that over the last twenty years Gustavo has been an inspiration to us; he has taught us ways of seeing and what constitutes the tap root of liberation theology. Whenever we have felt bewildered or discouraged, it has been Gustavo who has given us fresh insight and heart. I have written this article with special gratitude to him and with a strong hope for the future of liberation theology.

In this article I shall try to develop, very briefly, the seven fields in which I think liberation theology has been most fruitful and in which I think it will find its strength in the future. I shall try to answer the fundamental question: *Where does our strength lie?* If we know where our strength really is, then we know where we should grow and where we should concentrate our work and hope.

1. SPIRITUALITY AND LIBERATION THEOLOGY

God lives and bestows self-revelation in the world of the poor and their struggles for liberation. This special presence and revelation of God in the heart of the people is liberation's theology deep root, whence it draws its strength and future.

Liberating spirituality is the capacity to live, experience, discern, and express God's presence among the oppressed. Liberation theology reflects in a systematic and critical way the God who appears in spirituality. If liberation theology comes to be broken off from its root in spirituality, it loses its purpose and dies as theology. Liberation theology can develop only from its root in the spiritual world of the poor: their silence, prayer, and joy.

It has often been said, and rightly, that what destroys our spirituality is not atheism but idolatry. Idolatry is the "spirituality of death," which invades everything today and radically perverts the meaning of God in our society. The fruit of idolatry is death; the root of social sin is idolatry. An important task of liberation theology is to distinguish between liberating spirituality and destructive idolatry: between the God of life and the idols of death. Liberation theology has power and a future to the extent that it succeeds in this discernment. Liberation theology is capable of this discernment only in the light of the spiritual experience of the poor. Liberation theology must elaborate theological criteria for this discernment.

Traditional theology is a theology that becomes more repetitive every day. It is empty, feeble, lacking in significance and—why not say so?— boring. It is a science cultivated in closed elitist academies. The world is not interested in this theology, and neither is this theology interested in the world. The cause of its sterility is that *the dominant theology has no spirituality, no God, and does not communicate God's word*. It is a theology confused by idolatry. Often it is a theology of death. Liberation theology can maintain its power and originality only if it is a theology of the God of the poor and a theology capable of hearing and transmitting God's word revealed to the poor. This is its strength and its future.

2. POPULAR RELIGIOUS AWARENESS AND LIBERATION THEOLOGY

The religious awareness of the people is a combination of many things: popular religiosity, indigenous religions, Afro-American religions, animistic traditions, magic. . . . The religious world of the people is an ocean too vast for anthropologists, sociologists, and theologians to plumb. For us it bears two important characteristics: it is an *alternative* religious awareness and in a certain sense it is an awareness *informed by the gospel* and *asserting the gospel.*

First, it is an alternative awareness to the predominant religion, and often an alternative to the religious predominance of a church of Christendom. It is a "popular" as opposed to "official" religious awareness. Secondly, it is an awareness to some degree colored by the preaching of the gospel. In spite of five centuries of conquest and spiritual manipulation, many seeds and germs of the gospel have penetrated the soul of popular culture and religion. Moreover, it is an awareness informed by the mysterious presence and revelation of God in the world of the poor. And the church of the poor's gospel-preaching work, from Bartolomé de Las Casas to Archbishop Romero, has had a real impact on popular religious awareness.

Liberation theology can have power and a future only if it succeeds in taking root in this alternative and evangelical religious awareness of the people. If it fails to take root here, liberation theology will be merely another elitist, intellectualist, and sterile theology. Only through the religious awareness of the people can we come *historically* to the God of the poor and discover the power of God's liberating presence and word. Liberation theology has its historical roots in popular culture and religion. It will never become a popular alternative to the religious system of domination, it will never have evangelizing power if it gives up its roots in popular religious awareness. Liberation theology has not let itself be carried away by the liberal, fundamentalist, "charismatic" trends that have tried to preach the gospel to the people in a way that is outside and against all their own cultural and religious tradition. Liberation theology maintains the relationship between faith and religion, faith and culture, faith and people. This is the necessary condition for it to develop, keep its identity, and have a future.

3. ECONOMICS AND LIBERATION THEOLOGY

By *economics* I mean here the safeguarding and continuation of everyone's life, but especially *the lives of the poor and oppressed*. Fundamentally life means: work, land, food, health, housing, education, environment, rest, and celebration (festival). Here I am not talking about a dialogue between theology and economics, or a theological reflection on economics. I am saying that life, especially the lives of the poor, must be taken as theology's rationale. I am not talking about the meaning of life or an economic or political program, but about *life* as a criterion for discerning what is *rational* and what is *irrational*; as the criterion for discerning *true* from *false*, *good* from *evil*, the *beautiful* from the *ugly*. What is rational, logical, true, good, and beautiful is that all, especially the poor, should have life. What is irrational, illogical, false, evil, and ugly is that the poor should not have life. Hunger, unemployment, malnutrition, illiteracy, and the destruction of nature is irrational, illogical, evil, and ugly. When we speak about economics and theology, we mean the epistemological problem of our criteria of rationality and truth. The great challenge for liberation theology is the life of the poor as the criterion of theological rationality. Real life is not just a problem of economic, political, or cultural reality; it is also a spiritual and theological reality.

Saint Irenaeus put it succinctly: *gloria dei vivens homo* (God's glory is the living human being). God's own glory and credibility are at stake in the lives of the poor. This epistemological option, this option for life as a criterion of rationality, truth, goodness, and beauty, is what makes liberation theology, at its deepest level, liberating. And its liberating power is what makes it theology, because God's glory is revealed in the lives of the poor. We are not talking about a purely sociological problem, but about the very nature of liberation theology as *theology* and as theology of *liberation*.

4. ECCLESIAL BASE COMMUNITIES AND LIBERATION THEOLOGY

The three previous points — spirituality, popular religious awareness, and the lives of the poor as the criterion of rationality — took us to the root of liberation theology. They are the *radical,* original, and originating elements of liberation theology; they are its spiritual, historical, and epistemological foundation.

But now we must pass from the root to the trunk — to keep the tree metaphor. The root is invisible because it is underground, but the trunk is what makes this root visible and gives it body. Liberation theology's trunk consists of the ecclesial base communities (EBCs). These EBCs keep liberation theology alive and liberation theology develops through them.

Here I do not want to define the EBCs. Neither am I assuming that they have a single or universal model. I am merely talking about a presence of the *church,* experienced in a *communal* way and firmly established at the *base.* The EBCs are not an ecclesial movement or simply a pastoral model. They are the church itself, the life of the church at the base, among the people. Whenever we have an ecclesial presence, of a communal type, established at the base, then we have EBCs, whatever their form or organization. By base, of course, I mean the human, geographical, social, political, ethnic, and racial base of the church. From its beginning, liberation theology has been identified with this historical expression of the church. This is where it was born and for whose sake it lives. The presence of Christians in popular movements and the reconstruction of the church in terms of popular faith have been the major events giving rise to liberation theology. Therefore, liberation theology is not just an intellectual or theological trend. It is a work of critical and systematic reflection within the church.

In what way have the EBCs marked the very essence and development of liberation theology? Let us recall first the specific way in which EBCs work and then let us see how this dynamic has put its stamp on liberation theology. The specific key strategic element of the EBCs is *participation* —

the participation of the poor and oppressed as active subjects, doers, makers of history within the church. The poor were always passive objects in the church of Christendom: objects of gospel-preaching, pastoral attention, objects of charity. Under Christendom, participation was always almost impossible. It was very difficult even for the middle, and upper classes, impossible for the poor, especially the most marginalized among them: indigenous populations, peasants, blacks, women.

Today the poor are irrupting into the church and they are doing so mainly through the EBCs. The poor participate now as active subjects and doers in the church. This has been possible because of the political, social, cultural, and religious awakening of the Latin American peoples over the last few decades, but also because of the church's own preferential option for the poor. It is the result of the church's liberating spirituality lived out in the world of the poor. It is the result of the evangelization of popular religious awareness and of the church's entering the world of the poor and oppressed, and taking their lives as its criterion of rationality and truth. Not only do the poor participate as active subjects in the church, their participation is creative. The poor participate by creating a new language, a new symbolism, a new "rhythm," new liturgical forms, new prayers, a new reading of the Bible, new ministries, and a new theological reflection.

This creative participation of the people in the church, which has begun only recently, is a creative participation from these oppressed groups' own cultural, religious, ethnic, racial, and human standpoints. This movement of creative participation by the people as subjects in the church has had a profound effect on liberation theology. Now there is a new doer, a new maker of history, in the church, and this new active subject is doing theology or at least inspiring new theological reflection in the church. The emergence of this new active subject, forgotten for centuries in the church, perhaps since the first century, is what is crucial about the EBCs and what is giving rise to liberation theology. From here liberation theology draws its power and its future. If one day liberation theology became separated, cut off from, this new historical subject in the church, it would wither and possibly die as liberation theology.

5. BIBLICAL HERMENEUTICS AND LIBERATION THEOLOGY

The most profound and important work done by the EBCs is what we call "popular Bible reading." Poor Christians are appropriating the Bible and stamping it with their own spirituality and culture. This practice is as old as the history of the EBCs but only in the last few years have we been reflecting critically on it and doing consciously organized and biblical work in terms of popular Bible reading. From this practice a *hermeneutics of liberation* is also arising. This is just the theoretical expression of the practice of Bible reading in the communities. Let us look now at the essential ele-

ments of this biblical practice and theory, and draw a few conclusions for
the future of liberation theology.

We can distinguish three moments in the hermeneutics of liberation: the
political, the spiritual, and the hermeneutic properly speaking. In the *political* the poor emerge as new historical subjects: it is they who actively pursue
the hermeneutic process. The poor are reading the Bible and interpreting
it from their own point of view. These persons who are now actively engaged
in the hermeneutic process, are the same historical subjects — the poor — as
those at the base and root of the production process of this same Bible.

Today we repeat enthusiastically that the Bible is the historical memory
of the poor — and it really is. But for centuries this was forgotten and the
voice of the poor was not heard. The Bible became the property of clerics
and intellectuals. Today the Bible has been restored to its rightful owners.
The poor take possession of the Bible today and read it from the point of
view of their own culture, awareness, and history.

In the *spiritual* — the second moment of the hermeneutic process — what
appears is a new experience of God in the world of the poor and oppressed.
Liberating spirituality is making a strong impression on biblical hermeneutics. There is an experience of God and God's word that precedes the
hermeneutic process and is more important than all biblical interpretation.
The Bible is read to discern this presence of God and God's living word
today in our history. God is greater than the Bible. The absolute in history
is God's word. The Bible is an instrument in the service of God's word.
The greater the experience of God and God's word in the world of the
poor, the better and clearer is their biblical interpretation.

Finally, we have the *hermeneutic* moment properly so called. Here there
is a struggle between different readings of the Bible. The Bible comes to a
people already interpreted, but the interpretation given is normally alien
to their awareness, culture, and spirituality. It is necessary to regain the
text and the history of this biblical text from the viewpoint of the poor.
Every moment of the hermeneutic process is conflictive and so we can say
that in the hermeneutics of liberation a political, spiritual, and hermeneutic
rupture takes place. First there is a political rupture with the dominant
system, ideology, and culture. Then there is a spiritual rupture with the
dominant idolatry, the idolatrous spiritualism of a system of death. Finally,
and most specifically, there is a hermeneutic rupture with an already given
dominant reading and interpretation of the Bible. There is no doubt whatever that we are seeing this triple rupture in the hermeneutics of liberation.
What distinguishes us is not a particular hermeneutical line but this rupture, which is explicitly political, spiritual, and hermeneutic.

If we assume the distinction between the literal, historical, and spiritual
meaning of the biblical text, we can say that the greatest creativity in popular Bible reading is taking place in the spiritual. There is a production of
meaning that is affecting the biblical text itself and the history behind the
biblical text. When the EBCs read the Bible to discern and express the

word of God in our own historical reality, biblical history and the text itself acquire new meaning. Over the last few years poor Christian persons in Latin America have read Exodus, the Prophets, Psalms, Gospels, Apocalypse. All these texts today have a new, liberating meaning for the people. They have become living texts, capable of reading our history and transforming our communities so that they become prophetic. This new spiritual meaning of the Bible is not arbitrary, because, on the one hand, it is rooted in the experience of God in the world of the poor, and it is also "controlled" by exegetic work that discovers the literal meaning and the historical meaning of the text. Likewise we are accompanied by the sense of faith in the church as people of God and the magisterial authority of our pastors.

Liberation theology finds strength and renewal in popular Bible reading. There is an unlimited field for its development here. In the future, liberating hermeneutics will be the main activity of liberation theology and will give it even deeper roots in the political and spiritual lives of poor Latin American Christians. In the near future the main literary production of liberation theology will be in the biblical field and here it will find a new impetus and development.

6. THE THIRD WORLD AND LIBERATION THEOLOGY

The world population in the year 1900 was 1,600 million. Today, there are 5,000 million of us. At the end of the century the earth will have 6,350 million inhabitants. Between 1988 and the year 2000 humanity will increase by 1,350 million. This is about the same increase as that since the time of Jesus until 1900. In this century there has been a demographic explosion never before seen in human history. But the most significant thing is that this growth has been mainly in the Third World—that is to say, in poor countries and among the poor in all countries. In the year 2000, twenty percent of humanity will live in the so-called developed world and eighty percent in underdeveloped countries (including China). Today, three out of every four inhabitants of the earth live in the Third World. By the end of the century, four out of five will live in the Third World. But the Third World is not just a numerical reality, it is also a human, religious, and cultural reality. The great religions with a written tradition (Islam, Judaism, Buddhism, Hinduism . . .) are Third World religions. In the Third World we also have the greatest wealth of indigenous culture, as well as immense riches in human values and qualities. The Third World is poor, but rich in humanity, religion, and culture.

The twenty-first century (and why not say the whole of the third millennium) will certainly be the century (and millennium) of the Third World. Humanity will be concentrated there numerically and also there will be the greatest human, cultural and religious wealth of the world in the future. Christianity can have a future and power only if it succeeds in taking root in this Third World. Christianity was born in Galilee and Palestine, which

was the Third World of the Roman empire. Later, it grew among the
poorest and most marginalized peoples. But from the sixteenth century
onward, it spread to Latin America, Africa, and Asia with the expansion
of Western colonialism. This did not prevent the gospel from being
preached up to a point in many regions and groups in the Third World—
with relative success in some places and disasters in others. But sociologically speaking, Christianity has a Western colonial past, and this stamp
remains on it today. The churches of Asia were the ones that suffered most
from this past and this stamping, and so they are the ones that most clearly
denounce the dominant Western colonial character of Christianity. Latin
America, as part of the Third World, is also becoming aware of its indigenous and Afro-American roots, and discovering Christianity's Western
colonial character.

The Catholic Church will never be able to take root in the Third World
unless it gets away from this Western colonial past and form. It is not a
question of radically breaking with the West but of dialectically moving
beyond this colonial past, so that Christianity can become indigenized and
take root in the Third World. Christianity must get back to its origins and
recover its identity in Third World terms, in terms of the world's poor
countries and the poor in all the world. The church can have a future only
if it succeeds in defining its place and mission in the Third World, where
the majority of human beings live and where humanity's greatest human,
cultural, and religious wealth is to be found. If the church ignores the Third
World today and does not manage to take root there, it could be due to a
Western colonial memory of the past. The decolonializing of the church
and its "going native" in the Third World means looking at its universality
or catholicity from a new point of view. The axis of Catholicity does not
pass through New York, London, Paris, Moscow, Tokyo, but through the
heart of the Third World countries with all their human, cultural, and
religious wealth.

If we take the Third World as Catholicity's new horizon and the place
where the church, most importantly, ought to be, we also take up the fundamental contradiction experienced by the Third World today. This fundamental contradiction is between the power centers basically situated in
the developed world and the poor oppressed masses of the Third World.
This is usually called the North-South contradiction. It is a contradiction
between life and death, between the Third World masses struggling for
their lives, and the financial, technological, political, cultural, and ideological centers of death situated in the developed world. The contradiction is
not with the inhabitants of the industrialized world, but with the centers
of power and death situated in that world. At world level the church must
increasingly become the spiritual force of the poor and poor countries in
their struggle for life against the centers of power and death.

As well as the North-South contradiction, there is the East-West contradiction, but this is not the more significant one for the Third World. On

the contrary, the East-West contradiction has been used to cover up the Third World's problems and justify domination of it. It forces us into a kind of geopolitical fatalism, in which opting for the West necessarily means being in contradiction to the East, and vice versa. The world struggle is presented as the confrontation of "democracy" (West) and "communism" (East). We are forced to enter this confrontation and thus we are made to forget the tremendous reality of death in the Third World. In the Third World we opt for life and we want to have the freedom to use what is best in both West and East for the sake of life in the Third World. Our struggle in the Third World is not against communism, but against poverty and wretchedness.

Liberation theology is perhaps the most mature product of the process of decolonialization and de-Westernization in the church. Liberation theology's future is also linked to this process. However difficult, one of liberation theology's fundamental tasks will continue to be dialogue with Asian and African theologies, and also with other non-Christian Third World religions, as well as the indigenous traditions of Latin America. Liberation theology must grow in the Third World; this is its own natural and "supernatural" cultural and religious space.

7. LIBERATION THEOLOGY AS "PROFESSIONAL" THEOLOGY

Liberation theology has its root in the spirituality and life of the people. Its organic development is in the base communities. But this is not enough. Liberation theology must also have a "professional" development. The word "professional" is not really very appropriate, but it would be worse still to use the word "academic." By professional development I mean that liberation theology should be pursued in a professional way by persons who devote themselves entirely to this task. This professional work must be completely rooted in spirituality, and its organic trunk will be the base communities. The spirituality of the people and the base communities must give life and strength to liberation theology, and liberation theology must draw sustenance from them. In this way, it differs from traditional academic theology, which is sustained and fed by an intellectual life cut off from the people and the ecclesial community. Liberation theology consciously tries to overcome the dualism between intellectuals and the people. We believe in the people's intellectual capacity on the one hand, and on the other we believe that all intellectual activity cut off from the people is sterile.

As a professional theology, liberation theology must fulfill various tasks:

1. *Systemization of the work that has been done*:

From time to time it is necessary to create a vision of the whole, which will allow us to communicate our theology to others, so that it can be studied systematically by those who study theology in a professional manner. This work of systemization is required for the sake of universal communication and dialogue. What is new is that this work is now being done collectively.

It is not a *summa theologica* composed by one author.

2. *Dialogue with other, non-theological disciplines*:

In the social and economic sciences as well as in art and literature, a liberating movement is taking place, which is very similar to liberation theology. In former times dialogue was carried on almost exclusively with philosophy. Today we must extend it to other disciplines, and this requires a lot of time and hard work.

3. *Insertion of liberation theology into the church's history and tradition*:

It is necessary to study, critically and systematically, all theological traditions from the viewpoint of liberation theology. Biblical exegesis, church history, the history of spirituality and theology, and many other traditional theological fields must be deepened by liberation theologians — and this also requires a lot of time and hard work.

CONCLUSION

Liberation theology's future is difficult but possible. Liberation theology is the only possible theology *in the Third World* and the only possible future for *theology*. All this is clear, but it is also a challenge to us. Our certainty in saying this does not come from ourselves but from God and poor, believing Latin Americans. Liberation theology has been given to us; it is a free and transcendent gift of God to our Afro-Indian oppressed America.

In this article I have tried to answer the question: Where lies our strength? This is a fundamental question to prevent us from making mistakes and growing weak in the future. I hope that this article has given a humble and tentative answer to this question. At any rate it represents my deepest conviction and is the result of many years' reflection and experience.

To conclude in a few lines, we can say that liberation theology's future lies in its spirituality, its root in the cultural and religious life of the poor, its commitment to liberation in Latin America. It is the experience of the God of the poor, the freely giving, transcendent God who comes to meet us in the world of the oppressed, who obliges us to do theology, liberation theology. Here fundamentally lies our strength and our intelligence. Furthermore liberation theology's future lies in the EBCs and the rise of a new church model in Latin America. Our theology has always developed in the church, and in the reconstruction of our church as a church of the poor lies our strength and our future. I have also pointed out popular Bible readings and liberation hermeneutics as a fruitful area for growth and development of liberation theology. In the immediate and also the distant future, liberation theology will be above all a biblical theology of liberation. By appropriating the Bible on behalf of oppressed Christianity, liberation theology will discover new strength. The future and power of liberation theology also lie in its capacity for dialogue with Third World theologies, especially with African and Asian theologies of liberation; and with the great Third World non-Christian religions. This is the scope for liberation theology's universal growth. Finally, liberation theology must affirm its future as a professional theology, in dialogue with all the disciplines of liberation.

—translated from the Spanish by Dinah Livingstone

Contributors

PAULO EVARISTO ARNS is archbishop of São Paulo, Brazil. He is an active journalist and the author of many books and articles. He is a member of the United Nations Independent Commission on International Humanitarian Issues, Pax Christi International, and the Peace and Justice Service in Latin America. Among the honors he has received are the Nansen Prize from the United Nations High Commissioner for Refugees and France's highest honor, the degree of *Commandeur* in the National Order of the Legion of Honor.

GREGORY BAUM holds a master's degree in mathematics and a doctorate in theology. During the Vatican Council he was a *peritus* at the Secretariat for Promoting Christian Unity. From 1959 to 1986 he taught theology and religious studies at St. Michael's College in the University of Toronto. Since 1986 he has taught at McGill University in Montreal. He is the editor of *The Ecumenist* and a member of the editorial committee of *Concilium*. His most recent book is *Theology and Society*. Over the last decade or so his main interests have been political theology and social theory. He is an active member of the New Democratic Party, the Canadian equivalent of the British Labor Party.

MARÍA CLARA BINGEMER, a Brazilian lay Catholic theologian, is a professor of theology at the Pontifical Catholic University of Rio de Janeiro, and the Santa Ursula University. She is presently finishing her doctoral dissertation in systematic theology at the Gregorian University. She is regional coordinator of EATWOT for Latin America and is co-author, with J. B. Libanio, of *Christian Eschatology,* and, with Yvonne Gebara, of *Mary: Mother of God, Mother of the Poor.*

LEONARDO BOFF is a Franciscan priest, educated in his native Brazil and Munich, Germany. A professor of theology in Petrópolis, Brazil, Boff also serves as advisor to the Brazilian Conference of Bishops and the Latin American Conference of Religious. One of the major champions of the theology of liberation, Boff is author of *Ecclesiogenesis; Jesus Christ Liberator; Church: Charism and Power;* and (with Clodovis Boff) *Introducing Liberation Theology.*

ROBERT McAFEE BROWN is professor emeritus of theology and ethics at Pacific School of Religion in Berkeley, California. In many books he has tried to interpret Third World theological concerns to North Americans. Among them are *Theology in a New Key: Responding to Liberation Themes; Gustavo Gutiérrez; Unexpected News: Reading the Bible with Third World Eyes; Saying Yes and Saying No: On Rendering to God and Caesar;* and *Spirituality and Liberation: Overcoming the Great Fallacy.* His most recent book is *Gustavo Gutiérrez: An Introduction to Liberation Theology* (Maryknoll, N.Y.: Orbis, 1990).

HARVEY COX is Victor S. Thomas Professor of Divinity at Harvard Divinity School. His many books include *The Secular City; Seduction of the Spirit; Religion in the Secular City,* and most recently, *The Silencing of Leonardo Boff: The Vatican and the Future of World Christianity.*

MARC H. ELLIS (co-editor) received his doctorate from Marquette University and is professor of religion, culture, and society studies at the Maryknoll School of Theology, where he directs the Justice and Peace program. His books include *A Year at the Catholic Worker; Peter Maurin: Prophet in the Twentieth Century; Faithfulness in an Age of Holocaust; Toward a Jewish Theology of Liberation*; and *Beyond Innocence and Redemption: Confronting the Holocaust and Israeli Power.*

GUSTAVO GUTIÉRREZ, a native of Lima, Peru, was educated in Lima, Chile, and Europe, and was ordained in 1959. In his work Gutiérrez's theological training is joined with his experience of living and working among the poor of Rimac, a Lima slum. He is professor of theology at the Catholic University in Lima and advisor to the National Union of Catholic Students. His books include the classic *A Theology of Liberation, The Power of the Poor in History, We Drink from Our Own Wells: The Spiritual Journey of a People*, and *On Job: God-Talk and the Suffering of the Innocent.* His most recent book in English is *The Truth Shall Make You Free* (Orbis, 1990).

FRANÇOIS HOUTART received his doctorate in sociology from Louvain University where he is professor and director of the Center for Socio-Religious Research. He has done extensive research in Asia and Latin America and has published a number of books, including *The Church and Revolution; Genesis and Institutionalization of Indian Catholicism;* and *Church and Revolution in Latin America.*

PENNY LERNOUX was a prize-winning American journalist who worked in Latin America from 1961 until her death in 1989. She was the Latin American correspondent for the *National Catholic Reporter* and *The Nation,* and contributed to many other publications including *Maryknoll Magazine.* Her books include *Cry of the People,* on the changing role of the Latin American Catholic Church; *In Banks We Trust*; and *People of God: The Struggle for World Catholicism.*

ARTHUR F. McGOVERN, a Jesuit, is currently a professor of philosophy at the University of Detroit. He holds a doctorate from the University of Paris and a licentiate in theology. He has published numerous articles on Marxism and Catholic social teaching. The author of *Marxism: An American Christian Perspective* and co-author of *Ethical Dilemmas in the Modern Corporation,* his most recent book is *Liberation Theology and Its Critics: Toward an Assement* (Orbis, 1989).

OTTO MADURO (co-editor) was born in Venezuela where he studied at the Central University of Venezuela and at Louvain, from which he obtained his M.A. in religious sociology and his Ph.D. in philosophy magna cum laude. He has held academic posts in his own country and in the United States, where he is a visiting professor at the Maryknoll School of Theology. He has published four books on the general subject of religion and liberation, among them *Religion and Social Conflict,* as well as more than sixty articles and reviews in America and Europe.

JOHANN BAPTIST METZ is professor of Catholic theology and director of the Institute for Fundamental Theology at the University of Münster. He is a member of the Board of Foundation of the University of Bielefeld and its Center for Interdisciplinary Studies (including the projects of an Ecumenical Research Center). His many books include *Theology of the World; Faith in History and Society; The Emergent Church; Poverty of Spirit; Followers of Christ; The Courage to Pray* (with K. Rahner); *Religion and Political Society* (with J. Moltmann); *Our Hope: A Confession of Faith for this Time,* and *Toward Vatican III* (with Tracy and Küng).

ALOYSIUS PIERIS, a Jesuit, founder and director of the Tulana Research

Centre in Kelaniya, Sri Lanka, earned the first doctorate in Buddhist studies ever awarded a non-Buddhist by the University of Sri Lanka. He also holds degrees from London University and Pontificia Facoltà di Teologia, Naples. Pieris has taught at Cambridge University, Gregorian University, the Graduate Theological Union, Washington Theological Union, and Union Theological Seminary. An editor of the journal *Dialogue* and a member of EATWOT, he is the author of *Love Meets Wisdom: A Christian Experience of Buddhism* and *An Asian Theology of Liberation.*

PABLO RICHARD was born in Chile in 1939. He has a degree in theology from the Catholic University of Chile, a degree in Holy Scriptures from the Pontifical Biblical Institute, Rome, a doctorate in the sociology of religion from the Sorbonne, Paris, and an honorary doctorate in theology from the Free Faculty of Protestant Theology in Paris. At present he lives in Costa Rica and is titular professor of theology at the National University and a member of DEI (Ecumenical Department of Research). He trains pastoral workers for Ecclesial Base Communities in Central America. His most recent works are: *La Iglesia Latinoamericana entre el temor y la esperanza*; *Death of Christendoms, Birth of the Church*; *La fuerza espiritual de la Iglesia de los pobres.*

ROSEMARY RADFORD RUETHER is Georgia Harkness Professor at Garrett-Evangelical Seminary. She is contributing editor to *Christianity and Crisis, The Ecumenist,* and *Theology Today.* Her books include: *Faith and Fratricide; Sexism and God-Talk;* and *Contemporary Roman Catholicism: Crisis and Challenges.*

EDWARD SCHILLEBEECKX was born at Antwerp, Belgium, and was ordained in 1941. He studied at Louvain, Le Saulchoir, Paris, the Ecole des Hautes Etudes, and the Sorbonne. He became doctor of theology in 1951 and magister in 1959. Since 1958 he has been teaching systematic theology and hermeneutics at the University of Nijmegen, the Netherlands. He has received several honorary doctoral degrees and, in 1982, the European Erasmus prize for theology. He has authored many books, among them *Jesus, an Experiment in Christology,* and *On Christian Faith, the Spiritual, Ethical, and Political Dimensions.*

Index